FISHING WITH McCLANE

BOOKS BY A. J. McCLANE

THE WISE FISHERMAN'S ENCYCLOPEDIA
THE AMERICAN ANGLER
SPINNING FOR FRESH AND SALT WATER FISH
OF NORTH AMERICA
THE PRACTICAL FLY FISHERMAN
McCLANE'S STANDARD FISHING ENCYCLOPEDIA
AND INTERNATIONAL ANGLING GUIDE
FIELD & STREAM INTERNATIONAL FISHING GUIDE
McCLANE'S NEW STANDARD FISHING ENCYCLOPEDIA

BOOKS BY GEORGE REIGER

ZANE GREY: OUTDOORSMAN
PROFILES IN SALTWATER ANGLING

FISHING
WITH MC CLANE

30 YEARS
OF ANGLING
WITH AMERICA'S
FOREMOST
FISHERMAN

A. J. McCLANE

EDITED BY GEORGE REIGER

Illustrated by Roy Grinnell

PRENTICE-HALL, INC., Englewood Cliffs, New Jersey 07632

ISBN 0-13-319624-0 {A REWARD BOOK : PBK.}

Designed by Carl A. Koenig

10 9 8 7 6 5 4 3 2 1

Library of Congress Cataloging in Publication Data

McClane, Albert Jules
    Fishing with McClane.

    Articles previously published in Field and stream.
    Bibliography of the author's works: p.
    1. Fishing. 2. McClane, Albert Jules.
I. Field and stream. II. Title.
SH441.M323   799.1'2'08   74-32479
ISBN 0-13-319665-8

For my angling pals with whom the last
three decades have been shared in many
memorable ways and days astream . . .

DAN BAILEY	CHARLES LINDEMANN
LENNART BORGSTROM	DON MacARTHUR
RAY CAMP	BILL MacDONALD
DON CARTER	ARTHUR McCRYSTAL
GEORGE COOK	BING McCLELLAN
FRED CUSHING	TOM AND BOB McNALLY
HARRY DARBEE	VERNON OGILVIE
ARIE DE ZANGER	ED REDDY
GILBERT DRAKE	CHARLES RITZ
BOB ELLIOT	JACK SAMSON
ARNOLD GINGRICH	WALTER BEDELL SMITH
GUY KIBBEE	VICTOR SOSKICE
PETER KREINDLER	TED TRUEBLOOD
BERT LAHR	FRANK VALGENTI
PAT LANNAN	DAVID WAYNE
STAN LEEN	THOMAS. D. WHITE
TOM LENK	DERMOT WILSON

and, of course,

PATTI

Introduction

Tom McNally, outdoor editor of the Chicago *Tribune*, describes A. J. McClane as an angling innovator, casting engineer, tackle technician, skilled photographer, professional ichthyologist, master writer, and master fisherman. Arnold Gingrich, publisher of *Esquire* magazine, goes one better in comparing McClane's skill with a flyrod to Fritz Kreisler's mastery of the violin. Gingrich writes: "To me in my time, there are no anglers beside McClane."

A relative late-comer to the McClane fan club, I carry my adulation even further. For my vision of history sees this past half century's flowering of outdoor recreation in America in a small way comparable to the great age of discovery in Elizabethan England. In every sense of the word, we are living (may, in fact, have already lived through) an angling epoch. If this analogy is acceptable, I humbly submit that Albert Jules McClane has been our Sir Francis Drake and William Shakespeare rolled into one.

Right away I can hear some wag saying something about Shakespeare not writing his own plays and McClane not catching his own fish! Or, another wondering if I might be confusing the playwright with the tackle company. Not a few fishermen will be stunned by my placing a mere contemporary alongside an ancient venerated beyond all humanity. "What about Walton?" they'll ask, tugging at their forelocks with the same abject humility they reserve for the Bard.

Well, from my standpoint, Walton is to McClane what the writers of the medieval mystery and morality plays were to Shakespeare. *The Compleat Angler* reminds us of our origins and angling traditions the same way a performance of *Everyman* or *The Second Shepherd's Play* reminded a Jacobean audience of their theatrical past. But in terms of achieving peaks of excellence in their respective fields, you can't beat Shakespeare's drama, and you can't touch McClane's angling or his outdoor writing.

Both McClane and Shakespeare were well-grounded in the tradition of their fathers. As Shakespeare performed in morality dramas as a youngster, McClane was reared within the conventional angling forms of fly and plug casting. As theater became more realistic at the start of the seventeenth century, Shakespeare was able to adapt the morality formula and devise *Macbeth*. Similarly, A. J. not only witnessed the advent of spinning and spin casting, he was among the first to spread word of the new techniques with *Spinning for Fresh and Salt Water Fish of North America* (1952).

While A. J.'s writing is not of a kind with Shakespeare, common sense and forbearance are the characteristics most readily perceived in both authors. On a recent trip with A. J. to Deep Water Cay in the Bahamas, I watched a New York businessman/bonefisherman pester McClane with a hundred trivial questions all during breakfasts and dinners, and even try to push himself into A. J.'s boat for a day of angling. The New Yorker took flies from Al, asked him for free copies of his books, and even conspired to swap guides. Long after I would have lost my cool and been indicted for manslaughter, A. J. still suffered this horrible nuisance with patient grace. When I asked Al how he could put up with the man, he replied, "George, he is a dedicated angler."

Few outdoor writers combine technical expertise with a genuine feeling for words. McClane's descriptions of the passing of hickory and silk before the rise of fiber glass and nylon blend accurate reporting with poetry. There may be better fly tyers than Al, but no man knows the variety and uses of this genre better than McClane. Similarly, while there may have been better sonneteers than Shakespeare, no poet explored the possibilities (hence, discovering the limitations) of this literary form better than the Bard.

As for comparing McClane with a great voyager like Francis Drake, consider that Al has traveled the world over in pursuit of new angling experiences much the way Drake wandered the seas in search of gold and treasure. As Drake endured storms and war to follow his dream, McClane has survived a plane crash in Alaska, earthquakes in Peru and Chile, and revolutions in Colombia and the then Belgian Congo—all to keep his readers up to date on the most important of world events: namely, where the fish are and the best ways to catch them.

A. J. caught a 48-pound Atlantic salmon in Norway on what the average angler would have used to take a bluegill sunfish. Other memorable catches include a 132-pound tarpon on fly tackle in the Florida Keys, a 33-pound northern pike in Saskatchewan, and a 16-pound largemouth bass at Haw Creek, Florida. Tom McNally recalls watching him take eleven brown trout on eleven successive casts in Montana's Yellowstone River. Now that's angling!

In 1951, while working on the spinning book, Al took time out to show skeptics what lightweight tackle could really do. He flew to Walker Cay in the Bahamas and came back with a 44½-pound record barracuda on 8-pound test. A compulsive angler who feels that if it has scales and fins it can be caught, Al once spent an afternoon in Africa catching "tree-walking fish" by casting dry flies into the mangroves and onto mud banks.

There is one last way in which I find A. J. McClane comparable to the great Elizabethans. His life and writings are the kind that grow larger in the minds of future generations. Shakespeare finished his work, retired from the theater, and settled down in Stratford, content that no one beyond his own generation would be interested in what he wrote. His plays were only saved from oblivion through the intervention of a handful of friends.

In much the same way, Al does not see his life as extraordinary. He once did use the word *era* to describe the postwar decade of the 1950s when angling travel and exploration were at their peak. But he steadfastly refuses to see his contributions as anything exceptional among outdoor writers. "I am a reporter and nothing more," he says. When I point out that his *Practical Fly Fisherman* is already regarded as an angling classic, the first edition worth many times its original price—if and when you can find a copy—Al only shrugs and says something about the book having served its day and purpose. When I stress that *McClane's Standard Fishing Encyclopedia,* just out in a revised edition, is one of the most handsome and instructive of tomes, not only for the angler, but for editors, fisheries biologists, and even historians, Al smiles and says that he's pleased so many people find it useful.

Yet while Al eschews the limelight in his own generation, his reputation is the kind that grows with time. The next generation and the one beyond that will look back on all he accomplished, on the quality of what he wrote, and on the stature of the man himself with that special awe anglers reserve for their demigods: a G. E. M. Skues or Theodore Gordon.

An astrologist might have anticipated a great career in angling for young McClane. He was born under the sign of Aquarius, the Water Bearer, which of course immediately precedes Pisces, the Fishes. Although his birthplace was Brooklyn, New York, where he briefly attended Bushwick High School, then Richmond Hill High School after his family moved to rural Queens (at the time you could still hunt rabbits and trap muskrats along what is now the Long Island Expressway), he was already in motion by bus and train exploring ponds and streams as fas east as Montauk. Sometimes Al and his friends were so anxious to fish they couldn't wait to reach the end of the rail line. One day while his train stood unaccountably just outside the station at Babylon on a bridge over Swan River, Al spotted a big bass hanging in the shadow of the trestle. Quick as a wink, he rigged up his tackle and rather awkwardly dangled a popping bug out the open window. He hooked the fish about the same time the train started into the station. Despite the yells and encouragement of his fellow passengers and the conductor, word did not reach the engineer before Al's line dragged across the ties, and the fish dropped back into the water.

Beginning with his grandfather, who was one of the first engineers on the Long Island Railroad in the days of the diamond stacker, all male members of the McClane family were railroaders, and travel was literally a way of life. Grandpa William McClane retired at Hampton Bays in the twenties and this became a second home for Al, who at the age of ten had his own skiff and was hardly ever seen around the house from dawn until dusk. The road from Shinnecock to Montauk was in many places a one-lane sand affair which resembled little more than a pair of wheel ruts. Still the pot of gold at the end of the rainbow was always worth an expedition, for in addition to the unexcelled striped bass and weakfishing in the surf, Fort Pond (today called Montauk Lake or Montauk Harbor) was closed to the sea, and fat white perch, sassy pickerel, and largemouth bass were caught in abundance over its clean white sand bottom.

But these were also the years of the Great Depression, and even a young man of thirteen would decide that work was the common denominator. So bidding good-bye to his bewildered parents, Al hitchhiked to the Catskill Mountains. His vague plan involved a classmate, Harry Johnson, who had a sister working in a summer hotel somewhere around Arkville, and the two boys set out, confident that jobs were in abundance. By the end of the third day, with blistered feet and growling stomachs (and no idea where Miss Johnson was located), they met a farmer at the local railroad station who allowed as how neither one could milk a cow, room and board was the best he could offer until some skills became apparent. Their mentor, Basil Van Kleeck, was a flinty old Dutch farmer who cultivated those rocky hills twelve hours a day. Despite the presence of a trout stream running through the middle of the pasture, the only time Al could fish was at night or, on rare occasions, a declared holiday. After one week, Harry Johnson decided farming was not his métier and went home.

"Eventually, I worked for almost every farmer in Delaware and Ulster Counties," Al recalls. "The late thirties saw the demise of agriculture in that area. Margaretville, the town I more or less 'adopted' on the East Branch of the Delaware, was, unlike the charming, quiet spot it is today, a booming pivotal-point in the dairy and produce markets for New York City. At age sixteen I took a job with the Jenkinstown Power and Light Company as a second-class lineman which simply meant that I dug the postholes across an unending stretch of the Catskill Mountains.

"But these were truly wonderful years for me. I met and fished with many of the great Delaware anglers: Ray Neidig, Dan Todd, Mike Lorenz, John Alden Knight, Doc Faulkner and, sometimes, Pop Robbins and Reub Cross when they came over from the Beaverkill. Both the East Branch and the Esopus were tremendous producers in those days with 5- to 7-pound brown trout not unusual for somebody who knew the water. Despite the abundant daytime hatches of caddis and mayflies, the larger trout, and some of these were in the 10-pound class, were invariably taken at night on big wet patterns. Thanks to Doc Faulkner, I was the 'kid' who was allowed to tag along. He was such a fishing nut that when he broke his ankle—by getting his foot wedged under a boulder in fast water—the next day he waded in a plaster cast!

"Fortunately, I had an aunt who owned a hotel in Cresco, Pennsylvania, and occasionally I'd visit her to get a few days on Paradise Creek or the Brodheads. Both streams were in their prime then, but more important, there I met Lee Allen, a truly skilled fly fisherman (he only used one fly pattern, the Leadwing Coachman in all sizes, wet and dry), who took the time to polish my casting. Even Jack Knight, who didn't pass out casual compliments, considered Lee an artist on the water. He had total line control at any distance and could drop a fly within an inch of his target without rippling the surface."

With this outdoor and particularly water-oriented background, Al made a natural transition to the School of Agriculture at Cornell University in 1939, which at that time was staffed by pioneer fisheries biologists like Doctors Dan Embody and Charles Mottley. Al became a fisheries major and worked in the New York State Experimental Hatchery at Ithaca. Assigned to Dr. John Rayner (formerly Chief, Division of Research, Oregon State Wildlife Commission), Al quickly found the study of fish no less exhausting than running a farm. "I backpacked trout fingerling into a number of Finger Lakes tributaries. Each can weighed ninety pounds but after a mile, it felt like ninety tons. I helped John build a weir on Grout Brook to make a trout migration study. It washed away in the first heavy fall rain and we had to build it again. And again. I don't know how many poles we cut and pounded into the stream bed, but it was a frustrating project. That winter, in fact, a few days before Christmas, we nearly drowned on Skaneateles Lake when our boat swamped in a midnight storm while pulling a gill net. We made

[xiii]

night sets because the trout were more active inshore after dark. John and I walked naked in the snow to his Model A Ford and wrapped ourselves in the burlap sacks we used to haul fish in, and drove forty miles back to the hatchery covered with ice. It was prophetic, I suppose, because if you stay in the business long enough, little misadventures are inevitable."

Although McClane qualified as a fish culture aide, fisheries research technician, and finally junior aquatic biologist, events in Europe altered his destiny. In 1942 he joined the U. S. Army and went overseas with the 398th Self-Propelled Automatic Weapons Battalion, which was subsequently attached to the First, Fourth, and Fourteenth Armored Divisions. There isn't much to say that hasn't already been said about the trip from Normandy to the Falaise-Argentan Gap, Hatten, the Colmar Pocket and into Germany. Sergeant McClane caught a grenade fragment in the knee at Lunéville and was awarded the Purple Heart and Bronze Star. The irony of war, in this case, was that he had begun free-lance writing before going overseas and his first offer (some weeks en route) for a position as fishing editor at *Field & Stream* came from publisher Eltinge F. Warner while Al was digging a foxhole. He had sold a story to *Outdoor Life* in 1939 which finally appeared in September 1944 under the title "Bouncing for Trout." Its subhead reads: "When ordinary methods get you nowhere in the sultry summer days, try waking up the fish with a new, effective technique." By the time Al received his author's copy of this issue, he was far more involved with "new, effective techniques" for waking up the Jerrys than fish.

Al also sold a story to *Field & Stream* in 1942, but it was probably his article in *Outdoor Life* with a simple line drawing at the top of the page and one at the bottom showing how to "bridge your leader" that stirred his ambition to do this kind of thing full-time. After all, he shared the issue with *Outdoor Life*'s great angling columnist, Ray Bergman. There was also a good moose hunting tale by a free-lancer named Jack O'Connor and a great pronghorn painting by Francis Lee Jaques.[1] It must be wonderful to be associated with such talented people, Al thought, but how do I get back to 515 Madison Avenue?

All's well that ends well. The war stopped, and undeterred by the offer of a commission from General Walter Bedell Smith, Eisenhower's Chief of Staff, Al joined *Field & Stream* in April 1947. Dave Newell, who also

---

[1] Another aspiring young outdoor writer featured in this same issue was Sergeant Frank Woolner with a story about rabbit hunting in England. Today Frank is the editor of *Salt Water Sportsman*.

eventually joined the magazine, had been offered the job Al couldn't accept, but future editor-in-chief Hugh Grey actually took it until Ted Trueblood came along. "I'll always be grateful to Ted as he had a big say about who was being hired and I know he put in a good word for me." Yet there was one last hurdle: Warren Page and Al McClane arrived on the scene about the same time, and *both* were slated to be fishing editor. Publisher Warner, who had inadvertently precipitated the confusion, looked them over, snorted twice, and then named McClane the "fishing man" and Page "the shooter." It was a pronouncement destined to make outdoor-writing history. "I was the lucky one," recalls Al, "because Warren is every bit as skilled at fishing as he is at shooting. He's the ultimate outdoor writer in my book."

As for Al's initial efforts with the job, Tom Lenk, founder and president of Garcia Tackle, describes his reaction to the transition from Ted True-blood to Al McClane as fishing editor:

"I read *Field & Stream* avidly, for it was the only American outdoor magazine with a truly international flavor. When the editors announced that a mere youngster was going to take charge of the angling department, I was concerned. Could he do the job? But within two months, A. J.[2] McClane had won my wholehearted support."

From then to now, Al's many-faceted life has been a blur of activity which is itemized in the most recent edition of *Who's Who in the World*. Besides his regular column for *Field & Stream*, he wrote stories for *Esquire, Life, Gourmet*, and numerous other magazines. For a while he wrote and directed WOR's Rod and Gun Club of the Air. In 1950 Al even found time to court and marry Patti Murphy who has shared, along with their daughter, Susan Deborah, born in 1953, most of the McClane adventures of the past two decades. After leaving the New York office in 1953 to work in the field, Al proceeded to fish virtually every country in the world. In the jet age, angling horizons have expanded tremendously, and a trip from Argentina to Finland to Scotland and home to Palm Beach with a stop at the New York office is par for the course.

But from here on, I'll let Al do his own storytelling. His articles are not in chronological order but rather are arranged to bring the reader into the world of angling as though he or she were entering it for the first time. What kind of fish and how to catch them remain more fundamental ques-

---

[2] Al had his first stories published under the byline "Albert J. McClane." Eltinge F. Warner thought that was too formal, and since he himself usually went by the initials "E.F.," he suggested McClane do the same. Thus, from June 1947 to date, Al's official byline has been "A. J. McClane."

tions than where to go and what to wear. Making a selection has been difficult. At one point I was able to prune my list of favorite McClane stories down to forty, but Prentice-Hall insisted that twenty was all they had room to print. We both compromised, and here are the results. May you enjoy them as much as I have.

George Reiger
Heron Hill
Locustville, Virginia

CONTENTS

PART I: PUTTING IT ALL TOGETHER
1. Gear for the Barefoot Expert 3
2. Look, a Fish! 9
3. The Mysterious Mister X 17
4. Designing Your Fly Leader 25
5. Dry-Fly Fundamentals 33

PART II: BASS, BUGS, AND BLACK MAGIC
6. Secrets of the Bass 43
7. That New Black Magic 51
8. It Helps to Be Bug-Minded 57
9. Retrieving: The Real Art of Fishing 65
10. Ever Nod at a Bass? 73

PART III: FLIES, FLEAS, AND BEETLES
11. Upstream—Or Down? 81
12. Presenting the Muddler Minnow 91
13. Mr. Botz and the Beetle 99
14. Feather Merchant 107
15. The Art of Midge Fishing 117

PART IV: THE SPICE OF LIFE
16. The Fly Rod That Does the Impossible 127
17. The Lore of Night Fishing 135
18. Spinning Lure for Bonefish 145
19. The Fish Jumped Over a Spoon 153
20. That Old-Fashioned Wet Fly 159

PART V. SOME FAVORITE FISHES

21. Secret Life of a Bream Specialist 169
22. Sailfish of the North 177
23. King Permit 187
24. The Great Tuna Hunt 195
25. Wanted! More Salmon Fishermen 205

PART VI: HOW IT ALL BEGAN

26. Fishing With the Compleat Angler 215
27. The Golden Age of Tackle Making 227
28. My Old Kentucky Reel 235
29. Came a Revolution 243
30. The *Field & Stream* Hat Trick 253

Photos 267
Appendix A: Published Books 321
Appendix B: Published Articles in *Field & Stream* 323

FISHING WITH McCLANE

PART I

PUTTING IT ALL TOGETHER

1

GEAR FOR THE BAREFOOT EXPERT

In June 1947, Al McClane did an article called "That Spinning Game," followed by other pieces in 1948 describing the virtues of the fixed-spool reel. Today that's like telling people Campbell makes soup. But at the time nobody in the U. S. was manufacturing spinning tackle and just a handful of foreign imports were available. The first reaction to the new editor's article was to have the magazine's largest advertiser threaten to cancel all future ads unless McClane "writes something sensible" as nobody was going to buy that "junk." *Field & Stream* replied that business or no business, if the fishing editor believes in it, the magazine goes with it. Within eighteen months the tackle industry was revolutionized and McClane was writing about a refinement called "ultra-light spinning."

In 1958, with the experience of his daughter, Susan, to draw on, Al wrote "Gear for the Barefoot Expert," a light-tackle primer for parents. Al was well aware that most spinning reels carry spools with 8- or 10-pound-test line. With such welterweight gear, countless fishermen happily take on largemouth bass and pike, bluefish, and mackerel. The heft of the tackle may seem light to an adult angler, but too often he uses this same tackle on a pond or stream where 2-pound fish are lunkers. He doesn't stop to think that 8-pound line in such water is equivalent to using 130-pound line on striped bass—an unconscionable no-no for the sportsman. Even more disturbing is the thought that our fisherman may have in tow a youngster who will take all his angling cues from the adult. And what's the merit or future in an eight-year-old learning that it's possible to kill an 8-inch bream on 8-pound line?

GWR

GEAR FOR THE BAREFOOT EXPERT

If I were to name the most pleasant day of angling last year, it wouldn't be one of those spent looking for the big stuff in Peru or Arctic Norway, but a lazy afternoon on a small New York pond, casting for panfish with Bob Darbee.[1] It was a day when the clouds rolled like giant cotton balls over the hilltops, and the water lay clear as a cold martini.

We let our skiff drift aimlessly before the breeze and tossed our lures around stumps and yellow-flowered pads, searching for big sunfish. As things turned out, our trophies never appeared, but fat red-breasted miniatures of the 8- and 9-inch kind came rushing at our spinners. Sometimes a husky perch, painted like a Japanese print, rose from the pondwort and snatched

[1] Bob Darbee raises minnows and sells bait for a living. He is also the brother of Harry Darbee, master fly-tyer, about whom we'll learn more in Chapter 14.

the slow-twirling blade. Then, to prove that he still reigns as the wacky king of the weeds, a pickerel would bust into the lure and violently shake his head before leaping. Hardly a minute passed when one or both of us weren't playing a fish.

What made the game exciting was the fact that each of us was using a rod whose weight is a small fraction of your favorite outdoor magazine. Our lines tested a quarter of the weight of some of the pickerel we caught. Bob said he'd never had more fun fishing.

Hairline spinning tackle has three important roles. First, the gossamer line, the tiny lures, and the midget rod are the absolute refinement of practical equipment, and can be used effectively on civilized waters. Broadly speaking, ultra-light gear reaches its epitome under summer conditions on small streams and ponds where the fish have been thumped daily. There's no significant splash of line or lure to spook your quarry, and if they are willing to feed at all you stand a good chance of moving double-domed intellects like the brown trout—even in bright sunlight.

Using any reasonably light monofilament, you can cast worms, small minnows, hellgrammites, and those deadly inch-long crayfish to effective distances without weights. Hairlining isn't a method you can apply to big bass in weedy lakes or to the many-toothed northern pike. Nor, for that matter, can you use it in man-size rivers full of man-size trout—unless you are an expert and like to do things the hard way. Bear in mind, however, that a vast amount of our trouting is done on tame streams, where the average fish is creeled at less than 1 pound. Which brings us to the next point.

Secondly, the gear is so light that any small fish can provide fast sport. A fat bluegill or white bass, bucking against a 1- or 1½-ounce rod, will renew your respect for panfish. I have caught most kinds of the world's fish, and though I've never cared to have stuffed trophies on the wall, there's a space reserved over our fireplace for the first 3-pound bluegill I take. If he should be whipped on hairline gear, I'll probably install a spotlight and display him the way they hang ancestral portraits.

The wallop a sunfish packs is deceptive because he is built like a brewer's horse. Recently I caught an 11-inch pumpkinseed; typically, this sunfish was 10¾ inches in girth, or nearly as big around as he was long. My sunny scaled 2 pounds 2 ounces—which is about twice the average weight for a trout of the same length. There's a tendency among non-panfishers to underestimate all the muscle compressed between the nose and the tail of these spiny rays.

The third reason, and the one gaining popularity, is the personal sense of achievement you get in taking fish whose weight may be four or five times greater than the breaking strength of your line. Last summer my family made the annual pilgrimage to Bainbridge on the Susquehanna, where there are plenty of smallmouth bass. For the most part, large river bass are caught on crayfish and on minnows. Although we worked very hard to prove that theory, pound-size bass repeatedly took our baits.

Toward the end of the day I broke out my midget rod to liven things up. Using one of those new $\frac{1}{10}$-ounce bead-head spinners, dressed with a tiny pork-sliver, I worked it close to the gravel bottom. Though that tactic didn't discourage the small fish, it did finally hook a substantial bass.

The bronzeback rocketed about the currents and made one jump, which snapped the line. Judging by his bulk, the bass would have battered my top smallmouth for $\frac{1}{2}$-pound line (2 pounds 9 ounces), but that's pressing close to a six times ratio of test to weight. It's the same challenge as a three-thread sailfish in the over-seven-foot class. Comparatively speaking, every man can be a big-game fisherman with hairline tackle.

Behind these virtues is a dividend in practical conservation. With the growing interest in ultra-light gear, American trout ponds may be gradually relieved of specialized pressure as angling traffic switches to the invariably overabundant pan species. Countless lakes now teeming with perch and sunfish are earmarked for costly poisoning operations by fisheries managers simply because nobody bothers to harvest the crop. Yet these miniature fighters are a bountiful source of food and fun. I think parents frequently make the mistake of starting youngsters on hard-to-catch game fish when kids simply crave to hook something—anything. There's no better way of orienting a barefoot angler than on the village pond with child-size tackle.

A recent survey among the small boys and working fish cats in our neighborhood revealed that Mr. Rutherfurd's[2] lake was running amuck with yellow perch. I don't know how you feel about catching perch—but twiddling a spinner around the lily stems is high on my list of skills. Especially when the line tests $\frac{1}{2}$ pound and the lure is a mere $\frac{1}{20}$ ounce. Among the kids, though, the prime mover was the $25 prize offered by Bob Darbee for the most perch caught by any lad under fourteen from a number of no-limit lakes.

Locally, perch dine on young brook trout, and Darbee generously contributed to an effective measure of control. (Many conservation-minded citizens have found the award incentive a boon in other communities.) Taking my place in the ranks of the jet set, I discovered first that kids fish with plastic worms. Gone are the days of honest toil in the manure pile.

[2] Hugo Rutherfurd, prominent angler of 1930s and '40s.

Modern worms appear in antiseptically clean cellophane packages—all colors and all sizes. Apparently these soft-molded replicas are every bit as effective as the real crawler. Then, not unexpectedly, I found that spinning rods, with open- or closed-face reels, have replaced the cane pole. My only claim to distinction was the small size of my tackle, which impressed nobody, since I promptly lost three perch.

I had previously recounted in some detail how certain perch on Cape Cod spurned my best efforts with hairline gear until I mastered the very slow retrieve.[3] Well, the Rutherfurd perch have been multiplying so fast that I had the sensation of casting into a high-speed Mixmaster. The striped villains struck the instant my spoon hit the water. The fish ran a uniform ½ pound and with a touch that would have Willie Sutton envious I soon had the knack of hooking them. They required a gentle nudge at the strike. After a dozen minor victories, I walked around the lake to a cove made boggy by spring seepage, where I hoped to find a school of larger perch. Within a few casts the frail rod was dancing to what felt like the world record.

For the moment a 19-inch male brookie with his fire-engine-red belly can create the illusion of a giant perch. The trout slammed my wobbler while still thirty yards out, then swirled, showing his colors. Had the cast been short, he probably would have popped the monofil. But the cobweb line stretched and the barb held fast. I kept the drag at a minimum and let the fish have his head—charging in wide circles and pounding the surface with his tail. An emotion the hairliner cannot afford is rushing his quarry to the finish. A green fish at close range has a more direct pull against the rod, and one sacrifices a proportionate amount of flexibility in the line.

It took about fifteen minutes to exhaust the trout; then I coaxed him to my hand. He registered a shade over 2 pounds, which isn't remarkable except that it proved to me how much a man can refine his tackle and still hold a trout under ideal conditions. The ½-pound-test line mikes .0031 inch, which is so wispy that I have broken it against the callus on my forefinger when casting.

For the practical angler and the youngster alike, a 2-pound-test line is about right. In most brands of monofilament the diameter will measure .0055 inch. I play around with the lighter stuff for my own amusement, and occasionally out of respect to a difficult fish.

However, I have found in teaching children to cast that the average nine-year-old is coordinated enough for advanced tackle. More so than many

---

[3] See pages 132–135, *Spinning For Fresh and Salt Water Fish of North America.* Prentice-Hall, New York, 1952.

parents realize. His quarry seldom weighs over a pound, and adult-size tools designed for wild water just make Junior's hand sore.

I started my daughter, Susan, at the age of four with a 4-foot-long glass fly-rod tip, to which I tied an equal length of line. This gave her the feel of casting and a chance to imitate other members of the family. A year later we taped a reel to her "rod." She caught several fish that way, using cheese for bait. This season she has landed quite a few, including three nice trout—although trout are no more important to her than sunfish. Based on my experience with six nephews of varying ages, a dozen of the neighbors' kids and part of the Scout troop, the next step will be a superlight spinning outfit.

Once past the awkward age, a kid deserves the best tackle you can afford. It's hopeless to provide mismatched or adult-size gear and expect the little trapper to have fun. One comfortable outfit would be a 4½-foot tubular glass rod weighing 1½ ounces—coupled with one of those midget spin reels. Such mills usually weigh between 5 and 6 ounces; so the whole rig hefts a feather-light ½ pound.

You can teach a lad to use the outfit very quickly and, whether he casts live bait or artificials, the tackle is tailored to his requirements. After a season or two of catching fish, you can start him on the fly rod. It's important to get the catching part out of the way first—otherwise the more complicated process of fly casting doesn't make too much sense to him. I expect that some proud papa will write and tell me that Junior has been double-hauling since he was eight, but, generally speaking, a boy takes a serious view of the fly rod at about twelve years of age. In the meantime he can explore the busy world of panfish with a high ratio of success.

The hairliner has never had a more diverse microscopic lure colony than that now fixed under the fish's baleful lens. Today there are spinners from ⅟₃₂ ounce to ⅟₁₀ ounce, plus a variety of wobbling spoons weighing from ⅟₁₀ to ⅛ ounce, and one plug that is the smallest and lightest ever made. It is a jointed wiggler that weighs ⅟₁₈ ounce, is just one inch long and comes equipped with two pairs of No. 14 treble hooks. I don't care for so much hardware even on a small plug; so I remove the forward treble and the lure works equally well.

Presumably, the dwarf minnow is the progenitor of more plugs to come; miniature poppers and darters would be effective additions to the hairline arsenal. In general, however, the panfisher can get along easily with just two or three different lures. My favorites are a ⅟₁₀-ounce spinner with an inch-long blade, which I prefer in brass and gunmetal finishes, and a ⅟₁₀-ounce red-and-white wobbler. I keep other patterns and sizes on hand, but these are the baits that produce best for me.

2

LOOK, A FISH!

Outdoor writers are frequently asked to participate in local fishing tournaments, because the tournament managers feel a "famous fisherman" will bring out a larger crowd. However, except for participating in charity contests, most outdoor writers avoid tournaments like the plague. With some, it's the feeling that competition isn't what angling is all about. But with many others, it's the recognition that no matter what the outcome, amateur tournaments are a no-win proposition for the professional angler. If he wins a prize, folks will shrug or mumble resentful words about a big frog fishing in a small pond. If, on the other hand, he fares no better than most contestants, many spectators will smirk at the "phony" outdoor writer.

Such damned-if-you-do and damned-if-you-don't results even overshadow an outdoor writer's relationship with friends and family. Famous anglers are constantly besieged by acquaintances who want to go fishing. They could perfectly well go on their own, but some fishermen feel a "professional" has an inside track on fish behavior the way a crooked bookie has a hot tip on Lost Cause in the fifth. Sadly, because fish are fish, outdoor writers sometimes fail their friends, causing severe depression, migraine headaches, and canker sores all around.

Fortunately, Al McClane has no hang-ups about his professional piscatorial standing. The day Dr. Stanley Seton came to Al brandishing a brand-new spinning outfit and hinting heavily that he was all set for the big ones, Al couldn't very well turn him down. Miracle of miracles, everything about the trip was perfect—but the results. However, the outing inspired the following story that gently but firmly acquaints the reader with the fact of life that there's more to playing a fish than cranking on the reel handle.

GWR

LOOK, A FISH!

When you went to the tackle shop, you heard that spinning gear makes the ideal outfit for almost any kind of fishing and that it's the easiest to master in the shortest possible time. So you decided to become a spin fisherman and catch some fish quick. You asked questions around town and found that spin addicts like one reel or another, rods of certain lengths, and, of course, light lines to throw very light lures. After assembling the proper tools, you discovered that the winged sandals of science are hobnailed after all, and that fishing results must depend on the experience of the fisherman.

Little boys and old ladies can fling a plastic minnow over the schoolhouse, and I wouldn't care to debate the proposition that either one might possibly cast the pants off you and me, but when you get down to short strokes in the heavy-fish division, it takes considerable talent to flatten a slugger. Playing a big one is not like snaffling a small one. Unfortunately, most people have to practice on the wiggling kind, and when their legendary Old Bosco makes his fatal error, they blow the game.

Not long ago, I went fishing with my neighbor Stan Seton. We had sampled several of our local streams with indifferent results, so I thought it would be a fine idea to take him to a pond high up in the mountains where I know there are plenty of brown trout. We brought a canoe along, and frankly, there was no doubt in my mind that Stan was going to catch some walloping old cannibals, because he chose to use his new spinning outfit. It was still early in the season, and under the cold surface water those trout would take a spoon seriously.

No reader under ninety-five will fail to agree that a thousand fishing trips go by, undistinguished from one another, and then suddenly one comes along that is fatefully perfect. The air invigorates like an Alsatian wine, the lake is a miracle of blue clarity, the clouds are like puffy snowballs. The fish—well, they came up their spiral stairs to tap my dry fly. Perhaps this was the wrong way to begin fishing. The trout nearly tore holes in the canoe when they charged at Stan's wobbler. He hooked one after another. "Look, a fish!" he would say, and with his glass rod bent like an umbrella stave, he cranked so fast that his hand was a blur. Perhaps you will find this hard to believe, but mine is a serious narrative. Although we stayed on the pond until darkness ended our fishing, neighbor Seton lost every trout that grabbed his spoon.

I never realized there were so many ways to lose fish. Each time I explained why a trout got off, he'd lose the next one some other way. But add them all up and the reason why Stanley Seton dribbled away the fruits of angling was that he had never taken time to become familiar with his tackle. The fixed-spool reel can be a disembodied remote-control unit in the beginning; when the brake is set too heavy, the fish pulls up tight, stretching the line and bending the rod into an agonizing arc. For a long minute, the question only remained whether Stan would outfumble the trout before his line parted or the hook pulled loose.

When he did learn to flip the clutch off, the brake was set too light. Then the fish would bolt for the nearest stump while Stan cranked madly, but ineffectively. Although spinning reels make an appropriate sound when line is being pulled out, this only spurred him to more frantic winding. I hastily explained how he could use his forefinger to control the spool at such times, and then the trout caught him with his brake still loose, and the anti-reverse off, so the pick-up mechanism whirled like a dervish. Neighbor Seton still has a pair of perforated knuckles. If the fish had been smaller, I don't believe he would have had so much trouble, but between the excitement of seeing one heavy trout after another and trying to remember which way to turn the wing nut, poor Stanley Seton lost his buttons. I am not violating our friendship in telling you this, as the good doctor is otherwise a thoroughly modern and enlightened young man. Today he sits in the golden pews of the redeemed, but in one hectic afternoon he disproved that most flogged of all whipping boy hypotheses—that catching big fish is just luck.

Now if you are taking up spinning, I would suggest that you spend an evening getting familiar with your tackle, especially the reel. You might mount the reel and line in your rod, tie the line around a doorknob, and go through the motions of hooking and playing a fish. Turn the drag from one extreme to the other while pulling back on the rod; feel how much strain your tackle will take. A 4-pound-test line, for instance, can withstand a terrific amount of stress provided the pull is made smoothly. This is the way you're going to lead a fish to net. Locate the anti-reverse button which keeps the reel handle from turning when line is speeding out. Decide *now* when and how you are going to use it. And make as many dry casts as possible. No doubt critics may intervene during rehearsal, but they will gather in knotty respect when you draw forth the sonorous chords of grating gears.

Many spinning-rod anglers believe that only one brake tension is necessary in playing a fish. They set the drag so that the line peels off rather stubbornly. This is safe for small fish, but it's an artless practice with large ones. I think the best parallel is in big-game angling, where "star drag," or slipping clutch, reels have been in use for years. An experienced man in the fighting chair will readjust his brake many times during the course of play, taking in line and letting it out, depending on how critical the situation is at any given moment. And so in spinning, two different tensions are generally used if the best results are to be obtained; the first is the fishing tension, the second is the playing-your-fish tension.

The former, which is deliberately heavy, insures the penetration of the hook. If the clutch is set light, a sudden rap at your bait will jerk line off the spool. Add to this the flexibility of the rod and line and it becomes apparent that the slipping clutch is working against the angler at the instant of a heavy strike. Of course, the second tension is to set the clutch light so that the line does peel off easily. This insures that the line will not be broken while the fish is being played. Once hooked, it's a simple matter to turn the drag off, keeping just enough resistance against his runs to maintain some authority. If the fish finds a trouble spot, like plunging toward a weed bed, finger pressure on the spool should be substituted for the mechanical brake incorporated in the reel. You can check him by touching your forefinger against the rim of the spool and pulling back on the rod. This has the same effect as a very heavy drag but eliminates the danger of a line break if the fish makes another violent charge. As long as you are able to cope with the sudden movements of a heavy fish, there is no danger of anything breaking— and this goes for any kind of tackle. Anglers who rely on a heavy tension, enough to bring a fish in when the reel handle is turned, are literally "fighting," not playing, their quarry. You should attempt to pry a fish loose from the water—no more.

Rough handling probably accounts for more good fish lost than any other factor. A small bass, for instance, can be dealt with quickly, because its weight is so slight in relation to the strength of the tackle. But when you get anxious and attempt to handle a big one the same way, something is bound to pop. Often as not the angler just pulls the hook out while trying to force the play. Don't be afraid to let a fish have line. With your rod held up where the tip can take a good bend, it will absorb all the bulldogging a strong bass can execute. It is especially important to hold the rod high when you snag into a blistering surface runner like the bonefish. The more line you can hold off the water, the less surface resistance will be created. When a fish takes about one hundred yards of light spinning line or forty yards of fly line plus backing, your rod no longer has full control of the situation.

I don't like the term "pumping" in playing a fish on spinning tackle. I think it conveys the wrong idea. Actually, it is more of a stroking motion —a gentle nudging that gradually exhausts the fish.

Assuming that you have a light but firm drag working all the time, when the fish shows signs of weakening, touch the spool with your forefinger and raise the rod slowly backward; then lower it quickly while reeling up the slack.

Naturally, this motion brings the fish toward you, and it eliminates the possibility of line twist. Reeling against a dead weight for prolonged periods will twist a line considerably. When I first started spinning for steelhead, our monofilament lines weren't nearly as perfected as they are today, nor was my technique for that matter, and on a number of occasions I simply wore my fish down by constant cranking. After playing one heavy rainbow for about twenty minutes, I led him into shallow water where he could be released. Holding the rod under one arm, I got my fish loose, and about

[13]

that time I felt something running up the back of my jacket. I think that spinning line must have sputtered off the spool for about five minutes before it finally expired in a heap.

In the final phase of playing a fish with the fixed-spool reel, you can tighten up on the drag again, setting the tension so that line doesn't slip out, or use enough finger pressure to prevent the weight of the fish from pulling line out. Personally, I prefer the finger control, because large fish often make a last-minute flurry, and I can give slack instantly. More fish are lost at the net than in any other area. A recovering fish flopping on the surface and jerking against a tight line is the one most likely to break free. Remember, the line is much less flexible at close range and your rod will be subjected to a series of rapid-fire blows. A properly played fish, on the other hand, will cruise slowly at the top or roll on his side, making your task easy. In principle, most of what I've said about handling spinning tackle applies to any other method of fishing. There are mechanical differences in application, but the problems are similar.

When I first began fly fishing, I read every book available on the subject, and one of the things that impressed me was that their authors always recommended stripping the line in by hand when playing a fish. This worked fine until I started to hook an occasional big one; then a fist full of line got me in trouble, because the coils sometimes tangled when the fish made a last-minute dash. One of the finest rainbow trout I ever hooked in the Esopus River came close at hand before really starting his fight. The fish rose to my dry fly at least twenty yards up the pool, and after hooking him, he simply swam downstream toward me. I stripped the line rather quickly, and soon the great fish was thrashing on the surface. Just as I reached out with my net, the trout suddenly decided to put on a show and dashed upstream again. His run was powerful, and a horrible tangle of line flew from my hand and stuck in the ring guide. This stopped my rainbow short, but he leaped a yard in the air and came down with a bang, snapping the leader.

I have continued to strip small fish in, as there is no danger of sudden complications, but strong fish require careful parrying, and these I play directly from the reel. This is common practice among salmon, steelhead, and bonefish anglers, but the average fly-tosser, trained on fish measured in inches, is usually unprepared when his big chance comes. Take the position of the reel, for example, quite obviously, it has to hang below your rod when casting, but the problem starts when you have to crank—should the handle be to the left or right, or should the rod be turned over so that the reel is up? I can't see what I'm doing when the reel is below, and often as not I get the line piled up to a point where it thumps against the pillars, so turning the rod over with the reel handle on the right prevents uneven spooling. Whenever I go after steelhead, salmon, bonefish, or similar fleet-finned gamesters, I mount my reel with the handle to the left below, so that it turns up on the right.

There are people who act vigorously and innocently in dispatching a fish by cranking in every last inch of line. With tip-top guide popped against the fish's chin, young Izaak then wonders how to get his catch aboard without poking the pickerel down his vest. I've watched many a greenhorn with a fat bass made fast to the end of a casting stick, trying to drop his airborne victim into a landing net. Stan Seton attempted to swing about four pounds of threshing trout into the canoe that afternoon. For a second, the fish was hanging clear of the surface; then the brownie kicked out hard, breaking the line. The idea, of course, is to play the fish to a point where a length of line just two or three feet longer than the rod is out of the guides. Then, with your net dipped under water, it's a simple matter to lead the fish into the bag.

A good many people advise that you lower your rod tip when a fish jumps. The thesis is that when a fish pops out of the water your rod is subjected to a sudden strain. I have always found the reverse to be true—even if the rod is held in an almost vertical position, it's more apt to relax. After sitting through many thousands of feet of slow-motion movies, the most striking similarity from one jump sequence to the next has been the belly of slack that a leaping fish throws into the line when he soars over the water. Perhaps the fish might bend your rod if he made a long broad jump directly away from you, but as far as I'm concerned, "lower your tip" is an overworked cliché. The same goes for the wizard who conceived the tactics of pulling a fish off balance at the peak of his jump by jerking the rod back. This charlatan passes through the outdoor reading of our day with practiced dexterity. The object of turning fish over is to tire them more quickly, according to the practitioners, but with anything short of heavy tackle, it's a sure bet to snap the hooks loose.

No matter how good a man gets at fishing, he'll never land every fish he hooks. There are too many wise old finsters paddling around who know all the tricks in your book, and most of them are lost in the first few seconds of play because they have the advantage of surprise. They are no more predictable than the collision of the earth with a comet. Some fish make as many mistakes as people make, however, and that's when experience counts. Take the case of two bass I met in Texas not long ago. The first one wasn't the biggest bass in Texas, but he churned out of the water, did a whipstall, and hung over Koon Kreek just long enough to make my eyeballs spin. The bigmouth hit for deck with his engines wide open, and before I could shut my mouth, the bass had jerked the line around a stump. I don't know why I told my guide to back the boat up and go ahead in the same breath—but he tried both. While I pulled hopelessly at the stump, the moss-back made a fast circle that hitched a few yards of nylon solidly, and he pulled free.

Now, there wasn't much I could do in this case. My mistake was in telling the guide to paddle through a jungle of stumps instead of holding the boat in open water, where we'd at least have a chance of maneuvering. The second fish lay right at the edge of a thick weed bed along the shore; being a high period, the water was actually some distance behind the weeds and up in the brush. The bass swallowed my little surface popper, then bolted straight back through the weeds, over a log, and into a submerged bush. At the very instant my fish bulled into the grass, I flipped off the drag completely and let him run on a slack line. It was an easy matter then to paddle along and pick the line out of the places it had tangled and finally, by taking the line in hand, gently lead the bass to boat. This was hardly an exciting encounter, but I didn't lose any tackle.

No doubt these words will fall upon many stony ears, because teaching young anglers how to play a fish is no less perfect than teaching the beginning artist how to paint. Older anglers know that the natural tempo of misfortune is but a proper contrast to the good days astream, and it is interesting to consider that the most nostalgic recollections are of the fish that got away.

3

THE MYSTERIOUS MISTER X

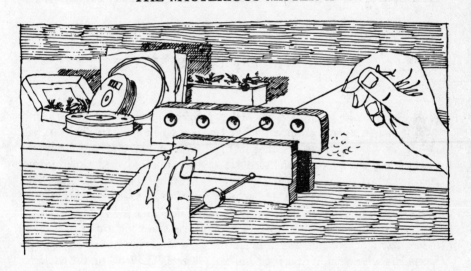

Now we're going to discuss X-ratings—not movies, but leaders. Probably no single facet of fly fishing has confused the beginner more and made him cringe before the Professor Corys of the sport than the mysteries of leader type, diameter, and pound test. Certain high priests of angling, to whom form is more important than content, seem to derive unnatural pleasure in subduing—nay, forever crippling—the confidence of breathless novitiates by spinning a web of occult nonsense about rod length, line type, and especially leader size. In recent years, some American manufacturers have attempted to clear the air by citing leader diameters in thousandths of an inch and pound test. But since the Japanese and Europeans prefer to measure their leaders in millimeters, the confusion can only be alleviated by digesting A. J.'s review and simplification of this most perplexing problem.

GWR

THE MYSTERIOUS MISTER X

While looking through the *Atlantic Salmon Journal* recently I came across a photo of myself hooked into a high-jumping steelhead. What a western trout is doing in that chaste publication is the editor's concern, but the picture reminded me of the unprecedented situation we faced ten years ago when all the quality silkworm gut had disappeared. The fish in the photo snapped my leader with no effort at all. I probably would have lost him anyway in one of the scores of techniques I have developed for losing steelhead, but that British Columbia trip was a nightmare of broken leaders. My stock of gut was prewar vintage, and obviously extracted from caterpillars who wouldn't eat their mulberry leaves. The label on the package simply read *Refina Superior*, over which somebody had inked the symbol *1X*. The handwriting showed the scholastic detachment that any dogface will recall in "Kilroy Was Here" or "Psst" or (upon entering some broken-down real estate) the classic "Off Limits." Theoretically, a 1X leader point should have stopped every fish dead in his tracks, but by using the term *Refina Superior* the manufacturer expressed some doubt about the worm's talent. He was saying fine diameter—but second quality. Unfortunately, when it comes to leaders, ignorance is not bliss. The only thing more important than a leader is the line, and both are more important than the rod. The fly is less important than the angler.

[18]

There exists in our TV-sodden era a mathematical system of estimating the popularity of various programs. A giveaway show having a rating of 25.5, for instance, may shake the advertising world but for you to get some basis for comparison you must also know that the President of the United States scored a mild 16.5 on his annual message to Congress.

Angling has a similar system, which is the emotional reason we never dropped the symbol X from the language of fly fishing. Try to imagine a hobnailed amateur who has just snaffled a 5-pound trout on 3X gut as he swaggers up to the bar with a sense of assured triumph and says, "I took him on a .007-inch point." Where's the impact? Nobody would buy him a drink. The mysterious X put meaning in cold figures. Any well-reared young man knows that 1X is heavy, 2X is lighter, 3X lighter yet, and anything finer than 4X is strictly for the pros. Or so it would seem. Actually, with modern synthetics, the demise of a 5-pound trout on a 3X point is not the glorious feat of yesteryear. Many nylons in a .007 diameter run 300 percent stronger than silkworm gut, and spin casters use drums of the stuff in subduing fish twice as large. The figures that have critical value to modern fly fishers are inch-increment diameters rather than the purely symbolic terms that muddle everybody, viz., X and —/5. Numerical diameters provide a precise description of a leader taper when related to strand length.

Back in 1949, I ran a series of leader tapers which many anglers adopted and were also later sold by Messrs. J. J. S. Walker, Bampton of Alnwick, England. I have no connection with the British firm, or any other tackle company for that matter, so the use of the name "McClane Tapers" is an arbitrary rather than a commercial reference. These leaders are discussed at some length in the book, *Still Water Fly Fishing* by T. C. Ivens and not unexpectedly in one of my own books. Mr. Ivens, however, demonstrated their value cross-sectionally, *i.e.*, if a diameter is doubled we multiply the momentum at a given speed by four; thus the ratio of wind resistance decreases, *ad infinitum*.

In Europe this is now called the Square Law Leader, but aside from these highly theoretical aspects of design, I never could find a perfect taper until I began thinking in terms of cross section and length. The mysterious X had me trapped in antique ideas. You can, for instance, use 6X points in modern synthetics and get results comparable to the 3X that made Grandpa a real hot rod. A quality 6X nylon can check out at 1.75 pounds, which is where 3X silkworm gut of top grade will pop. But before you buy a stock of lightweight leaders, remember one very important fact—the leader butt diameter must be at least .016 inch in the first five feet of a nine-foot taper, or you'll never turn the fly over. I would get to 6X with a forty-inch .018

butt, followed by .017 or .016 in the next three feet. Mass and weight are the ever-loving problems in getting a leader to carry itself to the point where momentum will straighten your cast out. I linger on this, as we are numbed by the habit of looking at X, when X doesn't tell us much of anything about a leader.

The popularity of X as a diameter symbol is about 200 years old. When watchmakers and jewelers made their own draw plates, there were three mathematical systems in use—the metric, linear, and Swiss ligne. To resolve their differences, the holes of draw plates were marked in an X progression, so that a 5X watch part would be the same in Switzerland as it was in France or anywhere else. A century later, silkworm gut was drawn on these same plates by pulling it through a mounted jewel bored to the desired diameter.

This requires skill and poses certain material problems. Caterpillars, from which gut comes, are not prone to assembly-line production. The raw material is extruded in different lengths and thicknesses. If the strand is .003 inch larger than the size desired, then it has to be passed through successive holes and gradually shaved to the correct diameter. From this we get the symbol —/5, which very few amateurs would recognize as our spook X in disguise. The symbol —/5, which we use for all sizes greater than 0X, is a basic draw-plate measurement (or point of reference) in that it is half X or half-drawn. Thus a ⅕ strand (.020 inch) is twice the diameter of an 0X strand.

As you know, drawing removes the outer surface of the gut, leaving it round and smaller in diameter; carried to its theoretical end, a natural .020-inch strand (which is about the caterpillar's maximum) could be reduced eventually by progressive drawing to a .001-inch strand, or a 10X point. It was "half drawn" in progression at the ¹⁰⁄₅ or .011-inch size.

This system of measurement is not only complicated but impractical. On the Continent, which is today a large source of our synthetic leader materials, manufacturers express diameters in hundredths of a millimeter. You have probably seen this on French monofilament spools marked ²⁶⁄₁₀₀ or ³⁰⁄₁₀₀ or whatever the size may be. Our system, of course, is in one-thousandths of an inch. Here again we can't get accurate conversion from millimeter to inch even after multiplying the European size by .0003937 (¹⁄₁₀₀mm.), because there is no exact metric equivalent. So we meet X again.

Spinning-line distributors have a safe out in that threadliners are concerned with pound-test ratings, and approximate diameters are good enough for their purposes. The rated breaking strain is also valuable information to the leader buyer when presented along with butt and tippet diameters. But for the man making his own tapers, a profile consisting of strand lengths in pound-test figures is too often inaccurate. You must work with a micrometer.

Before pursuing X any further, I would like to point out that silkworm gut is still widely used by fly fishermen in the U. S. Some of our best anglers won't touch nylon in fine sizes and will argue endlessly against synthetics. Personally, I never use gut anymore because caterpillars can't produce long enough strands to make the forty- and forty-four-inch leader butts I favor. I also make double-tapered leaders which jump .003 inch or more between strands, and with silkworm gut the safety factor in knotting materials of greatly different sizes is very poor. I further believe that a leader should float for dry-fly fishing, and nylon is much less dense than gut. There are other reasons, too; I find gut awkward to handle and keep properly soaked. It's more expensive and it deteriorates more quickly than synthetics.

Although I had trouble with slipping knots when nylon first appeared, there has been no cause for doubt since. For example, an 0X nylon can be used with perfect safety for trout in the up-to-15-pound class, and for Atlantic salmon in the 20-to-30-pound range. I would never consider comparable silkworm gut for the same type of fishing. By modern standards, a .010-inch tippet will test about 6 pounds, which is plenty strong for the man using a light fly rod.

The average bamboo rod reaches full strength under a 3-pound pull. Maximum stress before rupture varies, of course, depending on the taper, length, weight, and material of which the rod is made. You can break more leaders with glass rods, but any man who knows his job is not going to lean over backward to coax fish ashore. Nylon is more elastic than gut, and I believe it gives small dry flies, especially, a more lifelike float.

This is a vast improvement over the not-too-distant past, when the only synthetic leader material was Japanese gut—an Oriental fantasy made from raw silk passed through a boiling bath of animal glue and seaweed extract. The silk was reduced to an almost liquid state, then saturated with glue and hardened. Unfortunately, Jap gut had a strong tendency toward becoming unglued at the most embarrassing times, and matters deteriorated when frugal manufacturers started mixing cotton with the silk. This "gut" absorbed water and had the same characteristics as wet string. Pound-test ratings on Jap gut were reliable as long as you didn't fish with the stuff. For this reason, silkworm gut held a virtual monopoly on the purist market until nylon was developed. Us poor folks bought the cheaper Japanese product before World War II; I remember when ten yards of Jap gut sold for about ten cents, and one nine and a half-foot silkworm-gut leader sold for a dollar. Thus, the great bulk of tapered and level leaders were identified in terms of their

VITAL STATISTICS ON LEADERS

Trade name, diameter, breaking strength—here
they're lined up side by side for your edification

Silkworm Gut Classification	Draw plate gauge size	Diameter in 1/1000 inch	Approximate diameter in 1/100 mm.	Test in pounds silkworm gut	Test in pounds synthetics
HEBRA	1/5	.020	50/100	10–14.50	17–22
IMPERIAL	2/5	.019	48/100	8.75–13.50	16–20
MARANA 1st	3/5	.018	45/100	7–10	14–15
MARANA 2nd	4/5	.017	43/100	6–9.50	13–17
PADRON 1st	5/5	.016	40/100	5–8	11.50–12
PADRON 2nd	6/5	.015	38/100	4.50–7	10.75–11
REGULAR	7/5	.014	35/100	4–6	9.25–10
REGULAR	8/5	.013	32/100	3–4.50	8.50–9
FINA	9/5	.012	30/100	2.75–3.50	6.75–7.50
FINA	10/5	.011	28/100	2.50–3	6.25–7
REFINA	0X	.010	26/100	2–2.50	5.75–6
REFINA	1X	.009	24/100	1.90–2.25	5–5.50
DRAWN	2X	.008	22/100	1.75–2	3.50–4.75
DRAWN	3X	.007	18/100	.75–1.75	2.50–3.75
DRAWN	4X	.006	16/100	.70–.90	2.25–3
DRAWN	5X	.0055	15/100	.50–.75	1.75–2.25
DRAWN	6X	.005	14/100	.30–.50	1.50–2
DRAWN	7X	.0045	12/100	.25–.35	.75–1.25

Pound-test ratings of silkworm gut represent minimum/maximum of *Natural Selecta* after soaking in water for one-half hour. The range is given for twenty breaks per diameter. Ratings of synthetics are minimum/maximum dry test of one brand of platyl and those brands of nylon selected at random; each material was tested five times to constitute the twenty breaks per diameter. Fractional differences were carried to the nearest .25 pound in all sizes larger than 4X.

pound-test rating. This is not a very useful system today except for level leaders, and these have no value to fly fishermen.

There are several reasons why the pound-test system of leader identification is impractical. To begin with, we can't say precisely what 1X, 2X, or any other size of gut will test. Silkworm gut has a considerable variation in quality and the manufacturer would achieve nothing by break-testing them, since each strand came from a different caterpillar that was about to spin a cocoon but suddenly ended in a vinegar bath. Gut is classified by highly skilled workers on the basis of natural appearance: The perfect strands are *Natural Selecta;* the not-quite-perfect ones (which they will improve by a process known as mazantining) are simply *Selecta;* good second-quality gut becomes *Natural Superior;* while second-quality gut to be improved by mazantining is *Superior.* Finally, all third-quality gut is categorized as *Estriada.*

"Mazantining" is a polishing operation done with a linen cloth to remove slight defects in the gut, and it causes those familiar thin spots that drive the angler with a micrometer nuts. One lot of 3X gut might test .75 pound, while the next bundle can test 1.75 pounds. A 1-pound-test difference is not trivial, and if we failed to look for X in our conversion we could be talking about any diameter from 0X to 3X.

In Murcia, Spain, where the raw material originates, the five aforementioned grades of gut are further classified in nine different categories according to diameter. In the Esperanto of trade, our 3X might be a *Refina Natural Selecta* or a *Refina Estriada.* Without going through the whole classification (see table), a *Natural Refina* can be drawn down to 3X, or any other X size for that matter. Due to the plumbing of our leaf-chomping caterpillar, the maker knows that at .007 inch the gut will have a breaking strain somewhere around 1 pound. Now, here's where the whole X system goes to pot; a comparable nylon (or its counterparts) in .007 inch will test 3 pounds to 4 pounds. Although synthetics differ in test per diameter from one maker to the next, there is a redeeming virtue in that a single brand will be consistent. A uniform product results from the purely mechanical process. Horses' tails, pickled worms, and seaweed extract are less amenable to systematizing.

The angler who ties his own leaders from synthetic materials can experiment with different brands until he finds one that is superior, *i.e.,* stronger per diameter, with greater resistance to abrasion, more or less flexibility, and finish depending on his own ideas about color and gloss.

For no valid reason, synthetics permissibly measure .001 inch larger than drawn gut in sizes from 0X to 4X and some manufacturers use this standard but I have not indicated it in the table because gauge size is relative to the inch-increment diameter. Why bother your head with X, when he's an exploded myth, an exorcised hobgoblin for one hundred years? Has it occurred to you, gentlemen, that the angler who brags of a 5-pound trout on a 3X point doesn't deserve a drink?

Or does he?

4

DESIGNING YOUR FLY LEADER

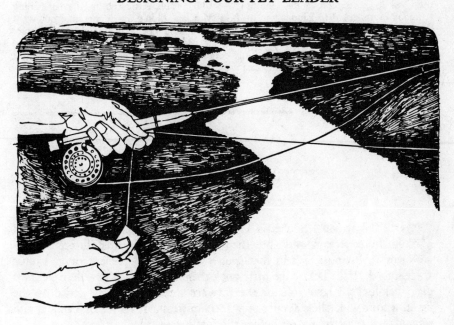

In 1954, Al and Patti McClane signed a lease on a 3,000 acre estate near Turnwood, New York. With one house already established in Florida, the object was to divide the fishing year so the cold months provided saltwater angling, while spring, summer, and early autumn were spent on fresh water. In either case "home" was to be a base for trips throughout the world.

When you look at a map of lower New York State, you find Turnwood plumb in the middle of some of the most historic trout country in North America. The Delaware, Willowemoc, Drybrook, Neversink, and Esopus all lie within easy driving distance, and the Beaverkill runs through the heart of town. A. J. fished all these rivers as a small boy, and in fact visited the Gould estate uninvited on more than one dark night in the 1930s since Drybrook flowed from it through the Van Kleeck farm. This occasioned an amusing moment with Kingdon Gould, heir to the railroad magnate's properties. A fishing pal, Brigadier Charles K. Lindemann, Counsel to the British Empire stationed in Washington, D. C., invited A. J. for a weekend on "some stream in the Catskills" as a guest of the Goulds—it was Drybrook. After the first day of fishing Kingdon commented to Lindemann on how McClane didn't waste any time but went directly to every good pool, even the barren-looking pocket water that everybody bypassed, where he caught and released trout after trout. "I believe that man could fish blindfolded," Gould observed. This comment was more accurate than Al's host realized. McClane had never before seen the water by daylight.

GWR

DESIGNING YOUR FLY LEADER

Early this season I hooked a 17-inch brook trout below a log barrier on our home stream, and since then have lost him on three different occasions. Moving a fish in that spot is difficult. To prevent drag, I must wade into the riffle below the little pool, then aim the back cast between two giant hemlocks. I have to shift the forward direction slightly and drop the fly in a foot-wide slick about forty feet upstream. It's a lot of trouble, and some days I snap the fly off before the cast is finished.

When everything goes right, the fly twirls around on the slick for several seconds, provided the line is slack, then bounces downstream. The trout, for some reason, always floats back, looking as though he had the fly balanced on the end of his nose. Nine times out of ten he will refuse the pattern and dash under his log. On rare occasions he will make a pass at it, but only when my tippet is refined to .0047 or .0031. I don't like to go below 6X, but apart from our original engagement, when the stream was flowing whisky-red after a rain and a heavier leader went undetected, my almost daily inspection tours have rigid requirements.

Although no leader can be completely invisible to a fish, it's evident that the finest tippets are less alarming. If I show my trout a pattern on .0094 or .0083 he doesn't even tip his hat, but the really hairy points puzzle him. Recently he followed a Guinea Spider on .0031 all the way to my rod tip, and after examining me with the indulgent gaze of a meat inspector at a livestock show he slowly swam off.

I was just as glad, because 7X is a feeble support for a widely hackled spider, and the chances are I would have popped him off on the strike. If I ever subdue that trout again, it will probably happen just at dark or after a rain, when I can sneak one in on 3X. However, that would take some of the fun out of our game. I'll feel chin-high to a beer keg until I can hook him in bright sunlight.

From an angling standpoint, a perfectly presented fly at forty feet is far more effective than an awkward splashing cast at forty yards. Complete mastery of the rod at normal distances from all positions and under varying wind conditions is the ideal most of us seek. I am also inclined to think, looking back over a good many years spent at fly casting, that a large measure of success that one experiences comes from paying careful attention to details, such as stretching the leader before fishing, or lengthening the butt section, or correcting the tippet size.

The leader is not only the connecting link between line and fly but the agency that delivers the feathers softly onto the surface. Even when a cast is checked high in the air, the weight of a falling line is sufficient to send out alarming ripples in calm water.

To make a perfect presentation, the leader must be designed correctly. Now a lot of people have different ideas on what makes a balanced leader, but that's because it must be tailored to the nylon, Dacron, terelyne, silk, or vinyl-plastic line being used and to the conditions under which it's fished. Even the modern knotless synthetics get altered several times a day when flies are cut off or new diameters added to suit the fishing.

If I start at the bottom pool on our home stream, I can fish up to the dam, a distance of about half a mile, with 3X or 4X tippets. The water here flows through heavy woods—big hemlocks, alders, and beeches—and its broken surface is constantly in shadow. Above the dam I have to wade knee-deep on an open sunlit flat. A fat log edging the bank is my favorite place, but that's only because of a past performance. Two years ago I caught a 19-inch brown trout that was rising next to the log, but I haven't taken a single fish there since.

The surface is so smooth and the water so transparent and shallow that the present tenant flees while my line point is still in the air. I concentrate on floating my fly along the edge of the banks at tufts of grass and tree roots, but for all my stealth and caution I don't take many trout on the flat unless the tippet is 5X or 6X and the flies are No. 16 or smaller. So when I reach the dam I always stop and rebuild my leader, then stretch it out perfectly straight with a piece of rubber. Because I've gone through this ritual so often, I know exactly how much ..0059 or .0047 my regular brand of knotless leader requires.

Most of the new wrinkles in accessories and equipment nowadays are designed to make fishing easy and pleasant to almost any degree one might want. They all work, but no item of tackle is ever perfect. There is always a drawback to offset an advantage. A knotless synthetic leader, for instance, is the epitome of simplicity when you recall the old days of Spanish and Jap gut; if the Spanish variety wasn't soaked enough it fractured at the knot or generally acted like a coiled spring. Jap gut had the same failing, and when immersed too long it fell apart like wet newspaper.

Nevertheless there is a very passionate school of anglers who insist on using Spanish gut. I don't believe that anybody can honestly say the silkworm leader is in principle better or worse than synthetics. Natural gut has a rigidity that some synthetic materials lack; I find that casting a completely limp leader is a handicap because it doesn't unroll smoothly. Some stiffness is needed for the leader to transmit the final pulse of energy that kicks the fly out.

Actually, developments in synthetic materials such as platyl and nylon have provided other advantages, and getting the best of everything is impossible. One must decide from personal experience. I use the knotless leaders regularly—rebuilding their tapers (which heretofore have been more or less uniform) according to what I need. Usually I find that ready-mades are too light in the butt and too heavy in the tippet.

I don't use level leaders at all. The level kind, which is uniform in diameter throughout its length, is used chiefly for bait and spinner fishing. This leader is a poor substitute for the tapered type in fly fishing, and considering the low cost of modern synthetics, it is no longer justified even by its cheapness.

The two main parts of a leader are the tippet and the butt. The tippet is the end section or strand of material to which the fly is tied; its diameter is determined by water or fishing conditions and the size of fly used. At the opposite end is the butt, or first strand, to which the line is connected. The butt is the heavier portion; generally speaking, it should be about two-thirds the diameter of the line point. Most American double-tapered fly lines are .030 at the end, so a .020 butt is generally correct. If you use any of the modern weight-forward lines made with a plastic coating, their points will measure from .033 to .037, and for these a .022 leader butt is necessary. My favorite trout lines vary from .022 to .025 at the point, so I begin all my leader tapers with a .018 or .019 butt. Being a nut on the subject of presentation, I stick to the lightest line sizes available—a preference that you may happily ignore.

The most common mistake in leader design is making a butt too light and too short. Some of the tapers in current fashion start at .014, which is a hangover from the days when gut leaders were the only kind available.

Mechanically, the oldtime leader maker was a conformist because of his material. When making a synthetic leader today, we can jump .002 between sizes without sacrificing strength—and go to sixty-inch lengths or longer if the design requires it. Equally important, synthetics can be produced in finer diameters than gut.

Generally speaking you will have to do a considerable amount of fishing until you find the leaders with which you can cast best under different conditions. They will vary from line to line, depending on their forward tapers and the length and diameter of their points. Once you get the proper leader, attempt to duplicate it in subsequent purchases. Of course, if you tie your own (and it's really very easy) the chances of learning exactly the right formula are much better. The basic design that I follow in making leaders can be formulated as 60 percent heavy, 20 percent graduation, and 20 percent tippet.

You will find this same formula in Charles Ritz's book, *A Fly Fisher's Life*. However, we arrived at this design independently; in fact, it was described in a book I wrote back in 1953. Charley uses from forty-two to sixty-six inches of butt section in his approximately nine-foot leaders. I seldom use more than forty inches, but follow it with a thirty-six-inch section of a slightly smaller diameter varying no more than .002 inch. I have to start getting some graduation in the butt end because I normally go down to 5X or 6X, whereas Ritz stays close to 3X for his fishing.

Basically, we both found that the long, heavy butt turned over better under most wind conditions. You may have a better taper, but if your present leader design isn't satisfactory our system is worth a try. Begin by using a bit more than one-half of the total length in heavy diameters, say from .020 to .018. After the heavy material tie in short graduating strands.

These stepdown pieces serve to reduce the diameter rapidly from .018 to the finer tippet sections you would normally use. With synthetics you can skip .002 between each strand and still hold the knots.

The tippet section should be from twenty to thirty inches long, the exact length depending on how well it turns over. Here's a rule of thumb: a fly that is proportionately large in relation to the diameter of the tippet requires a shorter tippet. A thirty-inch .0059 (5X) tippet, for instance, will roll over perfectly with No. 16 and No. 18 flies; if you tie on a bushier-hackle No. 10, the fly will tend to fall back over the leader. It will also twist in the air and weaken the tippet. This can be improved somewhat by cutting the .0059 down to about eight or ten inches, but it's better to replace the tippet with a heavier diameter. For a No. 10 fly, the tippet size should run from .0083 to .0094.

I have experimented below water with dyes of all shades, but my general impression is that a dull finish is harder to detect than a bright finish, and that color really doesn't matter. So many reflections exist in the soda-pop world of a trout stream that at times I even had difficulty seeing the feet of a nearby angler. A splashing line point or a wiry leader that floated in little hoops on top seemed to be the two most obvious indications that the fly was a phony. So, for my part, whether the leader floats or not is immaterial. I use an opaque or nearly translucent synthetic that might be called a dull mist finish and let the leader drift as it will. The important things are that the taper brings the fly down gently, and that it lies flat in the surface film.

There are four items that every serious fly caster should have in his jacket. The first, a small piece of soft rubber, is one you can't afford to be without. Cut out a two-inch square from an old inner tube and keep it in your leader pouch. This will earn more fish than a dozen new fly patterns. Before you begin fishing, rub the leader until it's perfectly straight and pliable. This will get some of the stretch out of it and prevent kinking. It takes only a few seconds to do this, and it will make a big difference in your casting.

You will also need a stock of leader material in various sizes, say from ⅖ down to 7X. These come wound on small, flat plastic spools and fit easily into a jacket pocket. There is a dispenser pack available that holds four spools of different sizes; the dispenser has a cutting edge that facilitates streamside alterations.

It's a good idea to keep a small scissors handy for trimming knots and poking the varnish out of flies' eyes.

The fourth item, a micrometer, can be kept in your tackle box or in camp. Mine is a Starrett No. 1010. This is an expensive precision model, but even a cheap one is better than no micrometer. It's impossible to build leaders if you go by pound-test ratings; these vary so widely in diameter that you may easily end up with light sections behind heavy ones.

It should be evident that the length and the weight of the leader to be used are dependent on the water conditions and the size of the fish. For instance, when the water is discolored and you're using a large hook like a bucktail, you can safely work with a leader on the heavy side. It doesn't have to be too long either. If you're casting small flies in clear water, the leader should be light and long; it's impossible to present a tiny fly properly on a short, heavy leader. I consider a seven and a half-foot leader short, and anything over nine feet long. I commonly use lengths of ten to twelve feet and have gone up to fourteen feet on occasion when fishing nymphs deep in mountain lakes.

In general, the leader for nymph fishing should have a very long tippet section to get the fly down fast and to remain as inconspicuous as possible. For most trout fishing I don't pay much attention to the pound-test ratings. On the average stream I seldom hook many fish over $1\frac{1}{2}$ pounds, and while I may break off on the infrequent heavier trout with 5X or 6X, I find that these tippets hold up to 3 pounds if handled gently. The fine stuff is a problem if the fish come big, but sometimes it's the only way to move them, and the higher ratio of strikes provides some success. In rivers where 4-pound trout are common (there are few such waters) I'd try to stay at 3X, but I wouldn't hesitate to go down to .0059 if the conditions required it.

Of course salmon, steelhead, and black bass are going to demand heavy diameters not merely because of their weight but because you must use much larger flies and lures. I once fished a river in Norway where 80-pound-test leaders were necessary to poke out No. % flies in a head wind. But this was sloppy casting in high water and not proper angling.

If you're a beginner, it's a good idea to spend some time on a very quiet pool just studying your line and leader. Make average casts from thirty to forty feet, using a nine-foot leader with fly attached. Remember to massage the nylon first with a piece of rubber so that it falls perfectly straight. Watch both the back and the forward casts. If the back stroke isn't rolling out straight to begin with, you have a casting problem. But if the line unrolls without humps and the leader flops around as though unrelated to the cast and falls in a heap on the water, then it's time to start building a new taper.

Here is one that is practically foolproof for honest H points of .025 or a shade heavier. Start with a butt of forty-two inches of .018, then add a second heavy section of twenty-nine inches of .016. This is about 60 percent of a nine-foot leader. Now add three 6-inch graduating strands of .014, .012, and .010. For the tippet, tie on twenty inches of .008. This all runs a fraction over nine feet, but after stretching the leader with a piece of rubber you'll be able to cast it with your bare hand. Any fly from No. 10 to No. 14 should sail out, turn over, and sit down daintily.

5

DRY-FLY FUNDAMENTALS

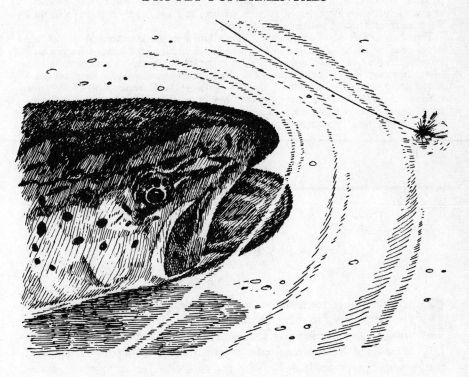

When I read the following story for the first time in 1954, I owned an oversize fly rod and an overpowered (automatic) fly reel, but had yet to try either in fresh water. My father had purchased this equipment in response to my craving for "sporting tackle." Obviously the bait-casting, boat, and surf rods I was used to handling on salt water were unacceptable since they so rarely appeared on the cover of outdoor magazines pictured alongside a supine fish. Thus, while I happily made a nuisance of myself by taking the fly tackle offshore to catch mackerel and bluefish—forcing everyone on board to stop fishing until I got my quarry under control—I had not yet taken this gear onto the ponds and streams where allegedly it belonged. The simple truth was I was afraid of looking foolish. I had had no formal instruction in the handling of a fly rod, and most of the material I read on this score, supposedly written to simplify learning, only made it seem more compound-complex. The business of what lines, leaders, and most of all, what flies to use left me gaping in reverent awe before the stentorian salesmen of Abercrombie & Fitch. Thus when opportunities to go bass or pickerel fishing came my way, I still packed along my trusty bait-casting stick. But one weekend when I was asked to visit a friend and his father in their cabin on a Vermont trout stream, I was unaccountably sick.

Then I read "Dry-Fly Fundamentals." Like a knight in shining armor, A. J. McClane strode into the midst of the murmuring cloud and with lucid strokes of his pen slew demons and dragons, trolls and witches, on every hand. Fly fishing was easy, he said. More than that, it was fun! Imbued with the spirit of this article, my brothers and I immediately planned an assault on the trout pool in the Palisades Amusement Park. Although we cheated on a few trout with bits of worm smuggled past the 25-cents-for-15-minutes ticket taker, we each caught at least one fish on untainted flies floating in the surface film. That afternoon and forevermore, my fear of dry-fly fishing was dispelled.

GWR

DRY-FLY FUNDAMENTALS

Dry-fly fishing furnishes an army of technical straw men for experts to strike down in their sermons. It's a remote temple, where men are heard mumbling in a void about insects that will emerge on St. Swithin's Day. Transfixed by tapered shafts wrapped and decorated with subdued mathematical precision, bursting with complicated tapers, graphs, and formulae, and facing tiers of colored feathers in their cardboard tombs on the walls of a fly tyer's shop, the modern dry-fly angler consists of considerably more human error and fewer interludes of perfection than the outside world might see. It's a glory game, the glamour game, a parlor game, a floating crap game, and it causes men to shout aloud, alone or in congregation. It left Skues rubbing bindings with Shakespeare, and Samuel Phillippe, builder of the first split-cane rod, is eulogized with a fanaticism rare in these lax times. Before you become complacently entangled in thread-line, let it be known that your purely mechanical assaults against the trout fall far short of the transcendent ecstasies hinted at in this book. The floating fly will give you a charge, a bang, a kick like a four-dollar shotgun, or ten straight passes, or taking a pair of teal flaring left and right.

Some people hesitate to take up dry-fly fishing because they think it is too hard to learn, and they are not sure about the end. Others think the tackle is too expensive and that dry-fly fishing is out of fashion. Actually, dry-fly fishing is easy, and the tackle is not expensive.

In the arsenal of casting you can find a conventional double-tapered line, which is better than a level line. But if you can't afford the tapered kind, a level one will do. I have caught hundreds of trout on level lines that cost no more than a dollar. The secret is to use a long leader with a heavy butt. This slows down your cast so that it doesn't slap the water. Any fly rod can be made to cast dry flies, but if you're buying a rod for the first time, get one weighing about 5½ ounces in an 8½-foot length with a trout action. Except for casting for very large fish, like steelhead trout and salmon, reels are not very important. Any light single-action reel will do. As to leaders, I'll say briefly that the beginner should have them in two lengths and weights—seven and a half feet long, tapered to 2X for casting on broken water, and a longer, finer one nine feet in length tapered to 3X for flat water. Add to this a few simple flies, a bottle of oil to float them, and the abstract air of a man devoted to a difficult mission; not a voice will be lifted in the length and breadth of our land to say that you are other than a dry-fly angler.

Some unexpected problems are ahead, but the only way a man has ever become good at the game is to fly-fish for as long as he lives, or as long as he feels like fishing. Come with me and I will show you why other kinds of angling are no more potent than a jelly bun, and let every young man observe what follows with attention.

You have read the casting booklets and practiced on the lawn, and you learned one fact above all else—that the various stages of a cast are not separate motions, but instead one motion, each part blending to create the whole, and you have practiced to make your casting look and feel like one smooth movement. The dry fly you know is almost always fished upstream, standing

[35]

on its stiff hackle and tail, and it will float at all times. A wet fly, with its soft, flowing hackle is fished literally wet, or below the surface, but insects are walking in the air today and trout will come up for them.

You are wearing fabric-topped waders that pull your steps up short, but you shuffle from rock to rock, picking a path out into the current from the fast edges and into the slower, deeper parts. A shadow bolts along the gravel upstream, so you make a slight circle to get on a patch of stones below the place you want to fish. There is a trout rising there, and two more are breaking water above him.

You are alone in the arena now with the complex and limited idea of catching a particular fish in a particular way, and as the electric shock of a tail-slapping fish courses through your nerves, you touch the fly with a drop of oil and throw it on the water. You strip out line, watching the nearest trout, pitching your back cast high overhead and then pulling more line off the reel as you snap your rod back and forth until it feels as if the fly will reach him. But the newly greased line sticks in the guides and the fly falls many feet short. You wipe your greasy hands on your jacket, wondering if you should wade closer before the trout quits. But the floating line comes back fast on the current, so you strip some into a few coils of slack with your left hand and then half roll-cast the rest into the air to try again.

The trout is humping the water now, snatching things you can't even see into his mouth. You put a definite push into your rod hand this time, the pale green line rolling and unrolling, defying gravity in both directions. As your wrist speed overcomes those first probes through space, the line straightens out high over the water and your senses leap with the pull, because this back cast is right, and you feel it's right. Propelled by the invisible nylon, a bauble of tinsel and fur arcs swiftly over the water. You check it about three or four feet in the air and now, with all forward speed gone, the fly drops daintily beyond the trout. Your line quivers on the surface as unseen currents push and pull the length of it, but the fly cocks prettily, a bold challenge to begin the play. Yet in a fleeting instant the trout has vanished. Your perfect, straight, upstream cast threw the line directly over the fish and he was frightened by the snakelike silhouette turning on the surface.

But listen a moment, and we can improve this quickly. Never cast directly upstream if you can avoid it. The study of a stream for dry-fly fishing involves two factors: first, figuring out the spots where feeding trout lie and, second, determining how to present your fly so the fish will take it. That's all there is to it. Cast quartering across the river as you face upstream. This way the fish have a chance to see your fly before they are alarmed by your line and leader. Stretches of uniform flow are best adapted to this cast, but you can use it in broken water if you can cast a sloppy-looking slack line. The slack will compensate for the faster water between you and your fly and give a fairly good float without drag.

When a rise reveals the presence of a feeding fish, particularly in still water, be careful not to cast over him. It is better to use several casts, the first two or three a little short, than to make the first one too long. The line and leader falling over a good trout will put him down. Accuracy pays well in dry-fly fishing, however, and if you can make your first cast exactly right, your chances will be better. Ordinarily, the first cast is the best. If there is an actively feeding trout in a good spot you are more likely to take him the first time your fly floats over than on any subsequent cast. Each time the line and leader alight on the water there is that much more chance of scaring the fish.

But, to get on with the fishing, you are going to wade a little farther upstream now and try for one of the two trout you saw rising earlier. Swish the water off your line and fly as you move up by false-casting the line back and forth a few times. In many pools the current swings gently against a grassy or brush-covered bank. Wherever it does, you can expect to find willing trout—provided they are feeding at all—and there's just such a place ahead. Food is concentrated there by the stream, and insects fall into the water off the foliage. Sometimes it is hard to float a fly over such a location properly, because the current usually is swifter a foot away from the bank than it is right against it. Since the fly frequently has to be within a few inches of the grass to get results, the current might pull your line away too fast.

Keep in mind that your fly is supposed to imitate a natural insect floating on the surface. A natural doesn't cut across stream and throw up a little wake, like a miniature motorboat. Instead, it floats serenely along on the current. You should try to make your artificial do this. Sometimes trout actually prefer a dragging fly. But you haven't covered enough fish today to know just what they will or will not do, so keep enough slack in your cast to get a free float along that bank.

The trout is lying there in his neat mail-order suit. Not a very big one, but you can make out his shadow off the end of those ferns. I have taken some good fish there, but I have done some bad casting too, dumping the fly too hard on the water and hooking the line foolishly against a gust of wind. Now, without too much movement, get your cast to fall quartering upstream so that the leader angles toward the trout. Don't let him see the line. You are casting too fast for an accurate throw, but you slow down and let the line pull out better on the back cast. And there it goes, pushing softly through the

[37]

air, unrolling like the Indian's magic rope, the silken curve of flight predicted by your eye and wrist. In a blinding splash your floating fly is seized by a much larger rainbow trout that was blended on the gravel where you couldn't see him.

Here is the moment you waited for, the wild piercing essence of a grinding reel, the runaway, high-jumping, line-jerking, rod-throbbing jig of a slab-sided rainbow wheeling into the current to kick his tail. And as the first trickle of cold water wets your rear, you feel good because it's your fish and you worked for him. And what he does now pleases you very much, and you want him to live up to his name and not come easily to the net. He isn't a fish with a bloated belly and pouches under his eyes, but a red-blooded, hammered-silver, man-hating rainbow.

He goes running through shallows that remind you of a gravel driveway after a heavy rain and then circles off again, with the pale green fly line marking his run. Your pounding heart tells you to bring him back if you get a chance, because there may not be another one like him in the stream, so you crank up line and let him feel the rod's bend. This prods him into a great jump and you see his scarlet tribal mark reflecting the sun. And for once your game is played well, for the trout sulks and comes turtling inshore where you can feel the weight of him hanging in your net. You have caught two pounds of rainbow on a dry fly, and though he wasn't the fish you planned on, few large trout are caught by plan on broken-water streams. A formless succession of accidents and follies always works in your favor.

Usually you will not get such a positive strike at a dry fly that you can afford not to strike the fish back. The rainbow took hold hard enough to hook himself, but the next time remember to raise your rod deliberately a foot or so; this will pull the small, sharp hook into his mouth. You remember in your bait-fishing days how you pulled back hard when a bass ran off with the minnow. Well, in dry-fly work, with your line floating on the surface, it is much easier to pull your hook that short distance required to get the barb into a trout's jaw, so you must not strike too hard. Whenever a line is submerged you have to overcome its weight under water in addition to moving the hook. Also, bait strikes are usually made in response to feeling the fish after he has struck. In dry-fly fishing you see the fish, and always the tendency is to strike before he has closed his mouth on the fly. Slack line, in addition to giving your fly a better float, will help to prevent this.

The dry fly was created in the latter part of the nineteenth century in England and was popularized by Frederic M. Halford. Halford sent some of these flies to his fly-fishing friend, Theodore Gordon, who lived on the Neversink River in New York. But these Halford dry flies were soft-hackled, built to float on still water, and they sank quickly in Catskill streams. To Gordon, this meant that flies for American fishing had to have stiffer hackles, which is the part of the fly resembling legs and that part of the dry fly which supports it on the water's surface. So Gordon plucked the glossy, stiff feathers from rooster necks and began tying dry flies in the style we know today. His efforts were imitations of local buglife, and here began a legion of new patterns created by a small army of men with a knowledge of insects that would confound and confuse the most systematic entomologist. Scholarly anglers learned when to expect the little black stone fly, the red-legged March fly, pale evening dun, green drake, the ginger quill spinner, and countless more. The white-gloved howdy comes on our eastern streams on June 27, or nearly so, and this is a kind of information that will rub off on you and become valuable as you progress.

But in the beginning, too many anglers spend too much time worrying about fly pattern and not enough thinking about fly presentation. Admittedly, there are times when the trout are critical, and then it is important to have the right fly. But most of the time trout will take a surprising variety of floating flies, and a study of their stomach contents will verify this opinion by showing the number of different insects they have fed on. Even during a big hatch, when trout are gorging on one particular natural, you can catch them on a dozen different dry flies. If your dry fly bobs merrily along, unhampered by line or leader, floating as high and saucily as a natural insect, the odds are it will catch trout whether or not it is an exact imitation of the particular insects hatching at the moment.

Of course every beginner wants to know what patterns to buy, and here are a dozen that will catch trout under ordinary conditions throughout the country: Quill Gordon, Brown Bivisible, Light Cahill, Royal Coachman, March Brown, Brown Spider, Blue Dun Spider, Light Hendrickson, Adams, Ginger Quill, Blue Dun, and Black Midge. The Brown Bivisible is a high-floating fly and for this reason is especially good when you are first learning to cast. The Brown Spider and Blue Dun Spider are important when trout are indifferent and you want to tease them into striking by repeatedly casting over the same spot. The Black Midge is a very tiny fly, and you probably won't have much occasion for using it except when you know or see that the trout are feeding exclusively on minute insects. And even then it will take some experience to use it skillfully. The rest of the fly patterns I've suggested can be counted on to catch some fish most of the time.

Dry-fly fishing is never the same from one day to the next. The next time it will be raining, and the next time your good fish will rise just as it turns dark, and the next time they will be holding in the fast bouncy water, and the next time they take tiny flies easily in the flat water with just a faint pull. And you will remember how it was the last time in the stream around Dan's farm, and how the trout just came one after the other and you felt like beating them off with a broom. Or the morning you stood in the Gunnison above Black Canyon and worked for an hour over one giant trout. But best of all, you will remember that 2-pound rainbow, your first trout on a dry fly, and how you strode very loosely and with a slight lift, feeling the weight of him in the grass of your creel as you walked home. And you might remember how you were on the stream again the next day, before the dew was off the grass and the breeze started, trying for another one.

PART II

BASS, BUGS, AND BLACK MAGIC

6

SECRETS OF THE BASS

Many fishermen take up snorkeling, and quite a few become proficient with scuba (self-contained underwater breathing apparatus.) After all, anglers love. fish and water, and it's fun to see the world occasionally from the fish's point of view.

But how many anglers do you know use diving as a means of cataloging all the fishy hideaways in a given lake and then systematically study the different species' reaction to a variety of artificial lures? Well, this is exactly what A. J. McClane did over twenty years ago, and the lessons he learned are as applicable today as they were then.

GWR

SECRETS OF THE BASS

A long hulked bowfin with a hide like vulcanized rubber and tiny pig's eyes wiggled out of the weeds in front of me, and I could see that he had a badly healed wound across his back, probably from the slashing beak of a leopard gar. The bowfin glided across the sunlit hayfields of the river bottom toward the glowing white sand hole, where a school of blue shad paced nervously back and forth. As we went slowly forward and the grass parted, a cloud of translucent fry drifted over rows of bream, but the bream turned in jerky flight when they saw us. Coming out on a bed of whip grass, I saw a black bass eating a crayfish, like a puppy wolfing a bone, and then a huge leopard gar spiraled down from the flat, silvery roof of the surface. As he approached a school of bass, they melted into the weeds the way buck deer disappear in the forest. The gar looked puzzled, then loped away across the green plains. Way off in the distance, a surface plug was chugging and popping, spilling little drops of silvery bubbles as the plug head forced air into the water. As it passed in front of me, I saw that the drops looked like balls of mercury, and a bass rose from the grass to follow this trail.

I saw these things from the underwater compartment of a boat on the Rainbow River in Dunnellon, Florida. Few of us are satisfied with one-dimensional angling. A fisherman stares at the surface hour after hour until he is left obediently trotting to tackle shops at regular intervals for the pur-

[44]

chase of some new wonder lure designed to exploit a world he cannot see. My trip to Rainbow River was the climax of a study I began last summer on three eastern bass lakes, and now I can tell you something about angling from the fish's point of view.

For one thing, your lures look more realistic than you think. While sitting at the plate-glass windows under Rainbow River, I had three anglers fishing from the surface part of the boat, and they used forty or fifty different spoons and plugs, any one of which was a convincing attractor, as they all caused fish to follow them at least. Although not one of the anglers caught many bass, hardly a cast was retrieved that didn't bring fish scurrying from their hiding places. The two factors that discouraged them from striking were lure speed and depth. Many good fishermen acknowledge that it pays to retrieve slowly, but let me add to this thesis. In searching lake bottoms with an Aqualung last summer I found that both largemouth and smallmouth bass always hide under weed mats, rock ledges, logs, brush piles, and diving floats. All big bass like shade in the zone penetrated by the sun, and to make your lure visible and its pursuit worthwhile, you must allow frequent pauses in your retrieve, so that the fish realizes there is some chance of catching his food without wandering too far from home.

Bass are so addicted to their dens that we tried an experiment on Rainbow River with a fish conservatively estimated at fifteen pounds. This bass has taken residence under a thick mat of weeds several inches in depth which scums the surface along the river bank. There is literally no way of getting a lure at him unless some day some smart operator drops a weedless spoon at the edge of the mat and sinks it to the bottom where the bass might see it. The water is about six feet deep under the mat, and the fish has cleared a hole in the weeds where there is no sunlight. From the topside of the boat, I moved the mat with an oar blade, leaving my wife, Bob McCahon, and Art Ornitz[1] in the compartment as observers. Each time I lifted the heavy canopy of weed and algal scum and dropped it in a new direction, the bass dashed from sight. But about five minutes after the water settled, the huge bass reappeared under the shadow of the mat. He had no intention of leaving home.

So a lure to be effective must be worked slowly when bass are not feeding actively, and it should have as much vertical, or bottom-to-surface, flight as it does horizontal range. The mere fact that you throw a plug in the water doesn't mean that the fish will see it. I have stood among towering weeds in

---

[1]McCahon was, and is, a noted film producer. Ornitz, a cameraman at the time, is today one of Hollywood's most successful cinematographers.

twenty feet of water that were literally teeming with smallmouh bass while an angler cast his lure in every direction, and not once did I see the bait. On Rainbow River I had the advantage of being able to correct the caster.

I saw Bob's wobbling spoon hit the water fifty or sixty feet upstream. It arced silver through a stream of bubbles and then wobbled back toward the boat, at times looking almost translucent in shades of red, green, and blue as the blade caught the sun. He made ten casts, and each time the spoon was followed by two or more small bass. Small black bass, incidentally, school and drift in open water and show little tendency to remain concealed. Bob's retrieve was slow and steady, following a path about four feet over the bottom. He wasn't aware of the fact that fish had followed his lure, and he estimated that the spoon was working within inches of the river bottom. Shouting up the hatch, I directed him to let his spoon sink deeper and retrieve with long pauses.

In the next series of five casts I saw more bass rising out of the hayfields than I ever dreamed existed in that area. As the spoon sank close to the grass, pods of bass emerged from hiding. Bob brought the wobbler back in a hopping action, and each hop caused a fish to rush at the lure, some of them actually striking or, more properly, nipping it, which Bob felt as an occasional nudge of his rod tip, as though the spoon was hitting weeds. This I corrected by having Bob add a pork-rind strip and tail hook behind the wobbler. I do not understand bass well enough to know why they nip at spoons sometimes. Even large bass will do it. But they take the rind trailer solidly, and you should always carry a bottle of strips in your pocket if you do much bass fishing. Thus Bob caught his bass, Art caught bass, my wife, Pat, caught a number of them, and I had the satisfaction of knowing why.

My second experiment was with popping plugs. Now a popping plug, regardless of the color, is extremely realistic from underwater. It somehow fits in with the pulsing rhythm of aquatic life. The trio of anglers working topside were using 5-pound-test monofilament lines which were invisible against the flat, silver roof above me. The only parts of the plugs I could see were the parts that rested below the surface. At each pop a stream of bubbles filtered down in the river and curved to the surface again. It was this bubbling trail that caused bass to come out from under their grass beds and brush piles. I am not certain of the extent to which the sound of the plug activated them into striking. I guided the boat on Rainbow River along stump- and weed-thatched banks, often stopping within five feet of a good bass, and although the anglers above popped and gurgled their plugs around these bass dens, none of the fish moved until the lure passed in such a position that the bubble trail showered in view. But they picked up this like hound dogs on a scent.

While sitting at one end of a weed mat about five feet under water, I saw a bubble shower fall in the sunlight on the far side of the mat, and a pair of bass came out of their dark retreat to investigate. One of them took the plug.

In using the Aqualung, I found that fish show no fear of the swimmer at all and are actually attracted to the stream of air bubbles coming from the outlet valve. Dave Goodnow[2] and I had a great deal of trouble in Doolittle Lake in Connecticut last summer while trying to make underwater photos, because the smallmouth bass insisted on swimming around our heads where they could stare at the escaping air. By the same token, most lung divers learn that a sudden and violent discharge of air will frighten fish, and it is probably the best insurance against curious sharks and barracuda. So the surface-lure question is left unresolved at the moment. From limited observation I would say again that it pays to fish slowly and cover the area well, as the bubble trail is an important, if not *the* important, factor in attracting fish.

One of the most revealing facts in my underwater study has been the abundance of game fish in lakes where very few fish are thought to exist. On one eastern resort lake last summer, I started wading from a shallow gravelbar, wearing an Aqualung and flippers, and as the water passed over my head at the drop-off, flocks of sharp-beaked perch rose from the grass. Off in the bluish light zone I could see smallmouth stacked up like DC-3's[3] over International Airport. They were all suspended in the shadow of a diving float. Diving floats and docks always have bass under them, even if people are jumping and diving in the water. Bass show no fear of boats or motors either, and I have often observed bass cruising in the bubble stream of an outboard.

Between where I swam and the float, a great pickerel lumbered out of his weed bed like some prehistoric monster and followed my bubble trail to the next drop-off. The bottom dipped away sharply like a ridge and I was soon drifting out over a forest of grass. There were the smallmouths resting in about twenty-five feet of water. I have never observed bass resting over sand, except for an occasional small fish or one that was actively chasing his food. The main school is always found in weeds.

Although smallmouths are considered fish of gravel-bottomed lakes, the illusion is more definitely related to water temperature in that lakes with large gravel areas are usually colder than purely weed-bottomed lakes. I have never found large bass on gravel patches unless there was an outcropping of rock or a log nearby that could be used for cover. On this particular day, I saw smallmouths that I estimated up to seven pounds in weight scat-

[2] A New York-based photographer with whom Al worked on a number of other *Field & Stream* stories.
[3] Bass don't change, but DC's do. You'll find more 7's in the air these days than 3's.

[47]

tered among the long fingers of weed that stretched across a submarine plain. They were deep and hard to get at—impossible to reach with ordinary sinking plugs—and as it turned out I managed to catch only two of them on a deeply fished feather jig later that day. This was one of those rare instances when live bait would have been more effective.

Even though live bait stands an equal chance against artificial lures, nearly 80 percent of the nation's prize-winning black bass in all divisions of the Field & Stream Fishing Contest are caught on artificials. The efficiency of live bait has been very much overrated in the heavy-fish league, except under specific conditions. Florida bass fishing, for example, is generally good from March through October, but when cold fronts start moving down from the north, the quality of the sport depends entirely on the weather. A prolonged cold spell will put the fish down, and casting with artificial lures produces relatively few bass. When the bigmouths get ready to spawn in February they move into the thick grass beds and the lure caster won't score on anything other than the small "buck" bass of a pound or two pounds in weight.

Those heavy roe bass are taken on large shiner minnows, which are still-fished over the spawning areas. The reason for this is easy to understand. The bass are resting in the thickest possible vegetation where a plug or spoon can't be left sitting still, and when the lure is moving the roe has no reason to chase it. The bass are not feeding and display no aggressiveness unless another fish sulks in the nesting area, and this is where the live-bait boys make their score. A six- or eight-inch shiner is tossed into the open pockets among the grass and left to tease the roe into striking. A plug or spoon, on the other hand, would be completely ignored, even if the lure passed right through the nest. Immature males, or young bucks who in Florida parlance are "on the hill," will strike artificials and thus mislead the angler into thinking that the fault lies with his lure. Roe bass are not aggressive and cannot be provoked into striking unless the live bait becomes such a nuisance that she wallops it out of sheer annoyance.

I recently spent several hours under water with an Aqualung in Lake Mangonia, Florida, watching roes on the nest, and these observations seem to check with the generally poor fishing that was had at that time. Prolonged cold weather is often coincident with the spawning period, as it was this year, and the longer this condition exists, the longer the roes stay on their beds. The habits of northern bass differ at spawning time in that the nesting period is shorter, and the fish frequently spawn in fairly open water, where the roe bass displays more aggressiveness in protecting her nest. These characteristics seem to balance nicely with the closed season on northern bass waters and the general no-closed season of southern states.

Although fishing is not permitted at Rainbow Springs, *Field & Stream* obtained special permission from the Florida Game and Fresh Water Fish Commission to fish there in order to collect material for this article. If you're headed for Florida I would strongly recommend that you visit Rainbow Springs and make the underwater trip down the river. It is an angling education.

7

THAT NEW BLACK MAGIC

In 1952 the McClanes bought a home on the inland waterway at Juno, Florida. The house was still in the heart of open country, with quail on the lawn and big snook and sea trout literally at their doorstep. But the building boom quickly swept in around them, and the McClanes packed up and moved to Palm Beach, where they live today.

When a writer first settles in a new location, his typewriter becomes a clattering dynamo as he races to capture the multitude of fresh impressions associated with new people, places, and experiences. The mid-1950s were, therefore, an especially fertile period in A. J.'s writings, and characters like Willie McKoosh, a retired Palm Beach fireman whose one great trip "north" was a visit to Tallahassee; Homer Large, the local police chief; and Jimmy Darr, manager of Bob Kleiser's tackle shop in West Palm Beach, all cross the stage to enrich McClane's narrative.

The following story is particularly interesting in the light of the angling upheaval created by the advent of the plastic worm. Fished slowly through drowned treetops or along old stream bottoms in the countless new impoundments that dot the American landscape, plastic worms in a variety of hues, but most especially black, have resulted in more big fish catches in a handful of years than any lure in history. The darn things even prove irresistible to the likes of tarpon and marlin! However, back in 1955, well before plastic wrigglers were on their way to dethroning the plug and spoon as the king and consort of bass lures, a spin-fishing underground was using their prototype with deadly effect. In fact, this article, which drew over a thousand letters at *Field & Stream* ("Where can I get the stuff?"), wiped out all available supplies of pigskin for months thereafter!

GWR

THAT NEW BLACK MAGIC

S ome months ago I told you that there would be a revival in the art of pork chunking. I didn't know at the time what form that revival would take, but this past summer a band of tight lipped spin casters invaded the Southland with one of the deadliest weapons since the scope-sighted crossbow. Jimmy Lynch pulled up in our driveway one morning and leaned out of his station wagon holding what looked like a midget black snake. This was the first time I ever saw or heard of what is now known as Black Magic. After unlocking my eyeballs I got Willie McKoosh on the phone, because Willie is an authority on hoghide baits. If you fished with Willie and turned in a bad performance using a chunk, you went down in his book as one of the *enfants perdus* living in the sinful contents of a posh tackle box. But the dictatorial Mr. McKoosh had been a victim of saw grass censorship, a peculiar phenomenon which surrounds this whole story. He knew nothing about Black Magic, and declared that if there was such a thing it was a Yankee-type bait and therefore no more than a cheap publicity stunt. Brother McKoosh was due for a shock, as you shall see presently.

I didn't tell Willie about Jimmie Darr, and how he caught twenty-five bass one afternoon using Black Magic, and how the pond he fished had been written off a long time ago. They said there were no fish left in it. And I didn't tell him about the snook fishermen who skulked around the tackle shop waiting for tourist customers to leave so they could buy the stuff unobserved. The bottled dynamite was delivered by a gent who acted like he was selling French postcards. As quick as the black jars came out of a carton they were snatched from his hands with impolite haste. I found that Darr had let the word slip to Lynch, but he couldn't remember who told him originally. When a tackle-shop operator can sell hogback at ninety cents a strip, it's understandable that minds will go blank. Steering me back to the broom closet, Darr closed the door and whispered how Black Magic is an overlong strip of pork rind, carved thick but tapered, between 8 and 9 inches in length, weighing about ¼ ounce, and dyed black. It is mounted with one hook, wiggles like an eel, and instead of being fished like an ordinary artificial, the angler casts and retrieves until a strike is felt. Then he lets his line go slack while the fish chews and swallows the strip. Brother Darr concluded by saying that the bait was so murderous it had to be kept a secret.

Orange Lake is in north-central Florida. It's about sixteen miles long, or 14,000 acres of turbid water full of floating plant islands, depending on which way you measure a lake. The sandy clay and limestone bottom is covered with layers of silt and plant detritus, a composition that spells big bass in Willie's country. There are two species of shad, crayfish, freshwater shrimp, crappies, and bream for the bigmouths to feed on, so it's no surprise to come up with an 8- or 10-pounder now and then. We used to have a guide there by the name of Sweet Richard, who was a tongue-tied Lothario but a real talker with the surface plug. His mute wisdom was in knowing that endurance is everything. When Sweet Richard operated on the marshes he just worried the bass into striking, a theme that paid off in several potgutted 15-pounders one spring. But stubborn dignity was no match for the McKoosh method of skittering a pork chunk, and that's the way Willie elected to pin my ears back that morning.

Willie is a sneak caster. He aims the bow of our skiff broadside to where the bass are feeding, then just before cutting the motor he makes a hairpin turn and snaps a cast off. His sense of timing is so keen that I always find myself looking at Willie's back while he tells me about the fish that is following his lure. Anyway, we started out that day probing the hayfields and me facing miles of open lake, an uncommon advantage for working pigskin voodoo, although neither of us knew it at the time.

The first thing I discovered about Black Magic is that it casts easily. I have a constitutional weakness for baits that sail through the air without flapping or holding back. Using a light spin stick and a 5-pound-test line, the hogskin doesn't need a split-shot assist, although I have used shot since when fishing very deep water and casting on wide rivers. Drifting with the breeze, Willie told me how black pork is no good, because the bass can't see it in thick water, and how chunks have to kick up a fuss, not crawl around on the bottom. We continued casting and Willie went into his early history of dyeing chunks yellow, red, green, and with polka dots. He told me how cracker boys soaked chunks in Mercurochrome and wiped them in shoe polish on the Altamaha, the big spread that pours from the Ocmulgee, and how the striped bass would ram a 12-inch strip of red rind but ignore any other color. What he said about dyes fit in with what I had learned from two leading rind manufacturers—that most dyes won't stay on pigskin. Unlike other materials, rind has to be dyed cold. While Willie was talking I was discovering the second thing about Black Magic. It doesn't stay black but turns a dull blue as it gets wet. I was about to tell McKoosh when a bass with a mouth big enough to hold a minnow bucket stuck his head in the air. He had swallowed the rind right up to the hook.

Some things about Southern bass fishing are grossly exaggerated. The publicity mills make it sound easy, which it is not, and while there are plenty of big fish to be had, you have to work for them. But the fighting ability of a Florida bigmouth needn't be questioned. He is a scrapper regardless of his warm-water environment. I have had 10- and even 12-pounders dance like their pants were full of 'gator fleas, and the best one I've caught so far, a 15-pounder, made nine headshaking jumps before coming to boat. This first bass to hit my Black Magic put on an aerial display that raged for ten minutes. Sometimes he came up as though shot from a cannon, with water grasses hanging across the line, and he'd pause in midair to kick, with his full belly shining white in the sun. Then he'd come up gently, pausing just before his gills rattled him into a movement no faster than the clouds that came across in the wind. It's these slow-motion jumps of a big bass that you have to watch. It may be the last time you see him. I kept my drag loose and worked the spool with my forefinger, putting the pressure on when the bass turned close. Willie never said a word until the bass was flopping in the bottom of the boat. Then he asked me the same question I was asking myself. How do they dye hogskin black?

The rest of the day was something special for me. I have no idea how many bass I caught and released, but there were more big ones among them than we ordinarily see. Willie stuck with his white chunk and made up for the defection with a procession of young mossbacks that trotted obediently behind his bait at regular intervals. It was clear to both of us that the guy who invented Black Magic was destined to become a person of great importance. The bait literally separates boy bass from men bass.

Although Black Magic is very similar to an ordinary pork-chunk lure, it isn't fished the same way. In fact, artful chunk procedure is epitomized by holding the rod high and literally keeping your line dry. Willie, for instance, reels fast enough to keep his bait splashing and breaking water. The black art is exactly opposite in performance. You must keep your tip down and retrieve very slowly, twitching the tip but not jerking it the way you would with a surface bait. There's been so much talk in years past about short-striking fish on pork rind that you will probably be tempted to add a treble hook in the tail of the bait. This isn't the least bit necessary. When you get a strike, just pause and let the fish swallow your rind before striking back. If you hit him instantly, as though using a plug, the chances are he'll have only half the porkskin in his choppers. Nothing will make the fish drop it, because the bait has a natural texture. Some of our local bass experts, like Homer Large and Peaslee Streets, twitch their Black Magic directly on the pond bottom and let the bass pick it up and swim off before setting the hook. Peaslee said his bass come up with mud in their mouths when he's working the rind correctly.

Black Magic isn't always effective this way. One morning below Wilson Dam, on the Tennessee River, Ed Bussey and I found that the smallmouths, all fish over 2 pounds in weight, hit the strip so hard that they had to be hooked on the strike. On the Mississippi, near Prairie du Chien, we fished below the dams for white bass and saugers as well as bigmouths, and here we found it was better to slack off after a strike if we wanted to hook whites. I haven't as yet used the bait for northern pike, but presumably old *Esox* would swallow the rind whole. Brown and rainbow trout will grab and swallow, so the strike must be delayed. On the Saluda River in South Carolina we tallied a half-dozen big browns one afternoon, all of them taking the lure so slow and easy that you'd think a catfish had the bait.

It may be that a good percentage of the fish coming to Black Magic hit across the head of the rind and are hooked instantly. I was casting on a peppergrass flat in Clearwater Lake one day when the sun was at just the right angle to light up the weed bed. I could see my lure fluttering in those S-shaped curves when a bass popped up behind it. He was an old bull of a bass with a huge head and belly to match. He swayed as he leaned forward with the pig eyes of his kind, unblinking, glassy, and rooted on the thing he was about to eat. Coming directly behind the rind, he wet his lips once or twice, then sidled past the bait, turned, and smacked it head on. I didn't hit back, but let the fish run a few feet before tightening up on him. He was hooked solid, wearing the black strip like a moustache when he came up.

I'm not certain what Black Magic imitates. It could certainly pass for an eel or a water snake. I do know that this overlong cut has a fantastic action in the water, a movement that you don't find in ordinary baits. Although it works well on the surface, the real advantage of the lure is in providing maximum action in deep fishing on open water. Furthermore, the lure is attractive to all game fish, both in salt water and fresh. The boys in Winterhaven originally designed this cut for eel-happy snook, but the possibilities of the bait are unlimited. One day soon you will be startled and possibly knocked over by a stooping creature, scuttling behind rod racks from one tackle shop to another as one pursued. Fear not. He is a victim of Black Magic renewing his vision of paradise in the search for bottled pigskin.

8

IT HELPS TO BE BUG-MINDED

Some years ago A. J. McClane introduced me to paradise. It was an indirect introduction, and Al was unaware he had rendered me this service until I told him about it. It happened that while I was teaching at the U. S. Naval Academy, one of my colleagues, a harassed electrical engineer by the name of Michael Greata, would disappear each June for two weeks and reappear in Annapolis with the most beatific smile that would linger through many weekends of tedious duty.

I was mystified. What kind of colossal fix could give a man such a sustained high? I was not at all shy in my determination to find out. Finally one afternoon, backed into a corner of his room at the BOQ with two sunlamps and a flashlight shining into his perspiring face, Mike broke. "Smallmouths," he blurted out. That was not enough. I needed to know where, what size, how caught. Mike caved in completely. He swore me to secrecy and then promised that next June I could accompany him. Thus began my intermittent love affair with the lakes of Penobscot and Washington Counties in Maine. It was also the first time I realized that fly rods were not invented for trout or salmon, as Ernie Schwiebert would have us believe. They were obviously preordained for the exclusive and exultant use of bass buggers who on chilly northern waters in June are sometimes lucky enough to jump fifty fish a day.

How does McClane fit in here? Very simple. One evening around the campfire, just after I had cut my forefinger to sign a blood pact calling destruction down on any member of our fraternity who breathed the precise location of the secret lake, I asked Mike and his good friend John Cadwallader how they had ever found this glory hole in the first place.

"We read about it in *Field & Stream*," John replied.

GWR

IT HELPS TO BE BUG-MINDED

Bass bugging is a mild form of insanity. All over this fair land, devoted husbands and fathers sneak out the back door for a few hours of casting on the local pond. Unfortunately, some gents forget to return before the milkman cometh, and our divorce courts would blush to tell you of the bass that have been named corespondents.

Among young men who could profit by moderation, the condition unaccountably becomes much worse. I know a fellow who fishes bugs until the ponds freeze. Louie is so hypnotized by the game that he drove 150 miles to a lake last year, hopped out of his car, and let fly a plastic popper which bounced *clunk clunk* over the ice. He really has 20/20 vision, except when he goes bass fishing.

[58]

One of the mysterious gifts of bug artists is their ability to have a hot spot stashed away in the middle of civilization. Gene Tunney keeps bass in his swimming pool. At heart he is an Atlantic-salmon fisherman, but big-mouths ward off the vapors and collywobbles besetting the lives of Connecticut commuters.

I don't know where your wife finds the calendars that hang in your kitchen, but the reproduction on ours is of a barefoot, freckle-faced fishmonger who is spurning the proffered coin of an adult bass angler. The four-color moral, underwritten by Herman Klotz, our butcher, is that cane poles and infant virtue triumph over all. This subversive introduction to the new year is a promulgated myth that all honest men will recognize at once. The easiest way to catch a bass is on artificial lures, and I bless the day my cane pole grew into a fly rod. Aside from unwashed artists and juvenile delinquents, nobody gets more enjoyment out of bass fishing than the bug caster.

I suppose the peculiar fascination of the sport is seeing a heavy fish rise from under the lily pads or come charging out from under a dense bed of weeds to smash at a comparatively tiny lure. Some days the fish knock the enamel off everything, and other days you have to sweat over each strike. Bass are not sophisticated, but stubbornly emotional.

To me, the ideal fishing country is one that has a trout stream and a bass pond; between the two you can savor the gamut of fly-rod experiences. I started my bugging career with painted corks and worked my way up through puberty, voice break, and Robert Page Lincoln to become a pop-bug artist. During a certain period in my life that I care little to remember, I fell by the wayside and cast bugs with a spinning rod. This took all the work out of casting, and that, oddly enough, spoiled the game for me. Also, I couldn't handle the really small poppers that our snobbish river bass prefer.

There is a prevalent belief that bugging sticks must be long and heavy—a point that always requires qualification. Any fly rod, reel, and line has a right to expect that each be endowed with the same measure of weight and personality to perform harmoniously. To create a happy bend in 9 feet of fly rod, the line needs authority—somewhere around the GBF or GAF sizes. The rod, of course, must be inherently powerful, bending all the way down into the grip. This permits slow casting to match the pace of highly wind-resistant bugs. A good bug rod literally waits until the line loop is properly executed before it takes a casting bend at the forward stroke. In a very broad sense, then, heavy tackle is ideal for the average man, if only to keep a hair frog out of his toupee.

But extra-large bugs are not indispensable. You can toss midget bugs at bass and get results that are often better and seldom worse. The secret, if it can be called one, is proper technique. For historical reasons the bulk of the lures marketed today are oversize and not at all advantageous in everyday fishing. I spent most of the last year on my bass ponds, using a 7-foot, 2⅔-ounce bamboo rod that was designed for dry-fly fishing. Coupled with an HDG line, the little stick propels No. 6 poppers to fifty feet without a hint of stress. Best of all, even a small fish puts up a fine performance against the light rod.

This kind of bugging wasn't practical in the old days. The bass tackle of Dr. Henshall's era and comparable tools today are materially different. Not only is the workmanship in bamboo rods superior, but modern fiber glass permits a wide choice of rod weights and lengths. At least one tackle company is marketing a good 7-foot glass bugging rod.

There are, of course, short-rod casters who inevitably go to pieces and get trapped in their own line speed. Bugging rhythm and *flick-flick* dry-fly work just don't match. Even a small bass bug is air-resistant. As with traditional 9-foot bug rods, you still have to allow a longer pause before you make the forward shoot. Beginners should try short distances first, and watch the back cast instead of the forward cast, observing just how long the lure takes to complete backward flight. On the forward stroke, start slowly and, an instant before the line straightens, gradually accelerate the movement of your rod. Successful bugging doesn't require extreme casting distances. Whether you work from a boat or wade, it is most important that you know where and how bass feed.

The wading fly-rod man tends to cast as far out into the lake as possible. (It is almost reflexive—probably for the same reason that boat anglers get in the middle of a pond and rip their underwear in reaching back to the bank.) In my experience, however, the great percentage of bass taken on bugs are caught within twenty feet of the shoreline among rocks, weed patches, down timber, and lily pads. For practical reasons, surface-feeding bass are shallow-water cruisers. I often get above-average results by wading parallel to the shore and working in an arc from the bank out. In fact, it's a good general rule to make your first few casts in ankle-deep water. Not only do bass hunt frogs, mice, and minnows along the marginal areas of a lake, but most insect life is blown there from the trees and bank brush.

Recently, while fishing one of those miniature, beach-bordered, northern resort lakes, I caught some beautiful bass by standing back on the sand and casting my bug in a few inches of water. The fish were feeding methodically on bluegill fry that they herded, then chased right out onto the beach. I cast my bug wherever I saw a disturbance and usually, after a minute or so, one *blurp* of the lure would bring a savage strike. The biggest fish was a 3-pounder, but on my little rod he made the reel sing. I discovered that this situation was not easy for wading because the water was extremely clear and my foot movements panicked the fry.

In recent years I have used popping bugs almost exclusively. I seldom use any other kind now, unless the fish ignore me completely. This may not be the most effective tactic, but small poppers are poison to bass if you work the lure right. There are many ways of fishing bugs, and experienced anglers have their pet methods. Most casters agree, however, that in general the slower you fish a bug, the more bass you'll catch. Covering a section of shoreline thoroughly, with slow playbacks, will usually make a better showing than sampling the whole lake fast.

This means you must drop your bug on the water and wait at least one minute before moving it. If there's any slack in your cast, lower the rod tip and take up line by hand so that the bug doesn't skid over the water. When you give the rod an upward swish, the bug should bury its nose in the surface and make a hearty sound. If you get nothing but a splash, you are doing it wrong or the bug is no good. It's as simple as that.

The pop artist has one obvious advantage: he can make more noise than anybody. If you think bass are not susceptible to noise, then you don't know bass. To a lunker who is dozing in his lily bed, the arrival and departure of an ordinary bug goes unannounced. But a bug that swims around in the outside world going *glub glub glub* is asking for it. Maybe the old cuss can't see a moving surface kicker, but his sonar will pick up the sound and he'll jump out of bed with his shirttail in the wind. Half the time his brain is addled, and he stops to gawk at the scenery like a GI tourist on a Paris street corner. One pop, and Mr. Bass suddenly becomes a press agent's version of himself.

If conditions are favorable, with plenty of stumps, pads, and bank grass around the pockets, you may not even have to pop your bug. Aim your casts so that the bug falls in the spatterdock and pickerel weed, then twitch it off. A hungry bass will bang it right then. One reason why I fancy dyalite poppers is because they really take a beating. My idea of casting is to bang the floater against logs, rocks, and other free-lunch counters along Bass Boulevard. Old-fashioned cork bugs and the early plastics flew to pieces. I still have to chuckle over a demonstration I gave on the St. Lawrence River one day.

I was trying to make a bug caster of my guide. Pete paddled me within easy distance of a rock ledge where a hefty smallmouth lay sunning himself. I said, "Pete, you are about to get a lesson in bugmanship." Sawing the air with forty feet of line, I measured the cast to jump my bug off the ledge. It didn't check right and the bug hit the rock over the bass' head. My popper exploded like a clay bird. The bare hook fell into the water and the bass swam over to take a look. Pete didn't say a word. I tied on a fresh bug and we went down the shore. There wasn't much doing until we passed a stump. I meant to cast next to the stump but overshot my mark, and a hog-fat bass inhaled the popper with the nylon caught over a limb. He took the bug and half the leader. Ever the diplomat, Pete sucked wetly on his pipestem and said, "Maybe you could just tell me about it."

Casting at solid objects is not without small troubles, but over the long haul you can get a satisfactory number of effective floats. I seldom hang up unless my mind is wandering, and as every bass fisherman knows, that's when you can kiss the bug good-bye regardless of where it lands. Tall, smooth-leaved pickerel weed will hold a bug until you are ready to shake it loose; broad, flat lily pads offer perfect platforms for jumping a weedless bug at the bass. By checking your forward cast over the target, you let the line fall without tension, and the lure won't spin or hit so hard that it gets stuck. After a little practice you'll get the feel of it—putting just the right amount of check into the line to make the bug fall dead. Roots and stumps are best attacked by bouncing the bug off them, and easiest of all is bank grass, especially along undercut riverbanks.

River bugging differs little from casting in lakes. You cast the bug to likely places, on ledges, bushes, and over boulders, then twitch it loose to drift with the current. Even when using poppers, I let the lure drift naturally on my first try. It may take several minutes in very slow current to fish the cast out. I work the second cast by twitching the rod tip but still without popping. If this gets no response, then the third float is a live show with plenty of noise.

Exactly why I follow this procedure isn't precisely explicable but it has proven an efficient routine on river bass—which are temperamentally different from other kinds. While fishing the Juniata River in Pennsylvania some years ago, I popped a particularly inviting boulder daily, and just as regularly a fine smallmouth appeared and tipped his hat. Finally, one morning I didn't pop the bug and my bass came out snarling like a bus driver. He weighed a bit over 3½ pounds, which is a pleasing size for river fish. So I've played bugs in the drift-twitch-then-pop routine ever since.

Where practical, the very best way to fish bugs is by wading. If the water is too deep or the pond mud-bottomed, I like to float on an inner tube. We don't have many lakes at home in Florida that I care to wade. I am a coward. For instance, the lake nearest town (which is now in the middle of a housing development) has a considerable population of alligators. To my subconscious, they belong back in the Everglades, although sober citizens occasionally meet one walking down the avenue after a rainy spell. I know they are reasonable critters but when one pops his head out and stares at me, it has an involuntary effect on my running muscles. I wade other lakes where there are alligators, but these are not Peeping Toms. I also do not care to suspend myself from an inner tube under these circumstances, as statistics on footless bug addicts are not available.

Next to wading, the canoe has more advantages than the rowboat. Two men can cast comfortably from a canoe without getting lost in a tactical jungle. If you are forced to use a skiff, then go alone, unless you can find somebody who will row the boat for you.

The only alternative is to invite another angler along. But when two pros fish together from the same boat you've really got a mess. Buggers can't be polite to each other and still think ahead. It took me years to learn the secret of bugging—to analyze the next pocket while fishing the one in front of me. The rhythm of the game is lost on the caster who sees his partner preempt the next three choice spots.

The ideal, of course, is to maneuver into bow position before you leave the dock. My sometime fishing partner, Willie McKoosh, advises that if you find yourself in the stern, brainwash the bow man by groaning each time he makes a splashy cast. After all, he is putting *your* fish down. McKoosh is a talented groaner and usually ends up with the other guy rowing the boat. Which is another problem if there is no soul-saving breeze to move the skiff.

But when everything goes right, even your wife will admit that bass bugging is an unusual game.

RETRIEVING: THE REAL ART OF FISHING

You learn to retrieve when you learn to cast. In fact, you can't make a second cast unless you've brought in the lure—namely, retrieved it—after the first cast. Thus many fishermen grow up with the misconception that retrieving is a secondary function to the fine art of casting—merely a way to get the lure back so you can demonstrate your teacup accuracy all over again.

Yet think back on the number of times you've come home from a trip mulling over what might have been. You were on target most every cast. And you did see fish. In fact, two Loch Ness monsters followed your lure to the boat before swirling away in disgust. Even in the shower, with the soap streaming in your eyes and no towel handy, you're kicking yourself for not trying a different lure—or even a different lake. Rarely do you put the blame where it all too often lies—on the speed and character of your retrieve.

Barring actually having A. J. McClane in the boat next time you're fishing your favorite lake, here's a checklist of all the major retrieving variations as tested and approved by the Practical Fisherman himself. Keep these variations in mind next time your strikes are few and far between. They really work.

GWR

RETRIEVING: THE REAL ART OF FISHING

There are two skills that distinguish the expert angler from the beginner. The first is his ability to cast accurately at all distances within the limits of his tackle; the second is his deftness in handling the retrieve. Retrieving is, of course, the recovery of the lure through reeling. Beyond that, though, it's the final touch of success—the delicate art of catching fish off their guard. Although technical advances have spawned a variety of nearly automatic baits that spit, hop, and whistle, there are qualities of action that cannot be built into a plug or a spoon.

Anybody who has fished often is aware of that classic angling paradox: Two men cast from the same boat, using the same lure, and one angler hooks fish to the point of monotony, while his companion feels like a charity case. I have been in both ends of the boat at one time or another. A casual observer might say it's "luck," but it doesn't take a genius to realize there is unending variation and novelty within a task that, to a duller eye, might seem mechanical. The successful angler knew how to work his bait.

Retrieving is the practice of innocent deceptions to make fish believe that

[66]

metal or plastic is edible—a kind of artful storytelling in which a plug plays the role of a tired frog, a leaping mullet, or whatever seems appropriate at the moment. The mere reeling of a lure is not enough. I don't know how many retrieves might be classified on the basis of distinctive movement, but I use four that I vary in speed and emphasis. Before discussing these, however, I'd like to clarify a few points about lure speed.

One morning last summer my wife and I fished Black Lake in northern New York. A thundershower had almost spoiled our plans, but the weather soon became hot and bright again. I took the stern seat while Pat worked from the bow. We both used a small, deep-running yellow plug designed to swim at the twenty-foot level. The lure, like many bottom-scratching baits, doesn't reach its maximum depth until the angler retrieves at top speed. The pressure against its long metal bill forces it downward.

I landed a nice pair of largemouths, then delicately suggested to my wife that maybe she wasn't reeling fast enough. We were facing opposite sides of the boat, but I could hear her cranking like a demon. I caught three more fish and she still didn't have a strike. Then it dawned on me.

I was comfortably retrieving twice as fast as she was at wrist-punishing speed. I completed two casts to her one. All this was no masculine distinction. It was due to my new bait-casting reel; not only was it filled to the pillars with line, but its gear ratio doubled that of the old enclosed-spool reel Pat was winding. Fortunately I had several other reels in the kit bag and we quickly put together a new outfit.

It made a difference immediately. She was able to retrieve much more rapidly, thereby pulling the plug down to fish level. I would guess that Pat had been working at about five feet below the surface, which is as far away as another planet when bass are hugging mud in deep water. Her old reel would probably have been effective if the plug had been a straight sinker with some weight, but our choice that day (and it was a good one) was designed, rather than ballasted, for a twenty-foot plunge.

All this brings us to the important question: What is a fast retrieve, and what is a slow one?

Different reels have different rates of line recovery. How many inches you will spool with one turn of the handle depends on (1) how much line is already on the reel, (2) gear ratio, (3) cranking radius of the handle, and (4) spool diameter. A very small reel with, say, a 2-to-1 gear ratio is going to recover much less line than a large reel with a 4-to-1 ratio. It's possible therefore for a man with the smaller reel to crank rapidly and believe that he is making a fast retrieve, whereas his actual lure speed may be less than half of what it would be with the larger reel.

Thus we have a considerable degree of variation in what constitutes fast and slow—mechanically speaking. I think the most workable definition of a slow retrieve is the minimum speed at which the inherent action of a bait will function. If it's designed to wobble, it should wobble; if built to flap a pair of aluminum arms, it should flap. By the same token, a fast retrieve must imply the maximum speed at which these devices operate. If the plug is "straight," or completely without mechanical action of any kind, then we might define a slow retrieve as the minimum speed at which you can activate the bait, a fast retrieve as the maximum speed at which you can reel. This usually means that the plug will skip over the water.

To determine the correct reeling speed on any particular day, it's a good idea to vary the retrieve every fifteen minutes, until you catch a fish or at least see one. On a fast retrieve, for instance, if a fish follows the lure for a long distance without striking, you can stop reeling and let the plug sit motionless on the water. There is a reasonable chance that he will strike when the plug is at rest, or when it starts to move again. If, on subsequent casts, more fish continue to follow without striking until the plug stops, you can assume that reeling at a slower speed with pauses is going to be more effective.

Conversely, you may get this response to a slow retrieve; if a fish swims along behind the bait without hitting, then a sudden increase in reeling speed might trigger a strike. Of course, you don't have much chance of seeing fish when casting deep-running lures, but it's worth remembering that we all tend to work at a medium speed, and it's usually the very slow or very fast retrieves that pay off when bottom scratching.

Now let's see how speed affects retrieving techniques. Popping is probably the most universal method of working a plug in both fresh and salt water. Fish can be attracted by sound—not necessarily a loud noise but a convincing one. I have seen many days when the *glub* of a surface bait was the only thing that attracted fish, and I mean everything from giant snappers of the Congo to Delaware smallmouths.

Popping is particularly effective when fish are hiding under bank brush where they can't be reached. They will hear the bait and come out for it. Or if they're loafing in a submerged weed bed in five or ten feet of water, the sound of a popper is often enough to bring them up. Popping is also the easiest way to get strikes in muddy water, when the visual search for food is limited by turbidity. It's effective too when schooling fish, such as white, black, or striped bass, are foraging on concentrations of bait fish. The sound commands their attention if you have to compete with a lot of panicky minnows.

[68]

A plug's ability to pop is built-in; the lure should have a slanting, concave face. When sitting on the water, most poppers float in a head-up position with tail submerged. A slight stroke of the rod tip lifts the plug to a horizontal position, and this causes the face to scoop water, creating a large bubble that breaks with a tantalizing sound.

The popper must be worked correctly. Its retrieve is slow, with long pauses. There is a tendency for beginners to pop themselves out of business, for many times too much noise will spook game fish rather than attract them. A good rule of thumb is to wait until the disturbance made by a popped plug has completely vanished—then count off ten seconds before popping again. Mild pops can be made with the rod tip moving upward and loud ones by using a sharp, downward jerk. If the plug flips out of the water, you are not holding the rod correctly in relation to the distance you have cast.

The correct rod position for any type of retrieve depends on the lure itself (its design and weight) and the length of line extended on the water. For example, a surface bait built to skip over the water calls for a rod held very high. A darter requires a downward-pointing tip to keep it weaving under the surface. And although you can begin all retrieves with a high rod on a long cast, you must gradually lower the tip to work many baits. It becomes increasingly difficult, for instance, to pop a surface plug when the extended line length is shortened, because the lure is eventually pulled over, rather than under, the water.

An experienced angler gauges the correct rod position with each cast. He tries to keep the tip at an angle from 45 to 60 degrees in relation to the line, whether he's working with tip up, down, or to the side. As much rod as possible should absorb the shock of a strike, yet it must never be so close to 90 degrees that he is unable to set the hooks.

The second technique I rely on is the whip retrieve. Essentially this is for the plug that has little, if any, incorporated action. The whip is most commonly used in salt water and in the South, but it's also effective on many occasions in fresh water. Starting with the rod tip at horizontal and pointed in the direction of the lure, pull the rod fast and forcefully in a 90-degree arc to the side of the body. The instant the rod stops, crank very fast to take up slack as you move the rod back to its original position.

When the rod again points in the direction of the lure, whip it once more. Repeat the process of reeling and whipping to give the plug a darting rhythm in a curved path below the surface.

Recently I caught forty-eight ladyfish on forty-nine consecutive casts with the whip retrieve. I began with a straight, fast return, and although the silver bombshells flashed behind my lure time and again, it wasn't until I started whipping the rod that I had my first strike. Saltwater game fish can be extremely selective in the matter of lure action and speed. Anybody who fishes for tarpon or snook regularly is usually a master of both popping and the whip retrieve.

My third method, one I learned from Pigmeat Johnson, is nodding. It's the manual opposite to whipping, and vastly different from popping. While the pop artist creates sounds and bubbles to draw the fish's attention to his lure, the nodder assumes that a fish is nearby, already watching the silent plug. The best time to nod is when you have located the lair of a big fish, or on those dreary days when the popper is left talking to itself.

Although you can nod with almost any kind of surface plug, the chances of a strike are greatly improved if you use the right type. The ideal is one with a propeller in the rear and a weighted tail section. The face of the plug should poke out of water so that it assumes the posture of a free-swimming frog resting on the surface. The idea is to tip the plug every few minutes so that it seesaws without any forward motion. After a reasonable length of time you can retrieve very slowly, with frequent pauses to let the plug nod again. This is a painfully patient method of bringing a bait back, but it pays off on smart fish.

I nodded a big lake trout last summer while casting for northern pike. This was unusual because the lakers were supposed to be out in deep water at the time. On another trip I nodded a 3¾-pound brook trout when I was looking for smallmouth bass. But yesterday was the payoff: I nodded a 10-pound gaff-topsail catfish in Lake Worth while casting for snook! Now, gaff-topsail catfish aren't high on my list of playmates, but this one was the biggest I ever saw, and I never heard of one being taken on a plug. I have caught blue and channel catfish on surface baits—but this gaff-topsail is strictly a garbage collector in our neck of the woods. All of which indicates that most, if not all kinds of fish, can be intrigued by a lure that literally sits and does nothing.

The fourth technique worthy of your attention is torpedoing. This is a refinement of spoon-skittering. It's faster than a fast retrieve—the plug should actually skip over the surface. There are several prerequisites. The lure must be long enough so as not to flip over your line. The rod must be long too, else you'll have to stand on a boat seat or a high bank to keep a maximum length of line above the water. And your reel must have a rapid rate of retrieve.

The idea behind torpedoing is to make the fish think that something good to eat is hightailing out of sight. Let me say in passing that although the days calling for a slowly worked plug outnumber the effective periods of torpedoing, this retrieve brings some of the most explosive strikes from reluctant fish I have ever witnessed. Invariably it stirs them to full speed with dorsal out, humping water behind the wildly skipping plug as though it were a last meal. It doesn't matter whether your quarry is a chain pickerel or a 200-pound tarpon. When the time is ripe, all predatory fish can be torpedoed.

The art of retrieving a plug is equally as important as good casting. In fact, anybody who can toss a bait twenty yards (and that's not difficult with modern enclosed-spool reels or spinning reels) may be reasonably certain of catching fish, provided he doesn't become addicted to automatic reeling. If a lake or a particular kind of fishing is new to you, it's worth the effort to ask the local boys how to manipulate their lures. Get the exact details. Most guides, pier operators, tackle dealers, and game protectors are reliable and generous sources of information.

And above all, if you find a piece of paper stuffed in the lure box, read it carefully. The manufacturer spent a small fortune in producing his bait, and he wants you to catch fish with it.

10

EVER NOD AT A BASS?

Pop, Whip, Nod, and Torpedo—they sound like an acrobatic team of dwarfs. But be honest: Which was the only one you've never really tried? You've certainly done a little popping and whipping in your time. Maybe in frustration you've even torpedoed an unproductive lure across the surface. But nodding? Have you ever really taken five whole minutes per cast to nod your lure home? Intrigued by the concept and utterly fascinated by the name of A. J.'s mentor, I went back for more information, and following is what I found. Incidentally, the sobriquet "Pigmeat" derives from the lavish pork barbecues Johnson was fond of hosting and in no way is intended to reflect unfavorably on his appearance or manners. Even so, his name gives Sirs Toby Belch and Andrew Aguecheek a run for their money!

GWR

EVER NOD AT A BASS?

After a rather successful tour of southern bass ponds several years ago, I ended my trip at Whistleberry Slough. My host, Mr. Pigmeat Johnson, was reputed to be the hottest bass fisherman in the Cajun country, an eminence which he'd attained with a homemade eye stopper that looks like a dirty silver cigar. The plug sits froglike on the water, its rear half under the surface. The real craft displayed by Mr. Johnson was not in his bait making, however, but in the way he brainwashed a bass.

The day started out well. We caught some 2- and 3-pounders, and once along a treey bank, where the sunlight shafted into the water, I saw a big one come up for a look, then dematerialize. I began experimenting with different lures because a bass of those proportions was entitled to the best I had to offer. But such activity was not for Pigmeat. He worked slower and slower, until finally he was just letting his plug float, nose above water. After what seemed like an eternity he twitched his rod tip and the plug nodded up and down. Then he stopped. I found myself watching his bait while I was casting. For some reason it makes me nervous to see a plug sitting in the same place doing nothing. I was about to ask Pigmeat whether he wanted to quit fishing, when his nodding plug disappeared into a deep gurgle. Pigmeat's old steel rod felt the sharp edge of success as the bigmouth lunged into the air for a shake.

[74]

There are many techniques in plugging. Bottom scratching with deep-planing lures lights firecrackers when your fish are down twenty-five or thirty feet. Torpedoing can be devastating if the bass are chasing schools of baitfish along the surface. Popping is traditional when the game fish are laying up in the weedbeds with full bellies. But nodding, according to Mr. Johnson, utilizes pure bass psychology. Before you can make a bass fidgety enough to wallop a sitting plug, you have to realize that the technique has a definite end. It's a competition in patience at first, for both you and the fish. "I don't imitate anything special with my plug," Johnson explained. "I just try to convince the bass that he's looking at something good to eat. When I leave my plug on the water that old daddy bass keeps his eyes open. He watches and watches and nothing happens. Then my plug nods a few times and that bass gets an itch. But he still thinks there's something wrong, and he decides to wait a bit longer. I let him wait a long time, then I give him a few more nods. Maybe another bass will come along and get him worried and there ain't nothing meaner than a worrisome bass. I believe that when two fish are around, this method works even better, because I've taken quite a few doubles when I'm nodding."

According to Johnson, he began nodding years ago when he bought his first casting outfit. "It sounds funny now, but I didn't know that plugs were meant to be reeled. I figured that they were like any other bait and the idea was to cast them out and wait for a bass to come along, the way you'd fish a minner. My son and I stood on the end of our dock one evening and caught twelve nice bass and a mess of shellcrackers without even moving the plug. We even left the plug floating while we tended to chores and we'd come back and find a fish had hooked hisself. When I finally did learn what casting was all about back in 1920, I found that I didn't always do so good when I reeled the plug so I nodded a mess onct in awhile. Some fellers think that noddin' is like popping a plug but they ain't alike at all."

Popping a plug or merely using a slow retrieve are not Pigmeat's techniques. For nodding, you have to use the right type of plug. The manufactured kind comes in three sizes: a ¾-ounce model with a 4-inch body length; a ½-ounce model with a 3½-inch body; and a ¼-ounce model with a 3-inch body. These all have propellers in the rear, which I think help when you finally get around to retrieving. The plugs are critically weighted in the tail so the snub-nosed face pokes out of the water. Some casters fish this bait with a slow, purring retrieve but its real attraction is the ability to tip up and down.

Next, you must have—and this above all—the patience to sit back and enjoy the sunshine while your bait does the fishing. This is very hard to do when you don't get results right away.

The difference between nodding and popping is subtle but distinctive. Anglers of the nodding school commence their exercises on the theory that a big bass is already nearby and looking at the plug. The pop artist creates sounds and bubbles to draw them from afar. Even a nearsighted bigmouth can find a deftly popped plug. The question asked by nodders is, "Will said bass sock a noisy bait?"

The obvious answer is "sometimes." Johnson feels, however, that if the caster is tossing his plug in the immediate vicinity of a bass the ratio of strikes will be greater for the quietly fished bait. Therefore, the success of nodding depends on how well the angler knows his water. "If you see fish hanging around the same place every day, you can bet your boots they'll be there right now, so why make a lot of rumpus with your plug? The popper works fine when the fish is in the right mood, but more often than not it puts them down and they won't strike anything at all."

To understand the mood he alludes to, you must first realize that surface plugs of any kind get their biggest play in shallow-water casting. Such plugs are made in a variety of actions, all aimed at disturbing the surface. They're usually designed to be most effective when fished very slowly. In using plugs that pop when jerked, it's customary to let them lie still after the cast, at least until the splash from their fall has subsided. Baits with a pronounced action (some pop louder or more violently than others) will bring fish from greater depths than those that make a mere bubble. When bass are bottom feeding in even ten feet of water they will sometimes come up for a noisy bait. If conditions indicate that very shallow water is holding fish, and this is usually so early and late in the day, the less-active plugs do their best work.

Pigmeat Johnson contends, however, that his nodding technique is a natural part of the sequence, in that bigmouth bass frequent the same areas whether or not they are actively feeding. "But when daddy bass decides his belly's full, he won't even follow your plug," says Pigmeat. "Anybody can prove that to hisself. If you ever get a school in clear water when you can see them, then cast a surface plug out. After it's been sitting awhile one will swim up and have a look. He has a halfway notion to take the critter just fell out of the sky so he's suspicious. Big minners don't drop from heaven. Most folks start reeling right away and ruin the whole thing. Now you just leave that plug there and that halfway notion will get to itchin' and burnin' his hide and the dang fool will come up again for another look. After he goes away again, *then* nod your plug just a bit. I've never fished with a man yet who could keep his eyes off my plug when I'm nod-fishing. The same goes for bass."

Pigmeat Johnson ordinarily fishes his plug for about five minutes in one spot. It seemed much longer to me, but I timed him. He gives the bass a few nods after two minutes, a few more at the four-minute mark, and then starts a feeble swim back to the boat. "I don't hold with the theory that an injured minner can swim the way most folks reel in a plug. All the hurt minners I ever saw just lay on the surface like they had been paralyzed. Onct in a while they give a weak kick but they ain't going nowhere. Funny thing is, though, you can't teach a man how to nod. Either he has the patience and knows what he's doing or else he's plumb uncertain and has to cast all over the pond." These casual, biting observations made sense to me but I didn't run into poor bass fishing until several months afterward.

Then Hamilton Jones and I were fishing a small lake in north Florida. We were on the water from dawn to nearly dark, catching not less than fifty bass, all of which we released. From the time we started fishing they struck indiscriminately at every plug we offered them. When bass are striking like that, it's foolish to draw any conclusions concerning methods of retrieve. Half the time they would hit the plug before we began reeling. We even caught two hefty blue catfish on our surface baits, which isn't too common. During the next few days I visited several other lakes nearby, and when I went back to see Hamilton he said the pond was in a slump. The fish had quit cold. We returned to all the same weedbeds and searched the creek mouths but the best we could muster was a few pound-size bass on the Black Eel bait. I think the eel would have dredged up more, and perhaps bigger, fish if I stuck with it, but the idea of testing Pigmeat's system appealed to me. Years ago, Jones's old boat livery collapsed during a storm and fell into the lake. The piers and lumber sank in from four to six feet of water and created some fine hiding places for bigmouths. This is where I went to work.

My first problem was the wind. The day I'd watched Pigmeat on Whistleberry Slough was one of flat calm, but now the breeze kept moving my skiff around and the plug wouldn't sit still because of the drag. I got out of the boat in my shorts and waded (an approach, incidentally, that I found most effective on subsequent trips). But changing the habits of twenty-five years of bassing is not easy. I tried hard to overcome the feeling that I was re- trieving much too slowly or not fishing in the right places. For half an hour I floated the plug over what looked like real hotspots, allowing five to six minutes for each cast. Hamilton came down to see what I was doing and while I was explaining the Pigmeat method of going crazy an old daddy bass swamped the plug. He burst up into the air with such a bang that Hamilton got to hollering like a parson and some tourists came down to see what the fuss was all about. Pretty soon we had collected quite a mob. The fish was no monster. It was about 5 pounds but full of spark and Hamilton took advantage of the moment to rent a few skiffs. I wasn't inclined to wade out of the pond in my polka-dot shorts, so I played the bass until he rolled over exhausted. I nodded only three more bass that afternoon but they were all twice the size of those we'd been catching before.

It's funny, you can't ever convince a fisherman that his theories are wrong, and it's equally hard to convince yourself that your new ones are right. But since that episode on Whistleberry Slough I've done enough nodding to believe that Pigmeat has discovered something worthwhile. So go to work on a bass psychologically, and you can fill in a few honor-badge applications.

PART III

FLIES, FLEAS, AND BEETLES

11

UPSTREAM—OR DOWN?

The practical fly fisherman stands between two extremes. On the one hand there's the dude who dresses as though he was designed by the consulting firm of Orvis, Bauer, and Dior. Everything is style for this cat. If you don't know the precise name and hook size of the fly you just caught a 3-pounder on, he sniffs as though you and the fish didn't exist. On the other hand there's the character for whom everything is content. He is a poacher at heart and wouldn't hesitate to use a hand grenade if he thought he could get away with it. Although the slob represents an undeniable hardship on fish, the snob works an even greater hardship on the sport itself.

The memory of one of the most satisfying brown trout I ever caught was tarnished by the jealous words of an erstwhile companion. He charged that I had not caught the fish *properly*. We had found the trout resting directly below a spillway in a New Jersey brook, and the force of the rushing water had precluded our attempts to present our flies upstream. Throughout the morning and by turns we returned to the run, but always with the same results: The fly would land, but even before the trout's brain had a chance to register the sight of food overhead, the line was swept back against our legs. Finally, in desperation, I went above the race and carefully crept out to a point where I could dangle my fly across the top of the swelling current close by the fish's nose. Pow, splash!—I nearly lost my rod when the clumsy knot connecting line and leader got caught at the tip. Only the spring of the rod prevented the line from breaking. However, my feelings of triumph were quickly dissipated by my friend's ridicule of the manner in which I had hooked the fish. Even though I was sensitive to his motives, his remarks did their corrosive work. Fortunately, A. J. McClane published "Upstream—or Down?" that same year (1960) and restored my angling equilibrium.

Actually A. J. had extolled the virtues of downstream dry-fly fishing in *Field & Stream* as early as March of 1951. And he has personally introduced many an angler to the deadliness of the downstream technique. Phil Clock, president of Fenwick Tackle, recalls how Al showed him the effectiveness of goofus bugs and grasshoppers fished downstream to the banks of the New and Green Rivers in Wyoming. In some cases, the fly was actually tossed up into the meadow and pulled out into the water as though the insect had just tumbled from the grass. "The fishing was nothing short of sensational," Phil recalls. "The only thing that marred the trip was the landowner on one side of the river riding parallel to us and carrying a rifle across his saddle. He said if we set one foot on his property, he'd kill us. Needless to say, for the two miles he kept pace with our raft, he was something of a distraction."

GWR

UPSTREAM—OR DOWN?

The kingfisher crouched on the limb of a gnarled petra tree and watched the river[1] below. For a moment we were partners in his tranquil enterprise. I could see nothing under the storm of tossing pearls that slapped my boots and rolled into black shadows, but the crested angler suddenly flashed over the water in silent pantomime. Then with a metallic *chr-r-r-r* he vanished into the Argentine forest. Perhaps what he saw frightened him.

My brown hairwing sailed below the tree with a feathery swish, and I felt the moths pounding in my stomach again. As the fly floated down the current, a huge landlocked salmon emerged from the shadows and cautiously swam behind it. This was his third inspection tour. I kept delaying drag by pulling more and more line from the reel, but after eighty or ninety feet the fly was sucked toward the tail of the pool. The salmon turned around and started toward his sanctuary with the gape-jawed weave of an old pro.

It was hopeless. I raised the rod and began cranking rapidly while pushing for shore. Just about the time my hairwing was churning across the surface like a miniature motorboat, that damfool fish came roaring back and smashed the floater flat. I won't belabor you with the explosive events that followed; suffice to say, a 10-pound landlocked salmon in swift water leaves nothing to the imagination. But according to the rule book I had committed two major breaches of dry-fly technique: I had cast downstream instead of up, and I had caused the fly to drag.

The fascination of angling lies in the fact that nobody can predict just what will happen on any given cast. But there's one cast in any sequence that I'll bet you have reason to remember on various occasions—the last one. How many times have you flogged the water without success and then, at the precise moment you decided to reel up and go elsewhere, had a fish bust the feathers?

A casual observer might call it luck, and many experienced anglers would agree. Encouraged, our angler goes back to fishing, but soon decides that he caught only the village idiot after all. That could be, but there's another factor: last casts are made with a complete change of pace. When a fly fisher decides to pack up and go home he forgets the rule book and does something that he has artfully avoided all day. Reeling in, he causes the fly to drag in abnormal fashion. Had he continued to work in a style comparable to the "lucky" cast (giving the fly real motion) more than likely he would take other fish.

Fundamentals, however, are difficult to ignore once learned. Ever since 1857, when W. C. (The Practical Angler) Stewart commanded purists to about-face and march upstream, dry-fly lore has become so narrowly confined that a modern caster looking downstream is about as well-oriented as

---

[1] "This was the greatest landlocked salmon river I ever fished," A. J. recalls. "It was known as simply Río Dos. There was also a Río Uno and Tres. (The map makers had apparently run out of names.) We camped for two weeks and caught salmon to 15 pounds, with many in the 10- to 12-pound range."

[83]

a squirrel without a tree. Except in the wild, tumbly rivers of western America —where everything goes with the current, including the angler—our felt-soled nobleman is a creature of habit.

Therefore, my semiprivate communication for this summer is to remind you that many fine trout will be hung on De-Liars simply because their captors flaunted tradition. I might add that while I'm writing primarily of trout, the same general principle also applies to salmon, smallmouth bass, grayling, or any other species that has grown antiseptic in its caution—or made the angler as blind as a bat.

Drag, by strict definition, is the condition that causes a fly to travel at a speed faster than the current it rides. Acceleration comes from the line, which is extended over currents of several different speeds. Partially caught in a swift flow, a portion of the relatively heavy line pulls ahead of the cast as a whole, dragging the sensitive fly along. This is evidenced in a dry fly when it suddenly goes skimming across the surface, or in a wet fly that takes off at breakneck speed on the downstream swing.

Unnatural motion seldom attracts spooky fish, and a dragging fly and line will generally send a trout running for cover. So it's important to know how to present a slack cast that will delay drag and get a natural drift. This is difficult when you're casting downstream, because the line tightens almost immediately. It's not only easier to eliminate drag by casting upstream, but you get other advantages.

Trout always position themselves with heads facing the flow. Thus the easiest way to stalk them is by coming up from behind, where their peripheral vision is limited. You can get closer to the fish, and when you present the fly upstream, it stands on the water quite naturally, twisting and turning with every subtlety of the current.

Although it's difficult for a beginner to manage a cast carried back toward him by the flow, he soon learns to keep the line taut by stripping in slack without pulling the fly. And he has a better chance of hooking a rising fish because his strike draws the fly back into the mouth on an upstream cast, and away from it on a downstream cast.

Finally, you disturb the water less when you fish upstream. Watch when a fish is hooked at the top of a small pool; he'll dash down and startle his neighbors with panicky acrobatics. If you're fishing downstream toward them you're in trouble. I have taken half a dozen fish out of a pool that would not have yielded more than one or two had I been casting downstream. By working up, nearly all hooked fish are drawn down with the current, which leaves the rest of the water undisturbed.

That is the whole argument for upstream fishing, and as a general stream tactic it can't be beat. But there are times when another tactic is called for, and learning to recognize those times is a valuable asset to the dry-fly caster.

We know, of course, that on many white-water rivers, downstream is the only possible direction in which you can work. A floater tossed on the slicks, even skipped over a custardy surface, can be amazingly productive. I have fished rivers like the Thompson in British Columbia where the very depth of the water demands going with the current.

The Thompson has whirlpools that suck down saw logs as if they were chips, and spit them up again a hundred yards downstream. Pool, in the angler's usual understanding of the term, is nonexistent; the Thompson is more like a giant wet road twisting along in streaks of froth that dissolve in those quiet places where steelhead lurk on summer evenings. Drag doesn't really matter on its broken surface, and letting the fly work slowly over one spot is the only way you can coax the fish into coming up. He probably has to be convinced that the floater will still be there when he reaches the top.

Shallow or calm water, particularly in rivers where brown trout predominate, is another matter, and the conditions for downstream fishing are more definitive. The obvious situations—a hat-lifting downstream wind or spots that can't be reached by casting upstream—are common enough. We also have the possibility of earning strikes by presenting the fly directly to a fish without showing line or leader, and adding an action to the floating pattern that puts drag to advantage. Ignoring my Argentine landlocked salmon, which came as an unearned dividend, we might examine these four downstream opportunities in more detail.

I can drive a fly line against very strong winds. When the m.p.h. reaches a velocity beyond comfort, however, I much prefer to work with it. A fierce downstream wind creates the conditions to move trout that wouldn't otherwise be caught. It limits their visibility in ruffling the surface, for one thing, and it also animates the fly. My regular summer-stream tools consist of a 7½-foot, 2½-ounce rod and an HEH line. This is hardly a breeze-beating outfit, but when aimed windward that line can do all sorts of tricks.

For best results, a long-hackled fly of the spider or skater type is necessary. Either one will move independent of the current because it stands away from the water without penetrating the surface film. A ten- or twelve-foot leader, tapered to 4X or finer, is equally important; its flexible length lets the feathers fly freely.

If you are on the river with heavier tackle when a wind starts, it's possible to get some results but the total score will only be proportionate to your gear; a heavy three-diameter line won't rise from the surface in anything short of a gale, and a short or heavy leader will only anchor the dry fly in place. And bear in mind that big floaters tied on small light-wire hooks do the most jumping.

We had a poor summer on the East Branch of the Delaware two years ago. Although the stream holds more large trout now than before, due to the cold bowels of the Downsville impoundment, a prolonged drought had shrunk the pools and the fish became dour. One morning the earth seemed like a furnace and a strong wind sent limbs clattering against each other. When the storm began I was about a mile above the Harvard bridge. I had covered the run thoroughly with nymphs and dry flies and taken two small browns. As the wind increased I decided to fish back to my car. I tied on a big skater-type dry fly and, wading deep, half-cast half-fed the line down the river.

The skater skated, bounced, and jumped in the face of the wind. Where the current breaks at the pool tail, a 16-inch rainbow belted the fly in midair. Typical of the deep-bodied trout inhabiting that watershed, he felt heavier than his 2-pound weight.

The wind continued to whip my skater about, and ten minutes later I rolled another rainbow in midstream, and he seemed much larger than my first. He wouldn't come back. A brooding black squall loomed over the hills as I hooked a second trout. I was holding my rod high, letting the long-hackled fly flap up and down, when an eager brown snatched it on an up flap. It took at least fifteen minutes to lead him into shallow water where I could punch a tag in his jaw. After the trout was quiet, I De-Liared him at 19½ inches and 3¾ pounds. I stroked his belly for a moment and we parted friends. It hadn't been a great morning, but a brace of good fish from the East Branch is ample reward.

The second situation—covering spots that can't be reached any way but by downstream casting—offers interesting opportunities. For the most part these are awkward places that anglers habitually avoid or pass by. For example, I often fish a stretch of the lower Neversink that has a perfect hiding hole for large trout. At the top of the riffle along the far bank is a hemlock log jammed against a huge boulder. Not visible from the downstream side is a deep pocket of water that forms in front of the barrier.

During my first year on the stream I left many precious blue-dun patterns in the bark while trying to shoot one under the log. Today I don't even try for a lucky cast when fishing upstream. I work all the way up the riffle to a place where a gravel bar slopes out above the log jam; it means going to wader-top level on well-greased stones—which is not something one does casually when there are miles of easy water ahead—but it pays off like an

[86]

overdue slot machine. Periodically, over a decade, I have found lunkers in residence that were more than eager to seize a downstream dry fly.

I am sure fish feel secure there, but more important, they are removed from the daily parade of artificials. On all streams I always pay particular attention to bridge abutments, sharp bends in the riverbed, rows of boulders, and brush sweepers, such as old tree limbs, that dangle in the water. These invariably offer a blind side to the upstream caster. Brooks also provide a variety of tricky covers—tunnels under the willows, footbridges, fallen timber. Cocked and floating naturally, a dry fly will invariably take at least one good fish when sent with the current to such hidden places.

The third opportunity for downstream casting is one that involves individual fish—presenting the fly without showing leader or line. As a rule, all downstream casts put the fly in front of the fish before he can see more than a fraction of our terminal gear, but the problem we are solving here isn't concerned with wind or awkward places—the object is to hook a spooky fish in perfectly open sunlit water.

I'm sure you have experienced bright summer days when trout vanish while the line is still hanging in air. Maybe you find one rising in a quiet pool, and before the taper has unrolled he ducks for cover. Even though your cast is long, with the line dropping like a cobweb and curved away from his position, the next fish flushes anyhow.

This is the kind of day when you can take trout on the downstream drift, not only because of the fly-first presentation but because you don't have to cast into that aerial window. On some pools, like the one next to our summer house, which is fished every day of the season, the trout become so keenly aware of external movements, I am convinced, that we don't stand a chance of hooking anything more than a yearling with an upstream presentation. In our Home Pool, for instance, a smart angler can take fish consistently by going well upstream and letting the fly drift down. I put a tag in a 7-pound tiger trout that way, a fish that had been caught twice before and would instinctively dive for an undercut when anybody waved a rod near him.

Many years ago I used to fish a small stream in the Catskills called Rider Hollow. There was a limpid Guernsey-bordered pool at the end of the stream, where it entered Dry Brook. The pool was good for five or six fish when worked up; I always covered the shallow tail to remove any small brook trout that might flush and warn their elders. Released in back of me, they'd invariably dart under the bank. After a while I got to know every fish in the pool, and the largest of these was a handsome native brown trout that took a feeding position in midstream. Sometimes he would review

[87]

several different patterns, but usually one cast was enough to put him down. Obviously the fish had met anglers before. One afternoon, after taking my usual quota of easy trout, I was at the top of the water changing flies when the brown made a splashy rise. I marked the widening rings about sixty feet below and knotted on a Gold Honey Dun. Ordinarily I would have walked below a rising fish, but casting at this one had now merely become a courteous gesture.

I worked out about forty feet of line and dropped the Dun in his alley. Pulling more line from the reel, I shook out the extra yardage. It seemed like an eternity before the fly reached his lair—and then nothing happened. The spidery fly just sat quietly on the surface. I finally gave it a very slight twitch—and *blip* it disappeared in a wink. That timorous motion was enough to draw a strike. Although the trout probably weighed no more than 1½ pounds, he was sassy yellow with carmine spots—and really quite distinguished for Rider Hollow. More important, he made me aware of the possibilities in downstream presentation.

Correctly executed, the slack-line cast is aimed directly down to the position of the fish, but it should float about half that distance. In other words, if the trout is holding sixty feet away, you should drop the fly about thirty-five or forty feet downstream and cover the difference by shaking out more nylon.

There are several ways of making slack-line deliveries. The oldest, and perhaps easiest for most people, is to false-cast in the usual manner and, on the final stroke forward, stop the rod at a 45-degree angle; then, when the line begins to pull-shoot, simply wiggle the tip from side to side. This lateral motion will create little curves in the outgoing line.

Play with this technique for a few minutes and you'll find that you can make narrow or wide elbows of slack with no effort. For our purposes, seven or eight small curves should be enough. When you drift the fly down on a fish you don't want slack concentrated in one big belly, which would get caught broadside in the current and cause drag. As a tactical advantage, the initial presentation should be made in a perfectly natural float. After the cast is fished out, you can begin animating the fly against a dragging line. So the rod-wiggling must be timed to distribute the curves throughout the length of the cast. This brings us to a point that is almost completely lost in upstream casting, or at least doesn't exist with the same latitude on currents of modest speed—animation.

The fourth downstream opportunity is, as I have indicated, a very productive method at times when you're casting with the wind. Of course, a fly can be animated without borrowing the help of a breeze, and there are days—

particularly in the late summer and fall—when a few calculated strokes will produce exceptional fishing.

I believe there is a solid argument for the success of a retrieved dry fly that many casters overlook. Ordinarily a river surface is freckled with flotsam —bark, leaves, twigs, weeds, and whatnot. When all these objects are coming over the trout's head, the slightest movement from something alive draws his immediate interest. Both dragonflies and stone flies push their abdomens through the surface when trying to get airborne. They also paddle frantically with their feet, and in sunlight this creates a sparkling trail on the water. A grasshopper resembles a leaning ICBM trying to get off the pad. The spasmodic kick of a caddis fly is hardly noticeable from above, but at trout level it looks like an explosion. The big mirror is a world of inanimate and animate things and, as the old he-hit-a-cigarette-butt story reveals, the competitive fish must make quick decisions.

There is only a shade of difference between a natural movement and an unnatural one imparted to the fly. As I have suggested, on individual rising fish an effort should be made to get a dragfree drift on the first cast. The fly will reach a point in its float when the trout either accepts or rejects it, and in the latter case the angler must draw his floater back for a new cast. When working directly down on a fish, this invariably requires pulling it over him—a motion that is either going to excite a strike or put the trout down. You will rarely get a second chance, as you might in upstream casting when the fly dances away on tippytoes.

The retrieve must begin *before* the line comes near the fish. This is the moment when a fine-line point, long leader, and correctly hackled fly make a critical difference. On calm water in particular, coarse terminal gear is going to create a wake and spoil the whole illusion. Raise the rod slowly and begin twitching gently, bringing the skater upstream in short pulsing strokes. If the fly is standing up on its hackles and the fish doesn't respond after it has moved a few feet, lower your rod and let the skater drift near him again.

A keen fish sense helps at moments like this, but gradually you will learn to gauge the fly's action according to the response of the trout. A sudden wiggling of the pectorals or a change in his posture may indicate extreme interest. He may make false passes at it. But if nothing else works, try skimming the skater away at a steady speed. As last-cast reeling has repeatedly proved, a positive and continuous flight often triggers blasting strikes. Although mayfly lore more or less conditions our thinking in terms of delicate ephemeral flutters, the fact is that many other aquatic insects leave the surface like a scared coot.

On civilized waters fish can become practically immune to artificial lures.

Generally speaking, the similarity of baits and presentations reaches the point of monotony. If a particular spinning lure, for example, enjoys a rash of success on a heavily trafficked river, most anglers will continue to use it, and in a short time the fish will ignore its arrival and departure. This is less true of fly patterns, perhaps, but from the standpoint of presentation, originality is almost totally absent.

We wade to the easiest positions and cover the obvious places. If stream gravel could hold bootprints you would find well-worn paths on which angler after angler has made the same calculated casts day after day. Rare is the man who works from the difficult bank or takes the time to study each lair and vary his tactics to best advantage.

For all the years I've lived on a river, I'm still learning new ways of fishing familiar pools and enjoying the fascination of what is so clearly to be seen but utterly inviolate except by stealth and art.

12

PRESENTING THE MUDDLER MINNOW

The next best thing to creating an effective lure is to introduce one that becomes a classic. In fact, so obsessed are certain outdoor writers with this brand of immortality they spend untold hours at the workbench trying to come up with the Watson's Wattle or Don's Dangling Dun that will outshine all the rest. On other occasions they show themselves more susceptible to the latest gewgaw than even the most gullible of angling Clem Kadiddlehoppers. After catching one or two pickerel with Fred's Fabulous Furd Fly, these aspirants to the hall of fame pose with the lure and swear allegiance to it till death do them part.

None of this is A. J.'s style. Like most outdoor writers, he is offered his share of new angling equipment. Unlike most, he does not accept freebies. If he sees something that interests him, he buys it, then tests it. When McClane finally puts his blessing on a line or lure, his word is better than the *Good Housekeeping* Seal of Approval. Thus when he introduced and underwrote a drab-colored, bulbous-headed, ridiculously named streamer back in 1949, only A. J.'s reputation for honesty and conscientious reporting saved the thing from being laughed back to oblivion. A good thing it wasn't —there are few fishermen today who don't owe at least one lunker to the mighty Muddler Minnow.

GWR

PRESENTING THE MUDDLER MINNOW

I was sitting in Dud's Café one afternoon, working on a slab of watermelon, when the boys were discussing whether billy goats eat tin cans or not. Dud allowed as how he was an authority on goats and that they eat only the paper labels, to get the glue underneath. This turned the conversation to fishing in Lake Sardis, and as their voices settled into a flow of sound, a fat man with deep sour lines in his face said, "Muddler Minnow." I nearly fell off the stool. Coming as it did in Tupelo, Mississippi, I would have been less surprised if he had recited the Copernican system.

It seems this fellow had snaffled some big crappie on the Muddler, and as he spoke, the words echoed in my head. A few days before, a writing-type citizen had said "Muddler Minnow" at the Outdoor Writers meeting in Rolla, Missouri. And a week before that, a gent on the Chickahominy River in Virginia had asked me if I had ever used the Muddler Minnow. Did I ever use it? This lengthy catalog of backward glances does not unfold easily, but the name repeats and repeats with the same inflammatory rhythm of a rising trout. I am the original victim of the Muddler Minnow.

Now, it may be that all flies are effective merely as an end result of a primary truth—the automatic response of a healthy young trout to his victuals. But before I'm found in tar and feathers astraddle a fence rail, I'll tell you straight out, the Muddler Minnow makes fish want things they don't want. Tossing a Muddler on the water is like showing a He-trout a picture of a half-naked She-trout awinkin', with a banner across her butt that says, "Can't help but love a feller who eats Muddler Minnows." The fly makes blubbering idiots out of smallmouth bass, and if my enthusiasm tends to the superlative, let me say that I've suffered with it for five years.

Like the day on the Elkhorn in Kentucky when the smallmouths came so easily to the Muddler that except for the miracle of their numbers there was no excitement left in catching them. And there was that cold, rain-soaked day on the White River in Vermont, when the Muddler dredged one rainbow after another out of fast water. Like the gray, heat-haze day on the Spring River in Arkansas, when I stopped at a roadside stand for some ice cream. While licking a Kreamy Kustard, I saw a flock of cedar wax-wings skimming and diving over the lime-colored flat. The lady who ran the Kreamy machine said nobody caught much there except carp, buffalo-fish, and a few jack salmon, but the waxwings were having a ball, and I was sure bass would be near. Catching them was practically anticlimactic; like the birds, the smallmouths were feeding on newly hatched damselflies, and every eligible cast brought a strike. There was a day on Butte Lake in British Columbia when the Muddler had the same impact on the cutthroat.

But before recollection outspeeds my pen, I will simply state what every-one who was reading *Field & Stream* in the year 1949 knows anyhow, that we introduced a new fly pattern created by Don Gapen in Nipigon, Ontario. Now, after taking hundreds of fish with it, I feel safe in saying that the Muddler Minnow should find a place among the all-time greats.

To many of my friends, the beginning will be a twice-told tale, so I will make the briefest possible sketch of it. Guy Kibbee and I were beating a Quebec pond to a froth one morning with no luck at all. It was like trying to remove freckles with a gum eraser. Our flies must have passed before the eyes of twenty-five thousand trout presumably addicted to the use of food, but they lay around in stunned silence. Finally, I tied on one of Don Gapen's Muddler Minnows and slapped it on the water. A brookie came up for a look with the exploring hesitancy of a man walking on fresh ice. He touched the fly gently, then fell on it. Nothing essential to our mutual enjoyment was

[93]

left out. The squaretail kicked, dove, jumped, and careened around the pond like he'd gone berserk. Guy kept saying, "Man, dig that crazy trout!" We dug them.

For ten days we uprooted one big brookie after another. I estimated later that I had caught and released about twenty trout over the 4-pound mark. But when you desperately clasp fish measured in inches and then fondly pat them in pounds, there is a tendency to lose perspective. No angling-type citizen on the hills, plains, or the great river valleys is immune to spasms of success, and in estimating the reason we tend toward unscientific prejudice.

Ordinarily, I'm not really fussy about fly patterns. A well-tied Light Cahill, Hendrickson, or Quill Gordon, if there's enough light to see it, will get my vote every time. I like to use spider-type flies also, especially the Blue Dun Spider, when the stream is low and clear. But the Muddler Minnow is a form and substance completely unlike orthodox dry flies. It is long, slim, and makes practically no wake when retrieved over still water. To a fish, the fly probably represents four insect families: dragonflies, damselflies, the larger stone flies, and grasshoppers. There is nothing mayflyish about the Muddler. In fact, it is definitely less effective in fast-water streams where the mayfly form is dominant. This is a fly for big, quiet rivers and lakes, which means smallmouth and largemouth bass, brown trout, and squaretails. Lake rainbows are very partial to the pattern when fished dry, but prefer their Muddlers worked as a streamer fly in fast rivers.

Actually, Don Gapen intended the Muddler to be a streamer dressing to imitate the sculpin, darter minnow, or Miller's Thumb, depending on where you fish. Sculpins are really a family of forage fish known as muddlers, which live on or near the bottom of streams and lakes. They have large, fanlike pectoral fins and somewhat flattened heads. There is a northern and southern muddler, a spoonhead muddler, as well as a deep-water and slimy muddler. Yet one chap in the Ozarks told me this year that he never saw such a good imitation of a brook stickleback; another fellow on the Shenandoah in Virginia said it was the deadliest suggestion of a crayfish he had ever put in front of a smallmouth. The interesting thing is that the fly suggests many different aquatic foods to both angler and fish.

I must admit the Muddler isn't handsome when you first look at it. One Sunday night I stopped by to see Carl Hoffman[1] on the Beaverkill. In a voice somewhat muffled by mashed potatoes, Carl asked to see the fly that

---

[1] Hoffman, deceased, was a management consultant for McKinsey & Company. He wasn't the first angler to pooh-pooh the Muddler on first sight. Fly-tyers Dan Bailey and Harry Darbee both laughed aloud when Al showed them the new streamer.

I had been taking my trout with, so I carefully set one on the linen tablecloth. Carl stared at the Muddler without moving the fork from his mouth. Just then, Mrs. Hoffman arrived with the gravy bowl and set it on top of the Muddler. Carl's eyes rested on the bowl, then he shifted his gaze to the end of the fork as though it was the most remarkable object on earth. "Been doing any spinning?" he asked. I felt like pouring the gravy over his head. Perhaps Mr. Gapen carved an odd puppet, but the world is full of such things as platypuses, oarfish, flying foxes, and similar extravagances which are accepted without question, so the scorn seems excessive.

Ellis Newman[2] and I tried to improve on the dressing of the Muddler Minnow. We substituted every hair, feather, wool, and tinsel we could think of, but we wore out our nights in a devil dance of frustration. It can't be made prettier and still be effective. The tail is simply a fiber of turkey-wing quill and the body flat gold tinsel. The wing, which should be just about the length of the hook, is made of matched fibers of turkey-wing quill, with sparse bunches of white and black impala on both sides. The hackle is a bunch of deer hair placed on top of the hook, then secured to flare forward. Only a small amount of hair should flare, as this part is trimmed into a head shape. Ellis cements every operation in tying for extra strength, but the ingredients are rugged and the Muddler will take a real beating.

As a dry-fly design, the Muddler Minnow is quite different. The dressing makes good use of buck hair for one thing; instead of being in the wings or built up in the body, the hair is used as hackle. It floats like a cork. There is no body weight to support, and when tied on light wire hooks (I generally use No. 8, 4X Long, on 3X wire) the Muddler sits insect-fashion over the water. I put a few drops of dry-fly oil on the hackle and then stroke some of the buck hair out to give it that scraggly-insect look.

Although I seldom use the Muddler as a sunken fly, I always keep a dozen or so dressed on heavy wire hooks to fish streamer-style when the occasion arises. The fact that the deer hair tends to bob the Muddler to the surface

---

[2] Newman was caretaker of the Turnwood property. Al regards him as "the greatest wing shot and fly-caster who ever lived—bar none. Ellis regularly threw measured casts of over 200 feet, and his entire style of delivery—particularly the long, slow backcast—was breathtakingly beautiful." In the days when Al was hosting the *Field & Stream* Fishing Clinic at the National Sportsman's Show in New York, Ellis Newman was the anchorman for the distinguished casting team of Marvin Hedge, Joan Salvato (now Mrs. Lee Wulff), and Bill Taylor. Ironically, three of the great fly-casters of that era died tragically: Newman in a gun accident; Johnny Dieckman, National and International Champion, when a jet crashed at then Idlewild Airport, New York; and Jon Tarantino, also National and International Champion, was murdered two years ago in a San Francisco robbery.

makes it a perfect pattern for diving and bobbing, a type of retrieve that is most useful in lake fishing. To complete the illusion, it's important to use a long leader; mine is eleven feet long tapered to a twenty-eight-inch, .010-inch-diameter tippet section.

Ellis caught my enthusiasm for the Muddler Minnow years ago when we were fishing a lake in the Catskill Mountains. I needed a large trout for a photo project, and content in the knowledge of where such trout lived, we set out with a twenty-gallon aerated tub on the back of Ellis's pickup truck. Not only were we absolutely certain that the fish would be caught on spinning tackle, but we used only lures adaptable to a single hook with the barb filed off. It never occurred to us on what dubious basis this tub-filling would be accomplished. To say that our threadlining proved a blooper would be a masterpiece of understatement. In four hours of continuous casting we did not move one trout. Like most truly heroic conflicts of angling, this war against the fish was not won by the most ingenious permutation or combination of fishermen's wits. Ellis merely said, "The hell with it, let's do some fly-fishing." We did. And we Muddled brown trout in places that had been covered thoroughly with our spinning lures.

The most difficult fish in my Muddling career was a relatively small one, a brown trout of about 2 pounds. An idea of the astronomical size this figure represents is suggested by the fact that Crazy Man Brook usually produces trout in the less than ½-pound class. The brook touches the property of a rather eccentric farmer, who sometimes greets strangers as if they were country cousins and sometimes throws rocks at them, or sneaks up behind them and suddenly screams incoherent barnyard homilies. There was a big breeze snoring in the woods that morning and, as luck would have it, I saw my host dashing along the bank, shirttails flying and shouting, "Don't take too long! Don't take too long!" Then he laughed and ran away, which I presumed to be an invitation.

The trout lay up in the first long pool, which is formed by a ledge and bordered by sweepers of red moss. He spooked on the first cast, so I marked him down for later and worked upstream. There were no insects on the water and no rising fish, but I covered every dub and depression on the stream bed and picked up a dozen or so small brookies and brown trout.

Toward afternoon I walked back to the first pool, and there he was again, resting over a fan of gravel where the current tumbled down. Possibly the sun was in a better position for me; in any case he didn't spook this time, and the Muddler danced nimbly over his head. The trout turned and took it easily, as if he was certain nothing could be wrong. At the first sting of the hook he shot across stream and under the ledge. After a few minutes, the old brute came out of the ledge, groggy but with heavy power and rage in him, and I respected his strength. I told myself that he would glide to the top to put his head out and thrash like any small-stream trout and I would get my net around him. But he lit out of the pool as if he had his pants full of hornets. Naturally, the farmer arrived at this point, and there began the craziest episode of Crazy Man Brook. The old man leaped into the stream, shoes and all, to "catch" my trout. I do believe that he thought he was helping me, but at the time it was nip and tuck as to who would outrun whom. The trout and I finished in a dead heat.

The Darbee incident was, I think, more typical of my Muddler experiences. Harry is a professional fly tyer, and he examined the Muddler with a physician's detachment that afternoon. He said that he didn't want to fish but would paddle the canoe for me. He paddled for about twenty-five minutes. We went only a short distance from the cabin when I hooked the first trout. Five minutes later another trout came to the Muddler. After taking five brown trout one after another, I offered the rod to Harry, and presently he hung a beautiful fish that broke off under a stump. As the trout swam away, the pond became stale and gray, where only seconds before it had been bathed in a beautiful radiance. The brownie had my only Muddler in his mouth. Oh, we tried all kinds of flies for the rest of the afternoon, but not another fish hit. Sifting the light stuff of which this is made, one might say that the trout simply stopped feeding. I can't believe that; neither does Harry.

These, gentlemen, are some of my experiences with the Muddler Minnow. I heartily endorse the pattern as one of the most effective flies you can put over trout and bass in lakes or slow-flowing streams. The most useful sizes are No. 6 for largemouth bass, salmon, and steelhead, and No. 8 for smallmouth bass and trout. A No. 10 is sometimes productive, but I don't believe that it's necessary to go that small, because the pattern, after all, is meant to represent a rather large insect. For streamer-fly fishing, a No. 4 or No. 6 on 1X or 2X wire would be right.

13

MR. BOTZ AND THE BEETLE

The camp at Turnwood was part of the old Jay Gould estate, and the accommodations, although rustic, were built with the good life in mind. The dining room, a building separate from the main house and enclosed in sliding glass doors and perched over a branch stream, dominated the "Kitchen Pool," a strictly off-limits home[1] for some very large trout. It was the custom at dinner time to throw bits of ham, turkey, or cheese to the fish who splashed and surged in a manner calculated to astonish new visitors. With an 11-pound trout (a three-year resident and therefore a stellar performer) smashing through the guests' soup course, a napkin tucked under one's chin was prerequisite.

Naturally idyllic circumstances like these rarely remain exclusive for very long. Al and Patti invited friends who in turn invited friends, and Ellis Newman eventually created a shooting and casting school on the Alfred Hudson Marks property across the river. Some weekends A. J. had difficulty recognizing many of the people traipsing over the lawn or wading through the streams. He was surprised one morning to see actor Terry-Thomas emerge from one of the two guest cottages and immediately mistake McClane for the "gamekeeper."

It was on one such weekend that Al met Mr. Botz. All A. J. ever found out about the fellow was that he worked on Wall Street. But there was never any notion of throwing the gate-crasher out. He was the source of too much fun—and insight into the ways of trout.

GWR

MR. BOTZ AND THE BEETLE

For a number of years I have kept a fairly complete set of notes on my fishing trips, and one comment appears in the margins so frequently that I am beginning to think that the presence or absence of mayflies on American trout streams is highly overrated as a factor in angling success. The bread and potatoes in a trout's larder are, in my opinion, being neglected. As an experiment this past season I spent six weeks on the Beaverkill River, in New York. This stream is considered typical eastern trout water and has an abundance of insect life. Yet during the month of May and for half of June, mayflies were so scarce that they hardly played a role in trout diet and, contrary to all reports I heard of green drakes hatching up or down

---

[1] Arnold Gingrich describes the only fishing expedition ever made in the Kitchen Pool on pages 118–121 of *The Well-Tempered Angler.*

the river, no amount of searching revealed the drakes in their stylized fertility rite. The few that did appear, beginning on June 9, were eaten avidly by the trout. Perhaps this insignificant fact could be put down to conditions of the year. If so, I have been repeating myself for eight years on streams throughout the country. The point of this matter is that there are insect forms more important to trout than the mayfly, which cannot be imitated by fully 90 percent of the fly patterns you are carrying today.

I have already told you about the Muddler Minnow and how important it is when trout are feeding on stoneflies and dragonflies, so the story of Mr. Botz and the beetle must follow. You see, Mr. Botz was staying at the same fishing camp where I was eight years ago. He had an odd wrist motion, one found among quick drinkers and yo-yo players. Although he had absorbed the explicit standards set forth in modern treatises on fly casting, he unconsciously spoiled the meals of a large number of trout by the mere act of raising line from the water. His back casts would have torn the underpants from lesser men, and he waded as though directing somebody else's legs out of a saloon. In brief, Mr. Botz had not caught a trout by the summer of his second season.

Now picture if you can a quiet pool with trout feeding softly just below an old dam. It is the Elm Tree Run. These grim sentinels have preserved the pool among them by rendering movement in that narrow space forever unprofitable. The sun shines on the water for only a little longer each day than it might illuminate the bottom of a well. I have seen great casters, whose lines rose and fell like a lover's whisper, whose hobnails were muffled to the padding of a giant cat, stumble away from the Elm Tree Run with heavy hearts and broken spirits. But as paradise lay across the stony desert of Babel, there Mr. Botz found his Eden. The june-bug beetles were marching across the elms and tumbling over the dam to build a blinding blaze of hunger in the damp pit of the trout. The fish gulped these fat, brown, shiny-backed insects as a weakling does a patent medicine that promises virility. And for once Mr. Botz could do no wrong. He worked like a cat in a mouse factory. When his line wasn't in a tree, it was stretched from the maw of a trout. Mr. Botz cold-decked ten slab-sided rainbows before quitting his crusade in an unholy land.

Since that day I have always referred to a flood of beetles as a "Botz situation." My notebook is so full of them, on streams all over the country, that I feel there is a gap between entomological and angling truth which needs some filling. Most citizens will ignore a beetle as happy picnickers disregard the ants on a fine summer's afternoon. For several years at least, my notebook indicates that I also ignored tiny events on the stream which might easily have been epoch-making, if the catching of larger trout may be dignified by such an adjective. Unlike Mr. Botz, who was immune to the contagion of mayflyitis, I could look in the stomach of a trout and, finding no trace of drake, dun, or spinner, confidently pronounce that this was truly a bad season. During the recent Botz situation, I visited a fish camp where all the guests were on the front lawn playing baseball. Inquiry revealed that the "mayfly was off," and, believing that the trout wouldn't feed until it was on, they had dissolved into a group so corrupted as to be entirely unrecognizable. Great trout were feeding regular as clockwork just beyond their outfield.

The imitation of natural trout-stream insects depends to a large degree on the presence of those particular insects. I do not believe, for instance, that an artificial mayfly of any kind is very convincing to the trout unless it is presented at a time when fish are conditioned to looking for the natural. It doesn't occur to the fish eating them that there is anything other than delight in the fact that he is about to eat more, even though it may be your imitation; a fly designed to simulate some other insect may be regarded with suspicion. Conversely, when trout are feeding on grasshoppers, beetles, caddis flies and many other insect forms, the typical divided-wing dry fly is a transparent absurdity to old fish. Look for a moment at the stomach contents of the 17-inch brown; this is what I call an end-of-the-season trout. None of the foods found in his stomach can be suggested by anything but a bucktail or a large nymph pattern; nevertheless he grabbed a floating beetle artificial. This trout, and others, was taken during a period of very poor fishing as far as the dry fly was concerned. As the season closes, trout are conditioned to seeking large food forms and, I might add, active ones. A dry fly fished in slight twitches against the current or across a slow, deep pool will produce amazingly well as the cold weather approaches. I have seen September fish gorged on beetles, notably on western rivers such as the Snake and Deschutes. An incident occurred last fall with a trout and a beetle just below the town of Bend, Oregon, which would make even Mr. Botz think twice.

Coming to a long, glassy run I climbed up on the bank and made searching casts to the bank opposite. There was a series of dark holes dug under the meadow grass that looked promising and working the fly across, then slacking the line to drift down, I had fifteen or twenty feet of drift before the fly swung around. Not a fish moved until I had walked almost to the end of the glide. A large brown trout came from one of the pockets as the fly turned and he turned with it, stalking the beetle even as I twitched it back against the current. Just about the time his curiosity was satisfied, the beetle

[102]

had arrived at a gravel rib in midstream, where it stuck fast. The fool fish actually picked at the beetle, hoping to pry it loose, while I jiggled the line in an effort to help him. The trout finally lost patience and excused himself with a flip of his tail.

In the margins of my record book, I have made notations from time to time concerning the results of trout postmortems as compared to the type of food the fish appeared to be feeding on. I'll explain how this works. After leaving the Beaverkill in June, I fished north through Vermont, in the Black River, the White, Mad, Winooski, and Little Otter, taking rainbows that were pink-cheeked and newly minted into manhood, but it was on the pond west of Little Otter that my flies dissolved amid the grim hilarity of wiser trout.

The day started badly. My line wouldn't turn over smoothly and I threw knots in my leader. Fish after fish splashed along the shore, apparently chasing minnows, yet none of my bucktail or streamer patterns brought a strike. One tub-sized trout cruised back and forth, exploding bait fish in showers. Finally, I tried the Muddler Minnow fished dry, working it slowly around the old brush piles where he was feeding. He hit with a splash. This was an 18-inch brown trout. An examination of the stomach contents reveals that minnows were not his objective at all. The trout was taking beetles directly from the submerged limbs, as evidenced by the pieces of bark and quantity of beetles. The pursuit of an occasional dragonfly or two-winged fly accounted for the splashing, which in turn spooked the minnows hiding in the brush. For several days the Muddler and an imitation beetle paid off.

As early as the end of April, though, a Botz situation was brewing. The 15-inch brown trout was typical of these cold-weather fish. The mainstay of their diet was caddisworms, particularly stone caddis, which they ate case and all. But the nocturnal june bugs were making an appearance and every stomach examined showed at least two or three in evidence. In a random sampling of trout caught by me and other anglers during the forepart of May, in only one instance was the remains of a mayfly nymph found. Yet stream-bottom research indicated the mayfly nymph to be abundant. Gradually, june-bug beetles became an increasing item of trout diet so that by May 15, the 14-inch brook trout typified my samples—in exceptional condition, butter-fat and full of june bugs.

Oddly enough, the strike of a trout to the natural or artificial is very unhurried, without splash and often little more than a slight pull. The natural floats awash, like a half-sunk rowboat, and the trout apparently finds them easy prey, taking them firmly and holding them in a closed mouth until the fish has positioned himself in the current again. When casting upstream with a long line, my only indication of a strike was that the float back had stopped. This was with a deer-hair-body pattern, which absorbed just enough water to ride in the surface film. When casting in the still waters of a lake, I simply left the beetle to sink slowly and a gentle tug signaled the play to come.

Big fish seemingly eat beetles no differently than the small trout. One afternoon on Forest Lake, I was fishing with Francis Davis when my line slipped downward. We never saw the trout, but for twenty minutes he lay on the bottom, shaking his head until the leader snapped. By June 8, dragonflies became an item of trout diet, and the Muddler fished dry worked as often as the beetle. Beetles continued to be important all summer, however, and they're filling the bellies of big trout even as you read these pages.

There's no doubt in my mind that some of our standard wet-fly patterns, such as the Silver Doctor, Leadwing Coachman, and Black Gnat, are mistaken for beetles by the trout. The gaudy Silver Doctor has all the flash and color of an iridescent beetle, while the Leadwing and Gnat patterns are fat and dark. Many anglers believe that the Royal Coachman simulates some kind of beetle, and possibly under certain conditions of light it does. I do find, however, that a fly designed to represent the natural is a vast improvement over the could-be counterparts. There are a few on the market, and I have had good results with them and also with an excellent fluorescent-green plastic june-bug imitation. Although it is difficult to cast, it really gets 'em.

But fly tyers in general have done very little in devising imitation beetles, largely because the fat, shell-backed bug is difficult to simulate. If you build the body of chenille, it will soak up water and sink like a rock. If you build it of deer hair, the body alone becomes a laborious operation and not economical for a pro tyer, who has to sell in the regular price range. Rubber and cork have been worked to a lather, but no effective patterns that I know of have been devised in these materials.

Although I have spoken mostly of june bugs, there are many smaller aquatic beetles, as well as land beetles, which are heartily endorsed by the trout. The live june bug is a big insect, and you can't use any hook smaller than a No. 6 to get a lifelike representation. The other species, however, may be imitated on sizes down to No. 14. If you bear in mind that most of them are black, with highly iridescent green-and-red backs, you can probably work out a few good dressings of your own. The only feather I know of that is an exact duplicate of the beetle's back is found on Impeyan pheasant, but undoubtedly there are many others.

So I put it to you: the beetle is a highly desired trout food, and with the proper imitations an angler could get through long periods of otherwise dull fishing. I do not believe that any of the artificials I have used so far is out of the ordinary. There is room for improvement. Having talked myself into an epilogue, I might add that I can now face my notebook, content in the knowledge that the gap between entomological and angling truth was bridged by Mr. Botz—and, of course, the beetle.

14

FEATHER MERCHANT

Clifton Fadiman once suggested that profiling people is no less a literary art than writing a sonnet or a one-act play. The best profiles are entertaining, yet packed with information about the profilee's life, times, and particular interests. Such portraits let the subjects do the talking with little or no editorializing by the writer. Thus, in the following profile of a great fly tyer, we learn that Harry Darbee has had a running battle with the National Audubon Society over his determination to obtain the plumage of certain rare birds and the Society's equal determination to see such birds protected. Whatever, A. J.'s feelings on the matter are discreetly withheld. After all, this is Harry Darbee's story.

GWR

FEATHER MERCHANT

Although a President may change the date of Thanksgiving with no stress,[1] Harry Darbee would fall into infamy if he changed the hackle color of a customer's Royal Coachman. To a man who must keep an inventory of 200,000 fly hooks, who has made flies for twenty-four hours without stopping to eat, who has tied eight dozen flies a day for thirty days

[1] Once upon a time, Thanksgiving—a holiday kicked off in 1621 by the Plymouth Colony to celebrate its first successful harvest (with a little help from the Indians)—came on November 26th, regardless of the day of the week or whether the striped bass were still in the rips at Montauk. At least that was how President Washington set things up in 1789. Then Mrs. Sarah J. Hale got to Abraham Lincoln in 1863 with the notion that if Thanksgiving always fell on the last Thursday in November, enough government workers would take off Friday to credit Lincoln's administration with having created the 3-day workweek. This is how matters stood until 1939 when Franklin D. Roosevelt—always a man to do things differently—proclaimed that Thanksgiving should be celebrated on the third Thursday in November. Of course, this might merely have been a ploy to sidetrack Congress so that the President could sneak some other legislation through both houses while the men on The Hill were counting off days on their lips and fingers. Finally, after more than two years of intense debate, while prices went berserk, bread lines grew, and war broke out in Europe, Congress passed a joint resolution decreeing that forevermore, or until the next administration, whichever comes first, Thanksgiving should be celebrated on the fourth (or last) Thursday in November. This announcement was greeted by general rejoicing in all the deer cabins in Pennsylvania.

GWR

straight, who once filled a single order for 800 dozen wet flies, and now finds he needs a few thousand dozen in stock to get caught up, the world is a whirling hive of synthetic insects. Men whose decisions divert golden streams of dollars one way or the other wait at his side like members of the South African Diamond Syndicate while he creates with inexplicable alchemy those gems of tinsel and feather that look exactly like the hundreds of thousands he has made before. With a quiet, measured speech and spongelike mind, Darbee sits squarely among the best in his trade, behind walls that have been frescoed in tobacco smoke and spatterings of old varnish; walls that echo to the legends of Eli Garret, Pop Robbins, John Taintor Foote, Ted Townsend, and the fabulous Bill Johnson.

Darbee lives in the Dutch, Rip Van Winkle, rocky, short-legged cow country of the Catskills. "It's all sidehill," he says. "Even the hay riggings have two short wheels." At night you see the deer go off through the trees, then stand looking back at your headlights, and a grotesque parade of hotels marches over the ridges, so that tourists can find any atmosphere from South Sea Islands complete with papier-mâché palms and rubber coconuts, to Swiss chalets, dude ranches, and a native form of architecture best described as Early Nothing. The mountains are old in all senses and dimensions, for just a few miles beyond the Borscht Circuit, away from pounding truck arteries, the rivers are so natural that they can be traced like veins in the neck of a Catskill farmer.

The angler gets a wonderful feeling of continuity in finding that the Willowemoc flows to the Beaverkill, the Beaverkill to the East Branch, and the East to the West Branch where both pour into the Big Delaware. Men who derive their nourishment from a weekend contact with these rivers usually stop at the eight-room, two-story farm-style house with a high-angled green shingle roof, which stands nervously at the roadside where the concrete drops rapidly into the flatness of the Willowemoc valley.

"I don't mind the traffic out there," Darbee said, waving at the road; "it's the traffic in here that's killing me. I didn't get to bed until three o'clock this morning. At six o'clock two guys were pounding on the door, wanting me to tie some flies for them. I guess I can hold out until the trout season is over, though. Elsie tied until three this morning. She's out back now putting a new spring leaf in the car," he added proudly, "but tonight this place will look like Grand Central Station."

The attitude of the purist toward his fly dresser is one of remarkable devotion. When the home of Reub Cross burned down in Lewbeach back in 1941, his frenzied followers took up a collection to put him back in business, for the balding, corrosive, caustic-tongued wit of the Beaverkill tied trout flies like no other man. And there were those who couldn't fish without flies made the Cross way. But a professional fly tyer is also able to prescribe accurate remedies for local fishing conditions, tackle, the mood of the trout, the state of the nation, and will dispense blood-circulating medicines to clients who just crawled out of the river.

Darbee has not only survived twenty years in the feathered jungle, but has spent much of that time ferociously biting the hands of the Audubon Society. "Damn bird watchers are ruining our business. Last year they pushed through section 1518 of the 1930 Tariff Act, which is a general prohibition against the importation of feathers and skins, whether they're wild or domestic. That means that only 5,000 skins of gray jungle fowl, and not more than 1,000 skins of mandarin duck, can be shipped in during the year. Then we have to split up about 45,000 Oriental pheasant skins with the millinery trade. As the law stacks up now, teal, kingfisher, partridge, woodcock, starling, snipe, grouse, coot, and bronze mallard are gone.

"The bird watchers bagged Reub Cross back in the thirties," he continued, "but he got them all fouled up. Actually, they had nothing on him. The crazy horse-feathers law demanded a certified public accountant to itemize every feather you had, and all Reub had was some feathers that I had sold him. He wasn't even selling flies then. But the warden and the game inspector who made the arrest didn't know which feathers were on the banned list. So the whole business was dropped and the law was amended.

"Now they're riding herd on us again, and we have to keep a record of all purchases and be open to inspection at all times. Of course we're licensed by the state, but the Audubon creeps have us up a tree. I used to import thousands of necks from Japan—I'd buy them in bales. Most necks are no good; so it would take a lot of them to get the few quality skins I needed. I still get some necks from the big feather houses in New York City who supply the millinery trade, but my best skins are the ones I raise myself."

Darbee is most proud of his near-pure strain of blue dun roosters. The blue dun is a dingy, grayish-blue chicken that runs from light to very dark, and its neck provides hackles for such popular patterns as the Hendrickson, Quill Gordon, Blue Quill, Blue Dun Variant, Blue Caddis, and the traditional Blue Dun fly. Although the blue dun rooster wouldn't win a beauty prize in the barnyard, his hackles are the most sought-after feather in the fly-tying world, because no blue race of chicken runs true to color. The blue dun is a Mendelian freak, unless you want to spend twenty years in crossbreeding, which is what Darbee did.

"My buff rooster is just as likely to have blue chickens as a blue dun cock. But I've worked my present three hundred birds to a point where I'm reasonably sure of getting blue duns. I started my stock out of blue Andalusians. Always in a large hatch of Andalusians you'll find a few sports," Darbee observed, "and these might turn out to be natural blue duns, but you don't know until you raise them. Some Andalusian sports throw back to whites or blacks when they mature. It can be very disappointing.

"If you do get a few natural blue duns, however, then you have stock to work with. You can't breed them to a dominant strain like the White Leghorn unless you're going to use a black dominant, too. I found you can throw genetic laws out the window," he continued, "because we have very critical problems in fly tying. I've worked my blue dun strain up with recessives. A recessive white and a recessive black. I use Buff Leghorn for blood, and Buff Cochin Bantam for early maturity and narrow, stiff hackle. I tried pure Buffs for a number of years, but they made the hackle quills stiff. We have to have flexible quills for tying, you know."

The Darbee chicken houses range from old shipping crates to orthodox coops that are scattered down the hillside in back of his house. Unlike production-minded egg farmers, who keep thousands of birds, Darbee maintains two to three hundred choice roosters, many of which have to be kept in solitary confinement.

"I can't get the gamecock blood out of some of them. They have to be culled, because they cut each other to shreds. My natural duns aren't really cooped, you'll notice; they just stay behind wire, even when it gets down to twenty below zero. That makes a quality feather." Although the present market price on top-grade blue dun necks is fifteen dollars. Darbee doesn't figure that this is a very high tab from a cost standpoint. "My ratio of good dun necks now is about one in five. The rest will be patterned or rusted. It used to be one in ten. Cripes, I was up to my button in fried chicken then.

"All my naturals are sold a year in advance," he continued. "I've got orders now for twenty that I haven't even raised yet. I don't kill all my birds. They average three or four crops of hackle a year; so I pluck them whenever I need material. I had one bird who gave a crop every six weeks. Sure miss him. They say the Old English Blue Gamecock runs true to color. Maybe it does, but those I've seen had very poor hackle. Sooner or later they must throw back to some other color, because all blue races run out. Then the hens are more often blue than the roosters.

"I have people writing to me all the time about my birds—in fact, I've sold some chicks because I want to perpetuate the race," he added. "And if

[111]

you think fly tying is competitive business, I'm raising blue duns for half a dozen fly tyers right now. We don't compete, because first of all there's too much work and secondly, we all have different styles in our tying.

"It's a funny thing, though, if we had to have as much black hackle as blue dun hackle, we'd all be out of business. Good black hackle is extremely rare. The Black Minorca strain provides most of what we use, but it isn't stiff enough. The same goes for dark brown. The darker it gets, the poorer the quality. A real chocolate color that dresses so well on a Royal Coachman generally has hooked fibers. Wish I knew why. Furnace and badger are fairly easy to come by; but when you get right down to it, we can never get enough top-grade hackle of any color."

Fly tying as a business runs the gamut from part-time professionals who wrap feathers in the back room of a grocery store or gas station to the half-million-dollar enterprises run by venerable firms like Hardy Brothers in Alnwick, England, and the Weber Lifelike Fly Company of Stevens Point, Wisconsin. The big plants are conducted on a piecework basis, the Europeans demanding long periods of apprenticeship in single steps of tying, such as forming a wing or wrapping a tinsel body, whereas the American system prefers female tyers who can make complete flies.

"One chap up in northern New York made a time study on each operation in tying," Darbee said, "and then built a rotary table which a dozen women sat around, each one doing a separate stage of the same fly that took the same length of time. The idea was that for each revolution of the table one fly would be finished, but it didn't work out," he concluded.

The demand for artificial flies has always far exceeded the supply. Even with an estimated 250,000 amateurs making their own, a small corps of talented individuals scattered throughout the land work around the clock to keep critical anglers supplied. Professional fly tyers won't talk about their incomes, but presumably the best of them make $4,500 to $5,000 a year.[2]

In spite of the fact that Darbee is a regional specialist, his orders come from all over the world, the bulk of his foreign trade centering in South America and Ireland. On the prevailing market he tabs $5.40 a dozen for dry flies, and $9.00 a dozen for salmon dry flies. Salmon fishermen like American Airlines prexy C. R. Smith and John J. McCloy cause Harry to split his work with Elsie. "She doesn't like to dress salmon patterns. Too much work in sorting materials. That's where the real work is," he continued. "When we're turning out flies as small as No. 22 up to No. ⅝ Long Dees, we have

---

[2] This was not bad money for 1955 when the story first appeared. Today such an annual income wouldn't feed a family of gophers. GWR

to spend a whole day just laying the materials out, grading the hackle sizes, matching wings, and so on. You have to be systematic. If I stopped to pick out new materials after each fly, I wouldn't be able to do more than two or three dozen a day."

Odd orders bother Darbee during his busy winter and spring seasons. "There's always some guy who wants one of each of thirty or forty different patterns, and somebody who wants all his flies dressed with four wings so they won't land upside down. I like to do the work, but it throws me way behind. Year in and year out, we tie more No. 12 Light Cahill than any other fly. Good patterns aren't an accident," he cautioned, "and I think that's where amateur tyers go haywire. They work at freaks, you know, things they dream up instead of the standard patterns.

"Basically, all an amateur needs is practice, a good thread, and good wax. I use 6-0 Holland thread and a homemade wax which I make from beeswax, rosin, and paraffin in mixture; then I add a little castor oil to keep it from drying out. Putting the materials together is easy. Really easy."

Born in 1906 in Roscoe, New York, young Darbee grew up in what was then America's most fertile trout country. While still very young he made an attempt to go to Alaska, but went broke in Wisconsin and gradually worked his way back to the Catskills where he resumed fox trapping, a profession that Darbee pursued right up until the depression. "I could get six foxes in one night," he said, "but that wouldn't be unusual those days. In fact, it was easier to get the foxes than the bait. I used house cats. Small, well-aged pieces," he said carefully. "When money really got tight, I began commercial fly tying because fishing seemed to be the only business that wasn't too affected by the depression."

Anybody can buy the few tools and materials needed in the fly-tying trade, but it takes great personal skill to become popular enough to conduct a business. Darbee advertised in all the outdoor magazines during his first professional year to build up a clientele, and after a brief partnership with Walt Dette he met and married Elsie, who not only learned the trade in thirty days but is now skilled enough to whip out a wet fly in two and a half minutes flat. Regular customers agree that Elsie is the spark plug in the Darbee combo, as Harry is inclined to wander off to the Big Delaware instead of sitting at his bench. "I painted one side of the house once," he added reflectively, "but there's no sense in finishing now because they're going to widen the highway out front."

To help others to take over wherever he may be compelled to leave off, Darbee has taught his art to many youngsters in the Catskill area, and to further assist unborn generations of fly makers he has collected thousands of original patterns dating from Theodore Gordon to contemporary experts and filed them for future reference. In an art form that demands strict adherence to the rules, one would expect all flies of one pattern to be exactly alike. But even with the same ingredients no two fly dressers achieve precisely the same result.

"You can't really dress a pattern correctly from a book description. You've got to have the fly in your hand. Give one printed description to twenty different tyers, and you have roughly the same fly, but twenty distinct styles. It's like playing the piano. Walt Dette is more precise about selecting his hackle for length than I am," Darbee continued, "because I can spot his flies right away. Reub Cross cocks the tails on his flies and he uses a shorter body. Mike Lorenz brings the bodies of all his flies down around the bend of the hook. Del Appley over on the East Branch makes a larger, rougher-looking fly, whereas Herman Christian on the Neversink ties so sparse that his flies are for experts only.

"I guess most of us aim at sparseness these days. I tie what looks like a bulkier body than most. But actually I pick the material out a little. When we first started in the business, I used No. 11, No. 13, and No. 15 hooks instead of the regular 10, 12, and 14. People knew there was something different about my flies, but they couldn't quite figure it out. It was a good gimmick," he added.

Darbee's friend, ex-game protector Roy Steenrod, stands as a link between past and present in being one of few men alive today who knew and fished with Theodore Gordon. Steenrod, creator of the famous Hendrickson trout fly, used to visit Gordon in his Neversink retreat before he died in 1915. Eroded by the culture of the Gay Nineties, and with a tendency toward hermitage, Gordon had the foresight to develop American dry-fly fishing, and thus is remembered in a class with such other permanent benefactors of the human race as the inventors of the cotton gin, the light bulb, and the wireless.

"I wish I had known Gordon," Darbee said. "He actually changed the anatomy of the fly. He set his wings with butts toward the rear and placed his hackles at right angles to the hook. He was smart enough to use non-absorbent materials, which made a big difference. English dry flies at that time were nothing more than modified wets. They still tied their wing butts toward the eye of the hook. I have thirty or forty of Gordon's original Quill Gordon flies. That man had a beautiful style. He tied on slightly long shank hooks, which gave his flies a real mayfly appearance."

Darbee feels that it is bad for a man to love one country too much, and when the wind sweeps a gale down the dark valley in the winter he gets up from his bench once in a while and thinks maybe he will leave, or maybe he will go trap a fox, or look for the blind deer that almost knocked George Stewart into the Beaverkill. "Somebody should kill that deer. The poor beast is half crazy. The boys find him floundering in the river every so often. His eyes are as white as marbles. By rights, though, I guess I'll have to wait until the season opens, won't I?"

15

THE ART OF MIDGE FISHING

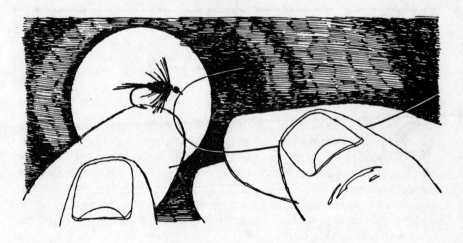

Ever been on a stream when brown trout were feeding around you like kids at a slurpy machine—and still been skunked? Even more dumb, did you know the reason why the fish weren't giving your flies a second look, but been too much a victim of the lazy, hazy summer day to do anything about it? Well, there's just one hope when trout are obsessed by the invisible. You must fish flies of comparable size on a comparably delicate leader. And this is easier said than done. For one thing, I get nervous not being able to see a fly so tiny it disappears five feet away. For another, it's difficult to pick up the rhythm of casting *nothing* after spending most of the afternoon casting *something*. Thus I'm one of those anglers who all too often succumbs to fate and mindlessly strokes the water with oversize flies while all around me trout are having an orgy. Yet if you'd rather catch fish than fantasies, this chapter is loaded with information. As usual, A. J. makes it sound effortless.

GWR

THE ART OF MIDGE FISHING

One day some summers ago, while I was fishing with Bert Lahr[1] on our favorite eastern mountain stream, the action was so fast that we lost count of the number of trout we landed and turned loose. We kept two fish each, and the smallest was a 19-inch squaretail that Bert took from a long, quiet pool. This is the kind of fishing you don't forget—especially in low, clear water where you must move from shadow to shadow while stalking the rise, then wait an eternity as the fly floats that immense distance of two feet in coming to the fish.

What made the trip memorable was the fact that all our trout were caught on No. 20 flies. I seldom use such a small size and neither does Bert, for unfortunately we don't experience many midging periods in our gravel-bottomed rivers. Some casters feel that the midge's absence is a blessing and that the insect well deserves a popular British epithet, "the fisherman's curse."

However one views the matter, the midge is abundantly bred in a stew of weed and silt such as we find in long parts of the Deschutes in Oregon, the Ausable in New York, the Housatonic in Connecticut, and just about

[1] Best remembered as Judy Garland's "Cowardly Lion" in the MGM musical *The Wizard of Oz*, Lahr was a long-time friend and angling companion of A. J.'s.

every other major trout stream or high-altitude lake. Paradoxically, one learns to cope with the midge or go fishless when a full bag is the potential.

There was a time when I thought miniature artificials were just curios that tyers made for their own amusement. As a boy, I often visited an elderly gentleman in our town who loved to talk about angling. His proudest possession was a framed set of wet patterns dressed on the No. 18 Redditch scale, which is equivalent to our modern No. 22 Model Perfect hook. I am certain he didn't fish with these, nor with any of comparable size, because silkworm gut has never been drawn fine enough or strong enough to make the tiny hook effective.

Of course, the story is quite different today. Synthetic leader materials have made the impossible practical. The present .0039 nylon tippet testing one pound may lose some fish, but it's a far cry from the silk leader, which comes out at twice that diameter for the same test.

Midge fishing is the least practiced form of our fly-rod art. At best one might say that it's a narrow specialty full of *mystique* and ceremony, more esoteric than a meeting of bird watchers. The natural midge is so insignificant in size that its artificial counterpart hardly looks capable of attracting a strike —much less holding the fish afterward. Yet members of the family Chironomidae, also known as gnats or punkies, are periodically more exciting to trout than all the larger insects that swarm over inland waterways. In fact, there are midge-rich lakes and rivers where only the tiniest artificials ever catch fish consistently.

The midge symptoms are easy to distinguish: Trout rise steadily all around you but will not take an ordinary dry fly. Usually the fish's back or tail breaks the surface and you see his lacquered flank flash in the sun, while others poised on easy fins repeat the roll again and again. Mouths open and close, the water folds back in widening rings, and eventually the game becomes one of snipping off the last pattern and trying a new one.

It's difficult to understand why trout, when taking midges, will not readily feed on larger insects that furnish more food. The fact remains that selective periods often occur when caddis or mayflies are drifting athwart the current in perfect safety. The angler is invariably misled by these floaters, because the largest of the thousand classified genera of midges is barely a quarter inch long. For all practical angling purposes they are invisible.

My first experience with midge-feeding trout occurred many years ago on the East Branch of the Delaware in New York. April can produce some tricky weather in that region: savage gusts smiting the water and whirling the line about, showers beating down from gray skies, and hands cramped with cold. Nevertheless there are rare periods in the late afternoon when

Gordon Quills hatch and for an hour or two you get excellent fishing. I have caught some handsome trout under a veil of snowflakes with the dry fly.

On this particular day mayflies didn't appear, but the fish went on a wild feeding spree just the same. I floated many dry patterns over them before switching to nymphs. Except for an occasional nudge at my leader there were no real strikes. Pounding the water until dark, I finally caught the village idiot on a fanwing Royal Coachman. Had I been more experienced, I'd have recognized the classic indicator of a midge rise—fish actually hitting the knots in my leader.

Why the trout, a fish credited with keen eyesight, will strike a leader knot is explained by the fact that a knot and a midge are about the same size. I must admit that this common-sense note is a contradiction to our first premise, but mystery is no small element of salmonoid charm. It may be that like the cat tumbling through space and twisting to land on its feet, a trout's first thoughts are reflexive rather than voluntary.

In speaking of the midge rise, we are actually dealing with three stages of the insect's cycle. The larvae, sometimes called bloodworms or wigglers, are little green, black, red, or brown worms about one-quarter inch long. Often you will find trout stomachs packed with these creatures. The pupal stage occurs when the larvae rise to the surface; pupae hang vertically in the water, head up and tail down, with their gills in the surface film. Both head and tail have distinctive hairy appendages, an enlarged thorax, and folded but visible wings.

Trout often take the larvae at the surface, and always come to the top for drifting pupae. This feeding sign is evident even in the subaquatic stages. The adult midge looks much like a mosquito, except that it holds its front legs in the air and is smaller. So, basically, you need imitations of two or preferably all three different stages. I have never found the pattern to be particularly important, but the artificial must be the right size.

Since that Delaware episode I have tried many patterns, both floating and sinking. I collected most of these in the British Isles, France, and Austria; the number of American dressings is very limited. The standard Gray Midge Pupa, Wetzel's Green Midge Pupa, and Harger's Black Midge pattern proved useful under most conditions. The so-called Doubs series of flies that originated in France make good adult imitations for surface fishing.

However, I finally settled on a perfectly simple dressing for the dry fly, using two tiny badger hackles on a No. 20 hook. One hackle is tied forward and the other aft, with only the black tying silk showing between. This was the pattern that Bert Lahr and I cleaned house with last summer. For imitating the subaquatic stages, I experimented with silk, fur, cork, nylon, quill, and raffia bodies before finally going back to silk again. It's the easiest material to work with on very small hooks and it makes a perfectly lifelike fly.

Such midges are simple to dress: Using a somewhat rough thread like Persall's rather than the very smooth Holland, I wrap the shank from the bend up to the place where my hackle is secured. The body is then coated with clear lacquer, which makes it durable and also gives it a dirty, wet look. Yellow, white, green, red, and black are all good body colors, and you should have a few of each.

Next I wind in the hackle, turning just enough to make a sparse collar. The hackle can be gray, black, white, or blue dun. It really doesn't matter because there's so little of it. I favor a yellow body with black hackle because some of the best necks for small feathers that I've found in recent years were natural blacks. That's all there is to tying a midge. The larvae, incidentally, are larger than the adult insect and can be tied on Nos. 16 and 18 hooks.

The midge is a significant trout food in both cold and hot weather. Rainbows and brook trout are especially partial to the larvae, and as a rule you will find a greater bulk of Chironomidae in their stomachs than in the belly of a brown trout taken from the same water. But when the brownie gets on the midge kick, he's your most critical customer.

A midge hatch may occur in the dead of winter, particularly on days when the water temperature rises to about 40 degrees F., or under the glare of a steamy August sun. Fished wet, the Black Midge makes an excellent pattern for opening day if the stream is running clear. On the Missouri River and the Yellowstone of Montana the midge is known as a "snow fly" and imitations are used for winter fishing. The popular sizes locally are tied on Nos. 12, 14, and 16 hooks, but these are 5X Short shank. The 5XS hook takes a dressing comparable to a regular No. 16, 18, or 20; it is similar to the low-water salmon fly in offering more gap to a sparse pattern.

I've carried a dozen of these with me for the past few years but never got around to using them until last June. I was fishing a high-altitude lake above a village in Norway. Here winter is in perpetual conflict with summer, retreating for a few hours at midday, then rushing back in a blast of snow by late afternoon. The lake water was frigid, but even at a distance I knew what to expect, for midges hung over the water in rolling clouds, and as far as the eye could see there was the recurrent dimpling sip of a trout taking the larvae.

I nearly disappeared in the soft silt bottom as I waded out to a casting position, but the fish worked steadily and undisturbed. There are two distinct ways of fishing a midge. If a dry pattern is called for, it is oiled and left floating on the surface. I usually let the fly sit quietly for some time before giving it a twitch. If this doesn't bring a strike, I retrieve the floater slowly with short pauses before picking it from the water.

However, the trout on this Norwegian lake were feeding on the larvae and pupae of the midge, which is a wet-fly operation. The idea here is to cast and let the fly sink, then make it behave like the larvae coming up from the bottom. Drag it slowly to the surface, then after a sufficient pause to let the midge sink again repeat the process. Sometimes trout will strike the instant your fly hits the water, and occasionally they'll hit a midge drawn across the surface, but the method I have described invariably produces results.

This day was no exception. I believe that I caught more than fifteen browns, standing in just one spot. The wind howled and the snow flew, but fish hit on almost every cast. It was interesting to note that several other people fishing the lake with spinning rods caught absolutely nothing. This is hardly testimony to any skill on my part, for the plain fact is that trout are really easy to catch during a midge rise.

There are also times when trout will grub for midge larvae along the bottom and you'll have to fish very deep for them. This takes a nice sense of touch because the strike will be no more than a slight movement of the line. I prospected for rainbows this way on the Dean River in British Columbia during a period when we weren't getting any large trout on the surface. Using a sinking fly line, I let the midge go down about twelve or fifteen feet. Sometimes the strike came when it was sinking, but usually when I made the draw.

The Dean is one of British Columbia's best trout streams, and the deep-fished midge really proved it. I suppose other types of flies would have worked under these same conditions, but for several days I had my hands full with rainbows in the 2- to 5-pound class. They were so stuffed that they spewed midge larvae all over the boat when I unhooked them. Many heavy fish popped my 5X tippet, and no wonder—this is the toughest way to strike trout on light nylon.

Presenting a midge on a leader tapered heavier than six-thousandths of an inch is seldom effective. A thick point destroys the illusion of a natural and prevents the fly from moving freely with the current. If you have a delicate hand, you can work safely with tippets from 5X nylon (.0055 inch) to 8X nylon (.0039 inch). These sizes are suitable for Nos. 18 to 22 hooks. I favor a 7X tippet for most fishing, and go to 5X only when the fish appear big or careless

At first glance you might think that such terminal tackle cannot hold large trout. Actually, the tiny fine wire hooks will slip into the skin of the

[122]

mouth and bite firmly. As a matter of fact, you will often have difficulty in removing the barb.

There is also a trick to using 7X and 8X nylon safely; never make your leader with a short tippet section. Most anglers believe that the less fine material they put in a leader the stronger it will be, whereas the opposite is true. You can feel the difference when unrolling a spool of, say, 1-pound test. If you take a few inches of the nylon between your fingers and pull, it snaps quite easily. Now roll off about forty inches and pull from both ends. The monofilament stretches and requires considerably more tension to break. So you should always add at least three feet of tippet, and on a twelve-foot leader I wouldn't hesitate to use forty or fifty inches of the 1-pound test for maximum elasticity.

The real problem in using a fine leader is in striking the fish, and this requires a little practice. You don't really strike at all. Just tighten on the line and keep a steady pressure with no wrist jerk. I know this is difficult, particularly for experienced anglers with whom an instantaneous strike at the taking of the fly is reflexive. The strike in midge fishing must be firm, but it must also be calculated between the fine tippet and the weight of the fish.

Fortunately, midge fishing is almost always done in relatively still waters, where you can see the trout rise and play him without the hazard of a wild current. Naturally, you will break off on some fish no matter how carefully you work, but if the number of breaks becomes excessive, something is wrong with your tackle and you should investigate to find out just what it is.

The tools you use in midge fishing are important. You cannot work with a heavy line or a stiff rod because either will snap a fine leader on the strike. The rod may be short or long, but it must be flexible. Some builders make extra-light wands specifically for delicate casting; for example, Paul Young of Detroit manufactures a stick called The Midge. This rod is 6 feet 3 inches long and weighs 1¾ ounces complete. For the specialist these are the ideal dimensions for a very light fly rod.

Your regular trout outfit might be perfectly suitable, however, and some idea of its ability can be judged by the size of line used. If the rod requires a line heavier than HDH for casting, you are going to have troubles. And larger size will offer too much water resistance for smooth striking with fine leaders. It will also prove a bit splashy for flat-water fishing. My personal choice for midging is a double-tapered silk IHI that is as light as a feather. As for three-diameter lines, I wouldn't use one larger than HDF or HDG. Although it seems hardly practical to select tackle on the premise that you

[123]

are going to spend the day casting small flies, bear in mind that the same outfit also propels standard sizes.

I got caught with my pants down last spring on the Trancura River in Chile. The stream is a fly fisherman's dream, with deeply undercut banks and long, slick runs that are incredibly pure. It's more paradisiacal than earthly, for at times the angler faces an endless train of rising rainbows as he drops from one run to the next. The average trout is small compared with those of the Enco or the Fui, but you seldom take one under a pound, and 3-pounders are common.

I planned the day's campaign to start by boat halfway up the river and finish at Martinez Pool. The weather had been wild, with a pampero blowing off the Andes; so I selected a 9-foot glass rod and heavy line. Considering the wind conditions, wet flies and bucktails seemed in order, but after working over countless rainbows I realized that something was wrong. As we glided down the main current I cast into emerald shadows behind the brush sweepers that fingered the flow. Fish came to examine my offerings like half-formed ghosts that dissolved at the moment of recognition.

Finally a small trout grabbed my bucktail and I sacrificed him for a post-mortem. He was gorged with green-midge pupae. There was no choice but to refine my terminal gear and follow the clue. They came to the midge, all right, but between my GBF line and big rod, I must have popped off on twenty or thirty fish. I landed one 3½-pound rainbow by dumb luck. It wasn't until we had drifted far down the Trancura to her white-water runs that I could raise trout on large flies. The problems of trouting are the same the world over.

Midge fishing may appear to be a long step from regular fly work, but it isn't. Casters who have the patience to polish their technique and make the conversion from heavy to light tackle will find greater pleasure in their days astream. In fact, one runs the danger of becoming an addict, for you are bound to improve your percentage purely on the numbers of fish struck. If for no other reason, this makes the miniature fly worthwhile.

PART IV

THE SPICE OF LIFE

16

THE FLY ROD THAT DOES THE IMPOSSIBLE

Al McClane's development of the flea rod (a term he coined for lightweight sticks under 7 feet long) probably began when he was teaching his daughter Susan to fish. In "Gear for the Barefoot Expert" we learned that she started with a 4-foot wand at four years of age. With an old-fashioned creel slung around her knees and a farmer's hat flopping around her ears, she'd wander into the woods along the deer trails and come back bearing trout. By the time she was seven, Susan was the unofficial guide at Turnwood. When Arnold Gingrich came up from the city, he'd always seek her out first to find where the big ones lay. Al was so impressed with what the little lady could do with a little rod, he wondered what an adult could do with the same equipment. Following are the results of his research.

GWR

THE FLY ROD THAT DOES THE IMPOSSIBLE

For many years I fumbled around like a bear cub with a basketball, trying to grasp what should have been a simple object. Now, any well-informed angler knows that the value of advice is always in direct proportion to the notoriety of the originator, and is in inverse ratio to the content of experience. This is an excellent hypothesis; it saves people from thinking too much. Not that Doc Faulkner[1] cared what people thought; in fact, he wouldn't pull a tooth during mayfly season. But he was such a hot rod locally that when he prescribed 7 feet of bamboo as a remedy for small-stream fly fishing, there followed a great stir and bustle as everyone donned hats and waders and filed down the brook with 7-foot rods. Unfortunately, when you are knee-deep in water with alder branches leaning on your chin, there's little difference between a rod 9 feet long and one 7 feet long. Observers agreed that Doc was on the right track, although the engine of progress had advanced only two feet. And now, after sweating in the jungle of a trickling trout brook, I see a bright new world of opportunity. To the makers of rods, this pronouncement may sound like the shriek of a bad hinge, but the remedy for small streams is a fly rod 3 feet in length, give or take a few inches.

One June day I sat on the bank of a miniature Catskill brook and watched

[1] One of the Margaretville, New York, angling society Al first got to know during his summer jobs back in the 1930s.

a gent pitch his fly line under a footbridge that was so low he had to bend double when he waded in to net his trout. We had both broken and blunted hundreds of flies against similar brickwork in years past, and when the black fish was lifted out in the sun, it was as if he had extracted a dragon from its cave.

Picking our way up the mountainside that morning, we had invaded the hitherto sacred privacy of impossibly placed trout. There was one under the helmlock bough; I caught it by standing on a rock and casting with my rod held at about 45 degrees below horizontal. And there were four trout I caught in a ledge-rimmed pool curtained by alders. In all the years I had fished Beecher Brook,[2] this pool was simply one to look at, because there was little more than a tunnel in which to unroll a back cast. Oh, there were bungled casts and lost fish, but Doc Faulkner would have done a flip if he'd seen Carl Hoffman standing under a mattress-branched hemlock tossing his dry fly forty or fifty feet upstream. A "short" 7-foot rod might have flattened the squirrels on the other bank, but wielding a rod made from a glass fly-rod tip Carl moved along the brook probing those cobwebbed corners like he was standing in space.

There is a pastoral charm to fishing small streams, and no matter how many rivers you wade there will always be the need for coming back to a brook. The current swirls, tumbles, and races full pelt down the mountainside, forming tiny pools where it hits against boulders or washes the hidden parts of tree roots. Trout scratch out a meager existence from the polished gravel, and they seldom grow big. Yet there are surprises: fish that come up the brook to spawn, and trout that want to escape summer's heat in the main stream, and fish that probably come to the source waters for reasons no different than the angler's. Here even a big trout is measured in inches, but my first 15-incher from Beecher Brook was no less a delight than my first 30-incher in Alaska. There was always an undercurrent of annoyance with the technical aspects of small-stream fly work, however. When a man has to concentrate on his casting instead of the fishing, he ceases to find pleasure in angling. I don't know why tradition set the length minimum of a fly rod at 7 feet. I have talked to many rod builders about this and they don't know why either. Possibly it is because of the nature of early-day rod-building materials.

Until the advent of glass an extra-short fly rod was impractical. Bamboo couldn't be used to advantage in lengths of less than 6 feet for the reason that such a structure would collapse under the stresses of accelerated casting

[2] A tributary of the Beaverkill.

with an ordinary fly line. In point, a glass-fiber rod of tubular construction is approximately two and two-thirds times as strong as a comparable weight of six-strip split bamboo. I realize that frail 6-foot bamboo rods were made many years ago; in fact, a craftsman by the name of Charles Mass made a six-strip bamboo rod just 16 inches long weighing $\frac{5}{16}$ ounce, and a reel to match. I have cast fifteen or eighteen feet with it. But these were of no value except as conversation pieces. The 40-inch rod I have been using will, with a double haul, throw the full length of a double taper smoothly and accurately, and it will whip a salmon as easily as a sunfish.

To my knowledge, there are no such rods manufactured today; possibly there never will be. But making your own is a simple process, and there's no reason why you can't fish small trout streams while progress overtakes tradition. All you need is the tip section of a tubular-glass bass-action fly rod, which will be from 36 to 54 inches long (depending on the original rod length), a large ring guide, and some tape to hold the reel in place. Personally, I use a 40-inch rod that was cut down from a longer tip section. I had a rod-building friend mount ferrules on it for two reasons. First, because the ferrule slows the rod's action down; secondly, it disjoints into two 20-inch sections that fit nicely in an overnight bag or coat pocket. Although the reel was taped in place two years ago, I expect that one of these days I'll mount a cork grip just for appearance's sake.

For best casting results, you should select a tip with a fairly straight taper. If there are any abrupt diameter changes the stick will flex too fast and throw a sloppy line, but as a rule, bass-action (or slow-action) fly rods are straight, with a linear average of variation approximating .030 inch per foot. When the tip is flexed by hand, it shouldn't vibrate rapidly, but it should rebound and stop with a feeling of authority.

Smooth casting with the short fly rod is easy to understand. Start with the basic premise that a man doesn't need a fly rod to cast and that any lever he puts in his hand will make the job easier. The longer that lever is made, the easier it will cast (up to the point where the man's wrist becomes inefficient); obviously we have a latitude from zero to infinity. Although most people never bother to find out, they can cast as far with their rod tips as they can with the entire rod—if they have good line control. The shortest levers require the greatest line speed, and using the double haul for acceleration one can lay out eighty or ninety feet or, without using the haul, half that distance, which is more than ample for small streams. The deciding factor is line control; the timing of the cast is faster, more positive, and requires practice to perfect.

An enlightening facet of short-rod casting is that you will find you can run through the whole alphabet of line sizes in level, double, and bug tapers with startling ease. One need only match his line to the job, and on small streams a forward taper with a *D* belly or a double taper with a *C*, *D*, or *E* belly is quite capable of reaching your target. This simply proves what we all know anyhow, that in fly casting it is the weight of the line that is being cast. The distribution of that weight assumes importance only when the casting distances involved become extreme or the bending capacity of a long rod is meant to take some of the burden off the caster. But now let's look at the short rod from a purely practical standpoint.

A very short fly rod would be of no advantage on meadow-type streams where the angler spends his day hip-deep in bank grass; quite the contrary. To work efficiently, without mowing the lawn, one must have a high back cast and, in places, no back cast at all; you simply reach out over the bank and dab the fly on the water. Too, the winds that come across an open meadow in trout country will force the line to drop, and an 8- or 9-foot length is none too long for proper line control in a gusty breeze.

But meadow-type streams are in the minority and pose less of a problem than the typical mountain trout stream, where trees squeeze down from overhead so that you are literally working in a tunnel. Such casting is done mostly from below shoulder level and usually while standing in the stream bed. The need here is a low back cast that can be executed between shrubs and branches in a tight line loop that will unroll and shoot without snagging the landscape. The short fly rod will do that.

This past winter I fished in a great swamp where the cypress and tupelo gum never heard the ring of an ax, where the coot shuttled through the eerie vastness making popping sounds as they punctured curtains of Spanish moss. Here the bass lay among withered stumps and nearly every cast was down long tunnels of gum sweepers and hanging moss. The 40-inch rod handled a buck-hair bug beautifully in traps designed for short casting rods and floating plugs. Undoubtedly there are other situations where the midget fly rod can be used to advantage, but of prime importance to most people is the small trout stream.

Ordinarily the man accustomed to a 9-foot fly rod would reduce to one about 7 feet long and feel that he was equipped for working a small brook. This, I beg to point out, is only the palest concession to that kind of angling. If we chop 4 feet off that, however, the remaining 3-foot length will permit casting from almost any position. I can use mine right- or left-handed, with the tip pointing almost at the water. Because of the length and essentially greater line speed, the rod throws tight loops, which permits casting under obstacles with relative ease. There is no tendency to "hook" casts off the target, as you most certainly must when casting with a longer rod in a purely horizontal plane. With a 7-foot fly rod, for instance, I rarely find enough space on small streams to work above shoulder level or below it. My casts either slap the water or hang in the elastic boughs of a hemlock. Casting in a purely horizontal plane throws curves in the line and leader that I don't want and am seldom able to correct.

One morning under the highway bridge on Pigeon Brook there was a nice brown trout rising in the sluice formed at the concrete foundation on the right side of the stream. Having a few feet of head room, I waded along the left side and flailed the air for fifteen minutes trying to get the fly to run back over the fish. Each time the line unrolled it flicked like a cow's tail, settling the fly several feet away from the trout's station. For all I know, that brownie never saw my floater. Yet I could have covered him easily with the short rod, using an almost vertical cast. The midget stick has cut the mustard in tighter places since.

One evening on the Rider Hollow stream, when the bank swallows were riding on a freight of mayflies, I worked into the hemlock forest above the Todd place. There under the claws of a stump lay a fat native that showed when he hit a grasshopper kicking on the surface. I have fished the Hollow since those roots were alive, and except for one freak cast years ago, I was never able to ease a bivisible on the current and work it down over the trout who always lived there. But on small streams we always stop at such places, where the slant rays of sun slip through the trellised bush and halo the dark pool, frothy at the top and hissing at the foot. I won't linger long at this pleasant turn, perhaps even a little nostalgically familiar to you. Nor will I tell you of the flies and leaders left hanging in the trees and how important it was to one day drift the fly correctly, even though the result would be measured by my hand. Back and forth the line sped between boughs and bushes until the bivisible fell bright and prim for that brief dance down to the stump, where it slipped into the trout's mouth. Never did I see a brookie more attached to his home. He jumped into the air to shake and then dove for the roots before fastening the leader on the bottom. I bent the fly loose without lifting him from the water. Although the fish was small, those few minutes contained as much action as one could hope for.

The bonus the short fly rod provides is that its size is in proportion to the fish being caught. Unmounted tip sections weigh from less than one ounce to less than two ounces, and a 10-inch trout will give you more sport than you ever thought possible. In waters where half-pounders are average you'll not only get more fun out of fishing but at the same time improve your casting skill. When you return to big rivers and longer rods, good line control will be an absolute certainty. I look forward to my annual small-stream safaris now, not because of the fishing, which I always enjoyed, but because my timing is sharper after a few days of short-rod work. And the real snapper is that such casting can be done off-season, indoors—a good-sized living room, hallway, cellar, or an office. This last is not recommended, however, unless the boss is a fisherman.

17

THE LORE OF NIGHT FISHING

You have to condition yourself to like night fishing. And this sometimes involves every kilowatt power of positive thinking in your head. When the sun goes down, Nature conspires to play tricks on all vertebrates with more cones in their eyes than rods—and this, unfortunately, includes man.

You'll stumble over rocks you would have seen by day and grip vines that writhe like snakes. You'll slip in over your waders at least once every five minutes and place your best casts on the shore when your line is not caught in the treetops behind you. The fish you finally hook splashes around like something ten times its size, and you're not at all sure that it won't turn on you next!

Years ago when my father was still making fishing expeditions to various parts of Florida and the Caribbean, one or more of his sons would usually accompany him. Night fishing was viewed as a special treat. During the day, Dad and his friends would wrestle with giant tuna, marlin, and the like and give us opportunity to do little more than act as a cheering section. The fact that we occasionally timed our encouragement to peak during the waning hours of battle when the angler's face was wet and white with purple blotches did nothing to endear ourselves to the human contestants. However, if we kept our sly commentary to a minimum, we were frequently rewarded with an after-dinner outing.

Mostly we haunted the docks or shoreline. But once in Bimini, we heard tarpon rolling—or so we thought—well out beyond the dock lights. Tony and I conned my father into borrowing a dinghy from a neighboring boat and taking us out. Naturally Dad did the fishing. But just being on the water at night was adventure enough. There was background music provided by the boys on the gasoline dock improvising the rhythm of "Sweet Bimini" on fifty-five-gallon fuel drums. And away from the lights, there was an overwhelming abundance of stars in the tropic heaven.

Finally Dad hooked something and diagnosed the massive weight as a jewfish. He then proceeded to bring all his blue-water training to bear and worked the whatever close to the dinghy.

"Light!" he commanded, and I switched on a three-cell flash we had brought along.

"Well?" he asked, his voice under some strain. "What is it?"

"I can't see—water's too murky."

"What do you mean, murky?" he roared. "This water is never murky!"

Then it dawned on me: I was looking at only part of the whatever Dad had alongside the boat. I flashed the light toward the bow, then back beyond the stern. Yes, it was a fish—a 13- or 14-footer.

"I think it's a shark," I offered.

"Well, gaff it!" Dad yelled.

Tony did. Several moments of terror later, we had lost the gaff and flashlight, sustained a broken rod tip and line, and suffered several major injuries to the dinghy which my father had to make good the next morning.

It was a most memorable evening, but Dad pretty much gave up night fishing after that. Like I say, it's something you have to condition yourself to like.

GWR

THE LORE OF NIGHT FISHING

A large segment of angling America will become nocturnal during the next two months,[1] because of the fact that many important species of game fish are now feeding heavily after dark. I suppose this simple observation might be construed as some kind of guarantee of a full creel, but such is not the case. Even in pitch blackness you still must know where, when, and how to operate your lures to be successful. The singular virtue of night fishing is that more and larger fish become active when the sun goes down, and this applies to everything from white bass to tarpon. However, any gent who fishes regularly knows that it's just as easy to get his wick trimmed at twelve midnight as twelve noon, and that's our semiprivate communication for the summer.

The influence of light on the feeding habits of fish is not perfectly understood. Periodically, all species are more active during the dimly lit hours or in total darkness. Increased nocturnal activity is often explained by the hypothesis that fish feel more secure from predation. Any man who has ever lived on a river is well aware that otter, mink, herons, and kingfishers accelerate their attacks when the water runs low and clear under a summer sun. After dark the fish can move out in the open with comparative safety, and then a big trout or bass has no trouble filling his belly. The clouds of moths and caddis flies that slam into porch lights with the coming of darkness reflect an abundance of nocturnal food.

There appear to be interrelated reasons besides security, however, that also affect the sunset-to-sunrise period: a greater availability of light-sensitive forage, such as the crayfish and the common eel; the cooler water temperatures toward dawn; and, for some game species, perhaps an owl-like tendency to avoid light. Nearly all chinook salmon caught at famed Campbell River are taken at sunrise and dusk. It's generally believed that fish, like birds, are guided in their migrations by light intensity, and research has already proved that spawning seasons can be accelerated by keeping a hatchery illuminated twenty-four hours a day. The mysterious influence of light is very great.

Anyway, veteran surf casters are working the night shift for striped bass, and bridge walkers are dodging traffic in the Florida Keys while waiting for a tarpon to explode in the moonlight, and white perch addicts are chucking minnows in black New England ponds. Their reason is that since man

[1] Originally published in the August, 1959, issue of *Field & Stream*.

[137]

first sought fish with a burning pine knot on a Scottish loch the compelling urge to take lunkers has been greater than the need for sleep. As a charter member of the sundown-to-yawn set, I may add an appropriate luminosity to what is taking place.

Although some points may seem contradictory at first, the ground rules for night fishing are fairly simple. When casting over bass or trout, for instance, never turn on your flashlight unless the beam can be hidden from view. These fish will panic at a roving light just as surely as if you tossed a rock at them. On the other hand, certain methods depend on attracting fish to a steady glow. Some of the most successful techniques of night fishing depend on using a carbide lamp or a gasoline lantern at the side of the boat.

In the Finger Lakes region of New York, a Seth Green[2] rig is effectively worked under lamplight. The glow attracts lake herring or sawbellies, and these forage fish can be dipped out of the water and sent seventy to one hundred feet down to catch the trout. On big southern impoundments the most popular hot-weather method for catching white bass and crappie is to dunk live minnows directly under the glare of the lantern. A half hour may pass before a school of panfish ventures into the light, but once they lose their caution it's almost impossible to chase them away.

Broadly speaking, then, the careless use of a flashlight merely announces your presence, whereas a constant glow is hypnotic to certain fish. Naturally, when you are casting artificial lures, the idea is to present a free-swimming target to a roving predator—and this has to be done in the dark. But in civilized waters never pass up the opportunity to work around permanent light sources. Even spooky fish can be conditioned to feeding under a lamp because it has a magnetic attraction for insects and minnows.

Al Pflueger, the taxidermist, took me to a Miami seafood emporium one evening. After we'd polished off a mound of succulent stone crabs, my host asked if I'd like an hour or two of fast fishing. He stopped at the car for his casting rod, and we walked around behind the restaurant. The building borders a mangrove creek, and at the end of the pier is a lamp that spotlights the water for twenty or thirty yards.

Al flipped a surface plug to the far side of the circle and worked it back very slowly. The lure hadn't traveled more than five or six feet when a fat snook came out of the darkness and walloped it. Al released the fish and I made a cast that promptly scored a ladyfish. Al took the rod again and

---

[2] Seth Green (1817–1888) is best remembered as the first man to cast a fly 100 feet and as the fish culturist who introduced *Salmo shasta* to eastern waters. The Seth Green rig is a type of dip seine he developed for use in his fish-culture work.

hooked another snook. We plugged for an hour and caught a ladyfish or a snook on almost every cast. Then the rubbery-fingered taxidermist snapped on a yellow nylon jig and for the next hour we caught lookdowns, panfish that pleased the Pflueger palate mightily. According to Al, the light attracts hordes of small fry—and the resident game fish droolingly wait for the lamp to be turned on each night.

I have found many similar situations in both salt water and fresh water in the past twenty-five years. Perhaps the best of my collection involved a dance hall on the New York side of the St. Lawrence. It illuminated an acre of water, and every bug for miles around flew into the building's screening and dropped to the water below. In a few hours there would be a windrow of moths on the surface, and if you listened carefully the dance music was counterpointed with the *glop, glop* of gorging mouths—fish that, incidentally, spook from a flashlight. The dancehall burned down eight or nine years ago, and the bass are back to earning an honest living.

Reflexive casting is almost essential to night fishing. A man who can handle his tackle with his eyes closed is eminently qualified to work in darkness. In this connection I suggest that novice casters use an enclosed-spool spinning reel and braided-nylon line. The reel won't backlash and the pliable braid will spool evenly when you're retrieving surface plugs. Leave the free-spool reels and monofilament lines to the experts, or you'll spend half the night untangling snarls.

Short, accurate casts are the rule with fly rod or casting tackle; there is considerable evidence that the range of fish vision is extremely limited after dark. It's not unusual to get a strike right under your rod tip at night. The only immediate problem is to keep your lure out of the trees. Much depends, of course, on being familiar with the landscape. It's a good idea to survey the lake during daylight hours and, as a matter of safety, always inspect an unfamiliar river before wading in the dark.

Ordinarily I work my plugs at night by casting toward the shore and retrieving very slowly. However, I'd suggest that beginners stay close to shore and cast parallel to it because there's less chance of snagging branches. Don't get the idea that all night fishing is done in shallow water. I think this is a mistake that many novices make, particularly when fishing for bass. By all means commence operations by plugging along the shoreline, but if that doesn't pay off, row out to deep water and work your lure on the bottom.

In night fishing we all have a tendency to favor surface lures because they can be seen or heard, yet much of the mumbo jumbo about rising and falling barometers and moon phases can be eliminated by simply changing your approach. Fish do not feed at the same time in the same place each night, even though a period of success might lead you to believe they do. Aside from a flexible mind, you also need four or five types of lures.

The popping plug is probably the most universal lure for night casting. When you jerk it on the surface, its sound can cause a night-hunting bass to lose his button. There's no question as to the general effectiveness of water-disturbing baits. I think the old injured-minnow and torpedo-type plug with propellers fore and aft would rank second with their wet, purring sound.

However, there are times when a perfectly quiet plug, such as the darter, will take more and bigger fish. The way I work a bait of this type is to cast toward shore and let it remain motionless for some time; then I retrieve slowly with long stops and pauses. If the popper, torpedo, and darter do not score in the shallows, try deep fishing.

My favorite subsurface bait is a jig-and-eel combination in southern waters and the old twin-spinner bucktail in northern lakes. Bottom bumping is particularly effective on bright, moonlit nights when bass are ignoring floating lures. I don't believe there's any inviolable law concerning lure colors. Many oldtimers follow the ancient rule of dark colors on black nights and light colors on bright nights. Still others rely on luminous baits. I like orange, yellow, silver, and black plugs, and use them according to my own whim.

Sound and movement certainly play major roles in alerting game fish to distant objects; this is true of all animals, including man. Once a fish becomes aware of something moving, he approaches it for a close examination or immediate disposal. I think the critical moment that makes the fish suspicious occurs when the angler overplays his hand and exaggerates the plug's action. The fact that a plug is black or white adds little to the illusion of reality.

I do not like to fish at night as well as in the daylight hours. My real satisfaction in catching fish is to see them strike and jump before rolling in the current, and except under unique circumstances, such as taking Atlantic salmon under the midnight sun, that visual pleasure is dimmed at night. Yet there are wonderful moments on the water after dark: summer mornings when a thin light streak shows along the eastern sky and you hear the far-off crow of a rooster, then the furious splashing of a trout chasing chubs; fall nights when the stars are small and frosty and you bless the invention of longjohns while you fumble for a thermos of hot coffee.

Autumn nights are probably the best of all for bass and walleyes in the mid-south. Your senses become razor-sharp when the world sleeps. In the past ten years I have logged 232 after-dark trips for a total of 3,365 fish, which averages out at 14.5 fish per trip. Naturally there were nights when I caught absolutely nothing, but there were others when an abundance of crappie or bass pulled the total score up. In perusing my notebook I find I can make some generalizations on these assorted nights of angling.

The most productive periods were from dusk to 10 P.M. and from 4 A.M. to sunrise. Those hours between 10 P.M. and 4 A.M. I'd rate from poor to fair when measured on a fish-per-hour basis. As for the moon, there's no apparent difference in my success from one phase to another except in salt-water fishing That can be explained by my own habit of going out on the full moon.

Most of these night trips were for snook and spotted sea trout in Florida bays. With the extreme tides occurring at full moon, many shallow flats where I normally can't run a boat become flooded and fishable. I also like to cast for tarpon by moonlight; so I practically eliminated dark nights by choice.

In freshwater fishing, however, my time was fairly well spread through all moon phases, and about the only thing I can conclude is that at some hour every night fish go on a feeding spree that averages about three hours in duration. I was completely or partially skunked on 22 trips out of the 232. Either I began fishing too late or quit too early—or I just didn't use the right method. Some of the failures are especially puzzling.

Last year when fishing fell into the hot-weather doldrums I happened to be visiting a mountain lake that reputedly is full of big brown trout. I could not catch the big browns, nor many small ones, for that matter. My morning exercise would commence with dry flies (although I never saw a rising fish) in various sizes and patterns; then I'd change to wets until I felt sure they were impotent. Next came nymphs on very long, light leaders, but again I could catch nothing larger than 9 or 10 inches.

Then I'd switch to deep-sinking streamers before locating the village idiot. There's always one befuddled fish that will strike at a marabou. I told my angling partner, Arnold Gingrich, that it was obvious that our big browns were feeding after dark. So for three sleepless nights we pounded the lake to a froth and caught exactly three trout—one each night.

I can think of a number of reasons why our nocturnal vigils didn't pay off, but the most obvious one is our personal brand of religion—fly fishing. Probably a live minnow or a worm fished around the spring holes would have caused a riot. For my part, however, I'll continue to work the fly stick after dark, because that's the method that gives me the most pleasure at all hours of the day.

For reasons that have never been perfectly explained, night fishing is not legal in all states. When in doubt, check with your local conservation agency before stumbling over a night-prowling game protector. In most states, however, the sport is considered a respectable occupation. For instance, the Michigan "caddis" hatches (really mayflies) are attended by countless stalwart citizens on such streams as the Boardman, Pere Marquette, and Au Sable. These stimulating insects bring the heaviest fish of the season to the surface, where they will take dry patterns ferociously. I have spent many a night floundering around Lower Peninsula rivers trying to hold fish that jumped with their bellies full of bedsprings after inhaling big floaters.

There are numerous patterns tied for Michigan night fishing, and inevitably fly boxes reflect a lore that is wholesomely local. We rarely have comparable nocturnal summer hatches of mayflies in the East or the Far West, but stone flies and true caddis occasionally create the same wild fishing. Then there is always the oddball sort of situation that I ran into several years ago.

Generally speaking, trout at night are not critically selective in the matter of lure color and size. However, I did record one instance of absolute selectivity in August 1956 that may be of some interest, inasmuch as the insect's appearance is an annual event. Breakfast began significantly with my wife's announcing that our porch was crawling with termites. I knew what to expect before seeing them.

The ancient hemlock posts that support our porch roof hide several colonies of wood ants. Once every summer they pour out of the crevices looking like a fierce army of termites about to level the house. Actually, these winged ants are merely being expelled from their nests by the nonflying workers that have carefully fattened them for their nuptial flight. In their bizarre cycle the male dies after mating, while the queen proceeds to lay eggs for the next six years or more—a fecundity that has pleased fish and confounded anglers for centuries. Unfortunately I had to work that particular day; so there was no chance of getting on the stream until evening.

Everywhere I looked, from the bridge to Home Pool, trout were scooping up ants. According to the highest scientific opinion, ants drive trout to paroxysms of hunger because they contain formic acid, and for the brief period that the insect is on the water, fish take them to the exclusion of anything else. The insects came from the old beech stumps along the bank and fell on the surface in sufficient numbers to keep the water splashing with fish. I played with them until dark, using a Brown Ant pattern that is an exact replica of the natural. Most of the trout were 10- and 11-inchers. When the stars were sharp as fresh-struck flames, I changed to a large wet fly with the idea of raising a lunker.

I have found that flies dressed on No. 2 and No. 4 hooks are most effective at night. They are tied with long, soft hackles and look like overgrown pan-fish patterns with fat chenille bodies. My standard procedure is to make short casts across and downstream, keeping the line fairly tight so that the fly moves along slowly. Drag is seldom, if ever, important; in fact, night-feeding lunkers will often smack a fly hanging stationary in the current. When the fly swings around, however, I give it a simple pulsing stroke before picking up for a new cast. That's the way I fished for the next hour.

I could hear some heavy trout working the flat below the bridge, but not a single one touched my sunk pattern. It finally dawned on me to try the little Brown Ant again, and once more I was back in business. A pair of 18-inch browns were my best for the night. It's fairly obvious that except for the fact that I was on the water earlier, I might have pulled a blank. It would never have occurred to me to use a No. 10 fly after dark, because large dressings almost always take trout. As I said, we all tend to channelize our methods.

The technique of hot-weather fishing is complicated by the phenomena of water temperature and light. Since a fish is cold-blooded, its body temperature fluctuates with the temperature of the water. In one year, a fish is subjected to as much as 50 degrees variation, and thus all its body processes —growth, spawning, breathing, and feeding—are to a large extent affected by the weather. Its ability to digest a meal is retarded when the water becomes too cold or too warm.

Sunlight is, of course, transformed into heat. In our latitudes about 14 percent of the oblique noon sunshine is reflected from the surface in winter, and only 2½ percent of the vertical sunshine is reflected in summer. Obviously, if the weather is hot the fish will go where it's cool, and if the water is illuminated under a brilliant sun the fish will feed at dark.

There is an immense range of variation, and no precise rule of thermometer will apply to all situations. One thing is fairly certain, however: the curtain of night brings food, security, and a touch of cool air in the dog days. Then a fish doesn't need any more urging to get out of bed and find himself a snack.

18

SPINNING LURE FOR BONEFISH

One afternoon on a Bahamian flat, long after I had all of the stage-setting photos of Al McClane bonefishing I needed, we spotted still another school. David, our boatman, moved us into position, and Al sent a long graceful cast snaking out over the shining water. Swirl—nothing. The fish were as skittish as mice in a kennel.

"Pick up that rod, George, and give them a try."

"I came to get pictures of you catching fish."

"I need a rest," Al lied. "Get up here."

Maybe spinning would do what fly could not. I had hardly set foot in the bow when David pointed excitedly off to the right—mud! That's exactly what we had been looking for all day. Bonefish making mud are far more likely to take a lure than cruising fish. Quickly I lobbed the lure into the cloud of marl. Smash! Zing!

Fifteen minutes later Al had taken a dozen shots of *me* with a bonefish, and we slipped the 6-pounder behind the rear seat. David wore a broad grin, and I could see he was drooling at the thought of fresh bonefish fillets.

Al took up his position again in the bow, and I put the spinning gear away. As I did so, for the first time I took a close look at the lure.

"Why, that's one of ——"

"——Dr. Cooper's marabou jigs," Al finished. "Except that one was made by a reader using a Colorado spinner as his steel base. It's the last one I have."

I opened Al's tackle box, popped off the jig and put it back in the box. I took out a plastic shrimp and began to tie it on.

"What are you doing?" Al asked.

I pointed to the marabou jig. "This one should be marked 'For Emergency Use Only.' "

When you read the following story, you'll see why.

GWR

SPINNING LURE FOR BONEFISH

Like most observers, I have long believed that bonefishermen need a psychoanalyst. Take those who frequent the Lighthouse Club[1] on Andros Island. You rise in the morning, and walk down to the pool and there's Eleanor Holm, maybe Esther Williams, and a bevy of similar-type quail stretched out getting a suntan. Who's behind the potted palms? Nobody. Every male worth his Dun & Bradstreet has gone bonefishing. If Jayne Mans-

---

[1] At that time owned by the Swedish financier Axel Wennergren, it is now a U. S. Navy research installation for submersibles.

field climbed on the diving board with a banner across her bosom reading "I love gents who love bonefish," she wouldn't have an audience.

Bonefishermen are dedicated. I know a man who spent a million dollars to buy an island and build a home in the middle of a bonefish flat. And another who profited with an inn on an island that the late Guy Kibbee described as Alcatraz in Technicolor. Bonefishermen crawl behind its walls every winter. Mine host can't keep them out.

Now, to bring reason where reason was not thought to exist, bonefishermen have acquired a consulting psychoanalyst. He is Dr. J. H. Cooper of Kansas City, Missouri. After systematic research extending from Cuba to the middle Bahamas, the learned doctor has come to the startling conclusion that it's the fish who need a head shrinker—not the fishermen. For therapy the doctor has devised a shock treatment which he demonstrated to your reporter last year, and one which I have not revealed for reasons that will quickly become apparent. The Cooper method gave me forty-one bonefish[2] the first time I tried it; so I decided the whole business must be a hallucination and went back to the swimming pool. Nine out of ten subsequent trips were most rewarding, though I have not had the energy for a bonefish marathon like the first. My poorest score was a trio of 5-pounders, and these fell to the Cooper method when live-bait fishermen couldn't get a bump. Spinning-type citizens may profit by the doctor's counsel.

Dr. Cooper discovered early in his clinical studies that *Albula vulpes* suffers from a neurosis induced by too many lures that do nothing. These usually originate in somebody's home workshop several latitudes north of salt water. The convenient theory behind these concoctions, simple and ingenious, runs thus: Bonefish always feed while standing on their heads, and therefore anything that drags sand at nose level and looks edible will be gulped. Both propositions are, of course, false. What left the doctor cowering on his couch was that, upon examination of the subject's environment, he found a maze of ribbon grass that dissolved any vulpian dream of gourmandizing on the lures sent his way. A bonefish would droolingly approach the "free-swimming" lure, only to discover it was a dollop of lead and hair hung on some weeds.

With one tentative probe, Dr. Cooper lay bare the innermost problem of man versus bonefish. It was this: There was no lure that would sink and

[2] Al says, "These were small Isle of Pines fish. Catching large numbers was no great feat. I think Ted Williams once caught forty-four. But fly is a different story: My best day in the Bahamas was seventeen fishing with Frank Valgenti, an outstanding fly fisherman and an attorney active in New Jersey conservation work."

retrieve slowly with a maximum of action, skip over weeds and coral heads, and at the same time have enough weight for long casts without being splashy. So the doctor went back to Kansas City and consulted with E. H. Branine, who, fortunately, never in his life had seen a bonefish flat.

"I needed an absolutely objective assistant," Dr. Cooper said as we strolled into the Bonefish Bar, "a man with no preconceived notions about lures and one who owned a home workshop. Mr. Branine was ideal. He could hammer out baits without compulsively sneaking in improvements. By the process of elimination, I had come to the conclusion that remedial success was only possible with the perfect shallow-water jig."

While our daiquiris sweated on the mahogany, I mulled over what our fact-gathering psychoanalyst was getting at—and it made sense. Earlier that morning I had been fishing one of the bays in the North Bight. Using Dr. Cooper's jig, I caught four bonefish simply by casting near tailing singles and letting the lure sink to the bottom. They picked it up and swam off like a bass with a minnow. Then a school of mutton snappers appeared, and after bagging two for breakfast I walked down to the tide hole and cast for groupers. Fortunately I had the foresight to tie on a wire leader; one fish was a 30-pounder. Then I ran into a school of barracuda, and by working the lure fast instead of bouncing it along the bottom I hung five big fish.

Jigs probably catch more saltwater fish in tropical waters than any other kind of spinning lure. A jig consists of a molded-lead head on a Z nickel hook, with a skirt of nylon, bucktail, or hackle feathers. The head can be chrome-plated or painted bright colors; most casters use a white or yellow skirt. Jig heads are made slanted, ball-shaped, bullet-shaped, coin-shaped, and keeled. For each shape there is a reason. A jig, being a compact mass of lead with very little air resistance, casts easily and sinks readily. It rides hook-up in the water and rests nose-down, which makes it nearly snagproof.

Presumably jigs are a fair imitation of bait fish when moved rapidly, not in the image sense of a plug but because of motion and color. Eskimos and South Sea Islanders use them, and commercial men all over the world depend on jigs for their livelihood. Yet if you fling most jigs onto a shallow flat, you toss eggs into the fan. Our crustacean-loving bonefish feeds in shallow places where rapid retrieves are impracticable. Old *Albula* has a short fuse and no sense of direction.

"You can image how I felt the first time I went to the Isle of Pines," Dr. Cooper continued. "I had made inquiries in tackle shops and they sold me all kinds of lures. It didn't take me long to find out that a lightweight jig would catch an occasional bonefish, but only with some luck. Why, the fish tailed in water that was barely eight inches deep! I would cast, and *plop*, there was my jig hung on the ribbon grass. Or down a crab hole. They just couldn't find it."

We sipped our daiquiris, and I thought about some of the flats I'd fished, and how so few of them were alike. The kind most people recognize are in the Florida Keys, around Marathon, Islamorada, and Key Largo, where the bottom is fairly uniform with marl and ribbon weed. Some of the ocean flats have paths of sand and you can work a jig beautifully on them. Southern Cuba has thick marl with heavier grass patches, and the tide runs way back from the drop-off, which would be bad if you didn't see tails. But the Isle of Pines area is full of head-down fish. Across the way at Grand Cayman you find both marl and coral flats like the southern coast of Puerto Rico.

The Bahamas have every type of flat, including creeks like Crab Creek on Munjack. Once you pass through the screen of mangroves, the creek winds narrow and clear like a mountain stream. Eight- and 10-pound fish feed in a few inches of water. Angel Fish Creek on Little Abaco is a broad, mossy flat, and unless your lure is designed exactly right you'll spend most of the day cleaning the hook. Creeks are fine places for trophy fish as a rule, because the ribbon weed grows dwarf-like, and some creeks have less grass than an egg has hair. However, big tidal creeks, like Cargill on Andros, sprout heavy weed beds, which may partly explain the vast schools of fish found there. But before you learn about flats, you must have some idea of what makes good bonefishing. It goes something like this:

You go to a place where there are flats with tailing and mudding fish. Not deep sand flats or coral flats where you can't spot the schools, but shallow ones with water up to your knees. You won't often see the whole tail of a bonefish, so don't look for one waving over the surface. Watch for the very tip of the upper segment wiggling like somebody's pinky poked out of water. At a distance beginners often mistake the tail for a minnow. At times bonefish just scratch the surface and people will pass a whole school without knowing it.

Should you get real lucky, you will see puffs of mud or the rippling of a school as it pushes water. If your guide knows his business, and there are plenty who do in Florida, he will pole a flat-bottomed skiff and not disturb the feeding grounds with an outboard or a round-bottomed skiff. Bonefish hit the panic button at the slightest provocation. Your guide is half the job in finding bonefish, which is why good ones can charge high prices and keep booked.

"I couldn't do much with the Cuban fish," said Dr. Cooper. "I'd see them tailing, but I had to reel like mad to keep the jig from snagging. Sometimes a big one would wheel after the lure, and I'd let it settle to the bottom. I felt like a man trying to ignite a sodden firecracker. It would be accurate to say that a hundred bonefish stared at my jigs. Bucktail is stiff and lifeless." The doctor made wet marks on the bar with his forefinger to emphasize the point.

"Now, sir, I've fished the Ozarks most of my life, and you'll understand when I state categorically that marabou makes the best streamer fly for smallmouth bass in clear water. I read that in your column some years back. It has inherent action. It literally crawls when retrieved slowly. It has everything bucktail doesn't have except durability.

"I surmised that what a shallow-water jig needs is a marabou skirt, because the critical moment in bonefishing occurs when you stop reeling." The doctor swept his hand across the bar and Ivan started squeezing more limes. "Watch. Here's the fish coming at the lure." Dr. Cooper walked his hand back with the studied lope of a 10-pounder. "Now he's directly behind the jig. Does he take? No.

"You are aware of Pavlov's conditioned-reflex theory? Well, the bonefish is conditioned to feeding on crabs. The fish pokes his nose in holes and under grass patches until he chases a crab out. The crab runs a short distance and stops to hide again. What does the bonefish do? He swims along behind and inhales the crab when it stops. Now, you stop the marabou jig a few feet from a tailing fish, or at the instant you see his shadow behind the jig, or when there is any surface disturbance around the jig, and *bang*, you have caught yourself a bonefish. Why? Because marabou wiggles even after touching bottom. It may not look like a crab, but the bonefish doesn't consider that—his reflexes associate food with movement at nose level. Not rapid movement. But stop-and-go-hide movement. I had Mr. Branine build different kinds of jigs to fit these requirements." The doctor looked reflectively at the black-wire bonefish swimming across the Lighthouse Club's walls.

"We tried dozens of head shapes and finally two of them turned out right. The solution came when we stopped molding a solid-lead head. Now follow this closely." The doctor paused. "Mr. Branine cut head designs from thin sheets of stainless steel. That made the difference! You see, lead is soft. Too soft to mold in wafer-thin shapes. With steel we could build the design we wanted. Then, by thinning and bending the edges, we could get a deadly fluttering action. By adding flux to the inside of the blade, and filling that area with lead, we changed the jig from a relatively crude lure to a precision-built bait.

"I went back to the Isle of Pines with the new marabou jigs, and my, what a difference! On Grand Cayman tarpon beat the bonefish to the marabou, and the loss of lures was appalling. I have not caught a really big bonefish on my jig yet, but I will, and that, as you know, sir, is less important in our sport than most nonbonefishermen assume."

A big bonefish, big enough to get your name in small print, would weigh 10 pounds. People catch 6-pounders and send them to Al [taxidermist] Pflueger. A real trophy would be over 12 pounds. Mort Tinker has the record for the Florida Keys with a 14½-pounder. Sam Snead tied the Bahamian record with a 15-pounder the first time out at Bimini. The biggest one on the books is an 18-pounder taken in Hawaii.[3] They grow as heavy in the Atlantic. Native hand-liners catch whoppers and eat them.

To get a trophy, you have to fish often or be lucky. Most of your bonefish will weigh from 4 to 6 pounds, and these are not to be underestimated if you use light tackle and artificial lures. I have caught bonefish in all weights up to 12 pounds. After the strike and first two or three runs, one size is as much fun as another. Most of the excitement is seeing tails, stalking, and placing the lure just right. Then the shadow and *blurp* when he opens the water wide, highballing across the flat.

"I am convinced," said Dr. Cooper, "that if a man uses light spinning tackle, say a 6½-foot rod of medium action and a 6-pound-test monofilament line, he can always catch bonefish with a marabou jig. Provided there are fish around. Even if you fish blind without seeing tails, the lure will attract them. When you see a bonefish coming at the bait, let it sit on the bottom for a few seconds and he'll grab it. That marabou paralyzes 'em. Of course, just wrapping marabou on *any* jig isn't enough. The jig head must have the right distribution of weight by mass to sink slowly and flutter gently when you retrieve. I have achieved that in two different shapes.

"There's no sense in saying my jigs are perfect. Bonefish will tear marabou apart. I figure each skirt is good for maybe ten fish. Then you have to tie on a new one." Dr. Cooper paused for a moment and continued thoughtfully, "But understand, I am not in the lure business. For whatever it's worth, I'm just giving you my analysis of bonefish lures."

We finished our drinks and walked out to the lobby. "There's one more thing," the doctor added. "Never use a leader with the jig. It spoils the action, and bonefish get suspicious. I tie my monofilament line directly to the swivel. A swivel is necessary; without it, you'll crank twists in your line when a fish is on. You won't break off if you play them correctly."

[3] "Larger bonefish have been caught since in African waters," says A. J., "but I believe these deep-water populations are a different species. I also think the small eastern Pacific bonefish are a different species, but nobody has worked up any meristics on these forms as yet."

Dr. Cooper stopped and offered his hand. "It sure was nice talking to you, Mr. McClane. I suppose you're going out fishing now?"

"Yes," I said.

"Well, I've had enough for one day," said the doctor. "I thought I might sit by the swimming pool for a while."

19

THE FISH JUMPED OVER A SPOON

Before you start thinking that A. J.'s expertise rests too heavily on fragile fly wands and little fuzzy hooks, let him tell you a few fundamental things you might not have known about the humble spoon. In addition to learning Omar Olson's secret retrieve for taking giant brown trout, you'll find enough tips on color, weight, and spoon shape to start a dozen arguments with your angling friends.

GWR

THE FISH JUMPED OVER A SPOON

It is often said that the national flag of Alaska consists of red and white stripes against a silver background. If you look toward the north country, you will see this brilliant pennant rising into the noonday blue with perpetual monotony. For here troops the tourist with a bagful of wobbling spoons and an unflagging devotion to hoisting them skyward. Alaskan fishes are so responsive to this kind of casting that a striped wobbler is considered the standard from which all other baits are measured. I saw a man button-deep in Brooks River one morning, with his nylon line stretched across the water like a frail cobweb dripping with luminous dew, and upon inquiring with which lure he had achieved these sweets of angling, he replied, "Geez, is there another one?" This, you must agree, is a difficult question to answer when the air is electrified by the sparks of a wild-eyed rainbow.

But Alaska is not the only place where spoon-twigglers have a ball. The wobbler is murder on pike, an invitation to suicide among trout, and deadly as a cobra in the the jungle of bass and muskellunge. Next to plugs, spoons are undoubtedly the most widely used artificial lures in America. They are fished with fly rods, by bait casting, spinning, cane poles, and trolling. There's no game fish who won't slap a wobbler, and since the advent of spinning mills, even the panfish are taking a thumping from those runt-sized teasers. However, there's an art to getting results with spoons, and every once in a while you'll come across a twiggler like Omar Olson,[1] who considered fly talk mere puppy yappings, because he was a wobbling-spoon specialist.

[1] Omar Olson was from Arena, a little settlement near Margaretville that is now mostly under the waters of the Pepacton Reservoir. (Naturally, this stretch of drowned

Omar would roar into town in his broken-down plumbing truck, and easing up in front of the drugstore, he'd wave the boys over to take a look behind the seat. There, stretched in their pristine glory, you could see two, maybe three, brown trout of a size that warned all comers that worms and minnows were just so many muddy-complexioned illusions in the hands of common men. Omar was the wind of success that whipped down Main Street, and people danced in his path like bits of paper. Old men wept and young men were thunderstruck. He probably caught more large brown trout than the whole town put together, and everybody was certain that he used live bait. Actually, he never said how he caught his fish, thus leaving a gap between moral and historic truth. But Omar was a spoon-twiggler pure and simple. He used a two and a half-inch wobbling spoon that he could pitch all over the river with a short steel bait-casting rod. One summer evening, when Dan Todd's hard cider had unmoored his convivial ship, Omar confided in us, allowing that spoons were better than live bait, and that he would prove it.

Now I've seen big trout follow my spoon like a sailor trailing a blonde. As long as the spoon ambled along with a little wiggle, the fish stayed right behind. But such sociability is seldom marked with success. When a real twiggler like Omar got on the scent, there was no trailing. He cast, and then dropped it down. Letting the spoon sink a few seconds, he reeled up slack and wiggled his rod tip so that the bait quivered with fear. He pointed his rod tip to one side, and jerked the spoon forward a full yard. He paused, then swung his rod tip to the other side and pulled some more. From the bank, we could hear Omar snarl as he worked. The spoon fluttered, wiggled, and wobbled while sinking toward the bottom, and then darted off in a new direction, shivering in agony at the sight of an oncoming fish. But Omar left nothing to chance; perhaps the trout would make an awkward assault and

Delaware used to represent the best trout fishing in the area.) Dan Todd, Margaretville's stationmaster when that town had a railroad, wouldn't even say hello to Olson as Todd was the purist of purists. Todd bought all his rods, lines, and reels from Wm. Mills in New York, and dressed his own flies to match the Delaware naturals. The assistant stationmaster, Ray Neidig, who lived in Arena near Olson, was an equally dedicated fly fisherman, and the railway station house looked more like a tackle shop than what it was.

Olson stopped by one morning looking for a shipment of plumbing supplies. Dan preserved aquatic insects for study, and a mason jar of caddis cases (the pebble type) sitting on his desk aroused Olson's curiosity. He asked Todd "What's them things?" Todd looked pained. "I just had an operation—them's my kidney stones." Olson stared at the jar. "God Almighty," he whispered. "No wonder you can't fish!"

It may have been the tenor of the times, but another railroad man on the Delaware, Dan Cahill, designed a now world-famous fly pattern which bears his name.

fumble the spoon, or perhaps the trout would have a change of heart and slink away. So he paused again and hopped the wobbler toward the surface with an overhead sweep of his rod, and down again, left to right, pulling and twitching the unbalanced metal into a fresh paroxysm of misery. That fish wanted to eat so bad that he jumped over the spoon, then snapped around, denting the wobbler with a sledgehammer blow. Although Omar had acted vigorously, Dan observed that he did very little reeling, except to take up slack. This adroit trick made Omar's success.

A wobbling spoon usually consists of a somewhat oval-shaped piece of metal, not unlike an ordinary teaspoon. It can be made in a variety of sizes and finishes according to the whims of the fish and the requirements of the angler. The tail hook may be single, double, or treble, and it can be feathered, covered with bucktail, or protected by a weed guard. It wobbles because the spoon has a calculated balance instability under induced spin, breaking actual rotation from one side to the other. Modern lure makers spend months calculating the relation of weight to mass in hundreds of curvatures before marketing a finished product. The end result should allow the spoon to travel with maximum motion through any speed range. But this was not so in the beginning.

Spoons are among the oldest lures in the world, their probable date of origin being around 3000 B.C. Originally they were made by primitive people from pieces of polished shell and bone. The modern spoon, as we know it, was alleged to have been invented by a young man in Vermont who accidentally dropped a teaspoon overboard while lunching on Lake Bomoseen. As the utensil fluttered down through the water, a fish seized it. Thus young Julio Buel conceived the idea for his bait business. Oddly enough, a butter-fingered butler in charge of a picnic on the Thames had lost a teaspoon from his master's punt just about the time young Julio's took the big plunge. Suffice to say, this teaspoon was reported to have been snatched by a pike. Laplanders in the far north of Sweden scoff at both stories, as they claim to have been using spoons for centuries. But the records show that Julio applied for, and received, the first patent for trolling baits in 1834, which qualified him as "spoon inventor."

Spoons probably create the impression of being small fish in the water, but I must confess I've never been wholly satisfied with this explanation. I suspect that many fish grab a spoon out of sheer curiosity. A white bass down in Kentucky demonstrated this quite clearly one day. There was a ball of shad minnows working on the surface when a school of whites got their range and shot them full of holes. I tossed a green-and-white wobbler among the bass, and one fish waltzed over to the spoon to take a good, long look. Remember, the bass had been dashing in every direction, snapping at the shad. I retrieved slowly, but he kept circling the wobbler, and it wasn't until the spoon was nearly under the boat that he made a lunge, missing the bait completely. Now, I don't believe that the fish believed my wobbler was a crippled shad. He would have blasted it without hesitation. Instead, he closed his mind to the shad orgy and followed the wobbler with an emotional detachment.

Wobblers range in size from spoons no bigger than your thumbnail to blades 8 or 10 inches long. The largest ones are used for muskie, salmon, and lake trout trolling, and may weigh up to 3 ounces. Most small wobblers are designed for casting with spinning tackle, and these usually weigh between ⅛ and ¼ of an ounce. Between these two extremes you can literally find a size or weight to fit every kind of problem. When casting for muskies and other large fish, it is not necessary to use 3-ounce trolling wobblers, for instance; you can take the standard ⅜-ounce bait-casting size and attach extra-strong hooks. By the same token, one of the most popular salmon and lake trout casting spoons today weighs ⅜ of an ounce, so the weight factor is relative to your fishing method. You can get a spoon 3 inches long that weighs ¼ of an ounce, or you can get another one only 1½ inches long of the same weight. Because of the greater blade area of the former, it will sink more slowly and work higher and faster in the water. From a casting standpoint, the smaller lure would also have less air resistance and thus cast more easily. So the argument for heavier spoons for the largest fish is as impeding to progress as a dozen square miles of mud. All wobblers do not perform in this same fashion, and it is a wise twiggler who gets the most of each.

My favorite color for a wobbling spoon is the all-brass finish. Next to this, I like a spoon that's silver on one side and enamelled with red and white stripes on the other. In third place, I'd put an all-silver wobbler, and then an all-black wobbler. Pearl and copper rank further down my list. There is no empirical evidence to support my choice, and such a listing might easily be reversed by somebody who fishes steadily in one area. When I first started tossing spoons years ago, silver was practically the only finish I needed. Walleyes and pickerel in dark, weedy water held the spotlight in those days. Silver is still my standby for saltwater fishing, but gradually I discovered that I was catching more and more fish on brass blades in fresh water. On a number of occasions in the past few seasons, I matched results with friends who fished an identical type of spoon in another color. Brass scored more consistently than silver, black, or copper under the conditions that existed, but on the days when black spoons were taken, they showed a much greater difference in the final score. Black is almost always attractive to bass, and both black and silver are excellent for fishing in discolored water, especially when they have a strip of pork rind trailing behind.

Pearl is especially good at times for rainbow trout and smallmouth bass. I am very partial to a midget fish-shaped wobbler that is pearl on one side and silver on the other. This bait scores heavily in northern clear-water lakes. In my experience, copper is the color for a lake trout trolling spoon, but in general, copper wobblers are more effective on western waters than they are in the East or South. I doubt if the color question has much relation to the predominant color of local bait fish where wobblers are concerned. Visibility, both to the angler and the fish, is probably the key factor. As a rule, bright spoons are more effective in dark water or on dull days, and the duller spoons are effective in clear water on bright days.

The spoon is as near to an all-round bait as you can possibly get. It can be fished in a variety of ways; you can sink the wobbler deep in a lake and work real slow along the weed tops. Often a slow, gravel-bouncing retrieve is the only way to take lake trout in the early season when casting from shore. You can fish at mid-depth with a jumping retrieve, letting the blade flutter to the bottom once in a while for largemouth bass and northern pike during the summer months. And you can use a wobbling spoon right smack on the surface, skittering style. Not all wobblers make good top-water attractors, but any of those with a reasonably curved surface will flap up enough commotion to draw attention. Of course, the real art is twiggling, an absorbing study with touches of unexpected detail. Like the day Omar's fish jumped over the spoon.

20

THAT OLD-FASHIONED WET FLY

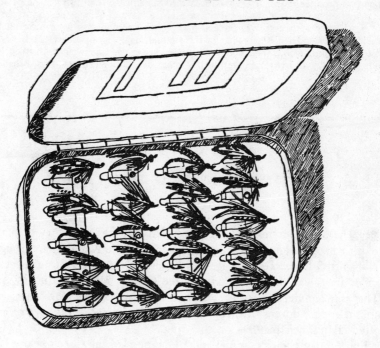

There is an ancient and honorable exchange of information between saltwater and freshwater fishermen. Because freshwater fishes generally live more cautious lives than their saltwater brethren, the freshwater angler has most often been a wellspring of new ideas concerning technique and terminal gear, especially lures. Saltwater fishes, on the other hand, lead faster, more reckless, existences. Consequently the chief contribution of the sea angler has been in the way of angling aids and the making of traditional tackle more hardy. The Great Lakes salmon fishery, for example, may refine the use of depth recorders, cable thermometers, star-drag reels, roller tips, outriggers, downriggers, and trolling boards, but the first inspiration for all this was the sea.

With this perspective, it surprised me some years ago when the Christmas-tree rig first hit the coasts to find some saltwater anglers blaming themselves or their kind for "inventing" such a contraption. Five, seven, sometimes as many as thirteen lures are streamed behind a spread of umbrellalike ribs producing, occasionally, an equal number of fish. The success of the rig lies in the simple truth that some days multiple lures on one line produce more strikes than one lure per line. Certain fish can be persuaded to attack a school of bait when they won't chase a stray. While the controversy raged over whether such gear was ethical, many saltwater converts were most anxious lest their freshwater friends get wind of the rig and make fun of saltwater's heavy-handed use of terminal tackle. Yet, with only variations in size and weight, thirteen lures per line have been *de rigueur* in freshwater fishing for over a century—as we shall see.

GWR

THAT OLD-FASHIONED WET FLY

The prettiest stretch of the Green River is the upper fifty or sixty miles where it edges Wyoming's Bridger Wilderness and flows through sagebrush hills, sweeping against the alders and willows in a succession of riffles and pools that hold some of the liveliest rainbow trout in America. This is magnificent dry-fly water, for when the trout are rising it's not unusual to see dozens of them working furiously across the face of a pool—often taking their mayflies on the wing.

But the day Elmer George[1] and I first sampled the Green below Cora the fish were obviously well fed. The river was covered with duns, but not a single rise marked the surface. We flailed hairwings over the best riffles; I zipped through twenty fly changes without stirring a fin. As a last resort I

[1] Auto-racing champion, now retired.

[160]

tied on a pair of wet flies and headed back downstream, letting the flies hang over the heavy run, lifting the rod every few seconds to make them dance. It wasn't long before the first rainbow came up and belted the tail fly. Then I took another, weighing about 3 pounds, which I kept for the cook. By the time I got back to our lunch spot the score was eleven rainbows, one cut-throat, and a brook trout. Two fish went close to 4 pounds.

I dressed out the one I killed, and not surprisingly its stomach was empty. Except for a dark smear, there wasn't a trace of anything in its belly. This doesn't mean that none of the fish were feeding, but it often happens that large individual fish will rise in heavy water for an easy-to-catch wet fly after ignoring a fast floating dry. The same phenomenon can be observed when using spinning lures—otherwise empty or nonactive trout will wolf some crazy spoon as it hangs artlessly in the current.

The old method in the Catskills—and historically this was the pivotal spot in the development of American fly fishing—consisted not of casting a single fly but rather two or three flies in tandem. This may seem like an awkward extravagance, but quite frankly the oldtimers knew a good thing when they saw it. A multiple wet-fly setup will catch fish when a single fly won't; even the shy brown trout will be tempted. This vintage violence was achieved by rigging the dropper fly high on the leader or snelling two of them at intervals, so that at least one "wet" fly would dance on the surface whenever the rod was lifted high. The angler fished a short line across and downstream, using the natural drift; then, as the flies completed their swing, he raised his line and leader until the first dropper was bouncing in the current. With quick flicks of the wrist the flies were kept darting over a likely looking hold until the angler was convinced that no fish was in residence.

I seldom use one wet fly when fishing for trout. If imitation and stealth are needed I use nymphs instead. I've proved to my own satisfaction at least that a pair of wet flies will double my chances of a strike. Perhaps the basic attraction is that the fish feels he can get twice as much for the same effort, or it may be the sight of one bug chasing another that excites his predatory instinct. I hedge my bets, however, and try to fish the flies in their cross- and downstream swing so that they drift naturally, without drag. When the line straightens out I may let the flies hang in the current for a moment, give them little twitches, or raise the rod and make them skitter on top, but I always let them remain in almost the same position for at least fifteen to twenty seconds. When using two flies, this "come-and-get-it" doodling draws a lot of hits.

A long fly rod helps. So does a long leader, rubbed perfectly straight with a piece of rubber, and a fine line point. The best wet flies have good entry;

that is, they are sparsely hackled and made of materials such as chenille, herl, and silk, which soak up water and sink fast. Many hair-wings are useless because they are too buoyant and won't go down when necessary. The ideal water for this kind of fishing is in fairly deep riffles and pockets; however, a pair of flies fished in the usual sink-and-draw manner is often effective in the quiet of a lake.

Although the primary purpose in fishing two wet flies is not to catch two fish at a time, doubles are inevitable. I seldom land both trout, but I must admit it's fun trying. Not long ago I worked a series of little ponds nestling in the slopes of the Madison Range at about 8,000 feet. As with so many isolated waters in the Rockies, the trout population is fairly uniform—in this case 10- to 12-inch browns—but I like to fish in the gin-clear water surrounded by wildflowers, with nothing but the wind and an occasional elk for company.

On this particular day I had a very poor start with the dry fly. The sun was terribly bright and the fish just wouldn't come up, so I changed to a pair of wets and worked the sloping grassy shores. I caught four trout near a little spring, and when I hooked the next one I saw several more browns making wild dashes at the trailing dropper fly. I eased the pressure on my hooked fish, and when he slowed down one of his mates snatched the dropper. Two 10-inch fish on a light fly rod can be quite a handful. I finally skidded both of them over the moss and let them go. With my Polaroids it was easy to follow the darting flashes of trout as they came out of the spring hole, and by playing each one gently I encouraged four more doubles, although I didn't actually land another pair. As proper angling this is pure monkeyshines, but it's rare that we actually get a chance to observe fish taking the second fly.

As fishing water I don't like the Madison River from Hebgen Lake down to Ennis. It is just one long riffle with very few pools or pockets—almost monotonous in its constant flow. Yet it holds some very large trout that rise well during the stone-fly hatch in late June and early July, and again at the height of the hopper season in mid-August. Between times you have to work for your fish, usually in the very bad winds that are common in July.

One afternoon I was trying the water below the new bridge south of Cameron, and after throwing a dry fly into the teeth of a downstream gale for an hour I finally gave up. My line wouldn't even stay on the surface. I tied on a pair of Black Gnats and took the easy way out, with the wind and current at my back. Nothing much happened until I came to a deep channel that curved into the bank. A small rainbow grabbed the dropper, and as I began to reel him in a brownie of at least 5 pounds came out of the channel. For a fleeting second I thought he was after the little trout; then the lunker shot straight into the tail fly and swerved back toward his lair, taking the rainbow with him.

This crazy quadrille lasted about three minutes, with the little trout hopping to the surface every time the big one came about, giving him slack. Finally the brown got his dander up and made one wild leap, falling back into fast water. The leader snapped. The rainbow was still skittering through the air when his buddy disappeared.

The wet fly is easy to work. Whereas the dry fly must ordinarily be cast upstream, giving the beginner a lot of trouble with the line, the wet fly can be fished downstream, thereby taking slack out of the line as it works with the current. True, the strike on a wet may not be as splashy, but anybody with normal reflexes can barb the majority of his fish if he watches the water closely.

Polaroid glasses are a great help in all kinds of fly fishing, and they prove their worth when you're working below the surface, where the slightest flash or movement may indicate a strike. In addition, I have favorite combinations of reliable wet flies that are highly visible in the stream. For example, I think the Royal Coachman and the Black Gnat make an ideal pair to fish because either the white wing of the former or the black body of the latter can be seen over any kind of bottom from pale gravel to dark moss. The Black Gnat with its light, slate-colored wings has enough contrast to be seen under any surface, as do the Leadwing Coachman, Wickham's Fancy, and Ginger Quill. But don't hesitate to try some of the following oldies: Orange Fish Hawk, Blue Dun, Grizzly King (an almost forgotten gem), Queen of the Waters, Parmachenee Belle, March Brown, White Miller, Scarlet Ibis, Professor, Cowdung, Pink Lady, Greenwell's Glory, Gold-Ribbed Hare's Ear, Montreal, Silver Doctor, Yellow Sally, Silver Prince, Mallard Quill, Quill Gordon, and of course the Light and Dark Cahills and the Light and Dark Hendricksons.

Try contrasting patterns for visibility, but if the trout display any preference for one fly or the other don't hesitate to give them a pair of the same pattern. You'll be surprised at how often the light fly or the dark one brings consistent hits.

Not long ago I was float-fishing with Forrest Wood[2] on Arkansas' White River, an insect-poor stream where the trout feed principally on crayfish and minnows. The popular lures are spinners, live bait, and rubber worms, but it's an interesting, though tough, stream for the fly-rod angler. I worked the water hard with streamers, dry flies, and nymphs and took an occasional

[2] A former Ozark guide, now president of the Ranger Boat Company in Flippin, Arkansas.

rainbow; then one day at Bream Shoals I began experimenting with a pair of wets—a Light and Dark Cahill.

In about three hours I caught and released twenty-six trout. Nearly all my fish hit the Dark Cahill, which I had mounted as a dropper fly. Out of curiosity I switched and tied it on as the tail fly, moving the Light Cahill up to the dropper. After that four out of five trout grabbed the tail fly. The logical next step was to use a pair of Dark Cahills, but to test the fish's apparent selectivity I added a Black Gnat to the dropper instead, and although a few fish hit it the Dark Cahill continued to draw most of the strikes.

This great discovery lasted all that day, but the next morning the fish wouldn't look at a Dark Cahill, nor anything else that Forrest could suggest. The daily rise and fall of the river level is a determining factor here in fly-fishing success, and during the night the White had swelled its banks at least three feet. But subsequently, each time we had low water a pair of small wet flies of one pattern or another would clean house. The trick is to take the time to wade the faster riffles and side channels that boat-bound hardware artists skim through—and pray you don't get torpedoed with a johnboat.

In Grandpa's day dropper flies were joined to the silkworm gut leader by means of looped snells. Rigging is greatly simplified today because of the security of synthetics such as nylon and platyl. To make a dropper strand, merely pull out one long end (about six inches) of the heavier leader section when tying the blood knot. The thicker piece will have enough rigidity to "stand away" from the leader, and even if it twists occasionally no harm is done. It's also important to keep the tail fly and the dropper well separated to prevent a twisting effect on the leader when casting. As a rule the two flies should be at least thirty inches apart.

Ordinarily I use ten- to fifteen-foot leaders, with my dropper forty to forty-two inches up from the point. If you want to use wet patterns of two different sizes, tie the larger one in as the tail fly; otherwise it will twist around the leader in a dropper position. Obviously you can't go too fine—down to 4X or 6X at the point—and maintain rigidity with two flies unless they are No. 14's or smaller. However, a pair of 14's are absolutely deadly at times and would be my first choice on hard-fished waters, east or west. The thing to avoid, and this applies to all fly fishing, is soft or flexible material in the tippet; synthetics with a hard finish turn over a lot better. The soft stuff belongs on spinning or bait-casting reels—not in fly leaders.

About a month ago I began to experiment with three flies on a fifteen-foot leader and have had some remarkable results with the rig, using sparse No. 16 Partridge Spiders and Gray Hackles. This is opening an interesting avenue for experiment, as the two tiny droppers have a wonderful action on the surface when danced over moving water. If this seems like heresy, remember that we're only catching up to Grandpa, and the angling literature he read advocated from nine to thirteen flies. One of the largest brown trout ever caught on the Beaverkill fell for just such a "strap"—and that happened in very recent times.

PART V

SOME FAVORITE FISHES

21

SECRET LIFE OF A BREAM SPECIALIST

Everybody is familiar with the bream, alias sunfish, alias—depending on species—shellcracker, redear, stump knocker, pumpkinseed, bluegill, and a host of other fond names indicating how intimately these bantamweight members of the bass family are associated with the American angling scene. Yet like .410 shotguns and .22 rifles, these feisty fighters are too often left to the kids. Once designated a "kid's fish," it's hard to get a more experienced angler to admit that fishing for these little guys is a sport and science all to itself. Yet surveys by the U. S. Department of Interior indicate that more than two-and-a-half million people joined the ranks of small pond fishermen between 1965 and 1970. By the time you read this, there will be estimated to be over ten million fishermen from coast to coast who find their chief recreation in the numerous one- and two-acre farm and roadside excavation ponds that dot the American landscape. So praise the catfish, crappie, and perch. But hail to the chief: the bream.

GWR

SECRET LIFE OF A BREAM SPECIALIST

Willie McKoosh was holding a séance for me one afternoon on the bank of the Waterworks Canal, trying to get a spirit message out of his fly box, when across the stream a bass began cruising in that jerky, tail-waving paddle they use for stalking in shallow water. As we watched, he beat his tail faster, coming toward our bank. He was bronzed as an autumn leaf, with a white mouth that showed clearly, and there was nothing clumsy about his quick, purposeful swim. A panic-stricken bluegill was running ahead of him. But the baby bream had no place to hide and when the old mossback was zeroed in, he hit with a whooshing sound that made Willie snort. You'd have thought the bass socked McKoosh in the belly. And in a way he had, because Willie's one of a breed apart, a bream specialist.

A coal miner digs coal, a sailor sails, a painter paints, a minister preaches, and a bream fisherman catches bream or he feels obligated to be starved into extinction. In an age when mechanical devices hurry the new crop of angling talent along like artificially ripened tomatoes, and with similarly flavorless results, it's interesting to find that absolutely nothing has changed the techniques of expert bluegill fishermen. In fact, young anglers might come from the very antipodes to study Willie's methods, for in the growth of any artist the essential element is the correct dosage of experience.

[170]

Take the matter of panfish bugs, for instance. These can't be a little too big or a bit too small; they must be the correct size. Spinners must also be exact in size and retrieved at a precise pace. Then there are lead jigs, and these must be hopped with just the right stroke. As to flies, Willie thinks they are the poorest attractors for big bream, and he will use only the McGinty or a fat herl-bodied Gray Hackle. With a record of seven bluegills weighing over 2 pounds taken last spring, he is justified in his opinions.

When Willie uses live bait, well . . . there's only one bait in the McKoosh method, and that is a red worm no more than one inch long. The worm is fished on a long slip float, as this type of bobber is very sensitive to nibblers. Willie paints his in red-and-white stripes like a barber pole for better visibility, although on open lakes, when long casts are made, he prefers an antenna float with feather vanes on the end. The vanes are fished below the surface, not above, in order to anchor the float upright and hold it steady in a breeze. All these articles of faith he abides by with the rigid resolve of a devoted disciple.

It would require supernatural aid to sing the praises of a fish whose rustic charm far exceeds his capacity for prolonged struggle. But when caught on very light tackle, there is a patent of nobility about the bream. A large bluegill will usually get your line over his shoulder and go off at great speed, shaking his head until the thing that is holding him snaps. He is too smart to jump, although he sometimes does when there's no other way of escape. After banging the line with his tail, he will try to outpull you by boring straight for the bottom, and if this doesn't work he will scamper in circles just under the surface. Spinning-tackle makers have largely ignored the kind of equipment that would make our bream a weighty game fish, but the day of hairline tackle is coming soon. Regardless of the kind of gear used, however, it should be as light as practical for real enjoyment. The thing to know about bream fishing is how to catch the bluegill, not play him.

One trait which many people fail to recognize about bluegills is that they very seldom eat minnows. Although bream are caught on minnows every day, the numbers taken hardly reflect the population present, nor will these fish be large ones. Bucktails and spinners are even less effective when worked as minnow imitations, yet both lures, if retrieved in a very special way, can be most efficient, and I'll tell you about this presently.

The bream family differs from other panfish in that they are principally insect feeders, and this is evident by their mouths. Except for the green sunfish, all other bream have small mouths. You can just barely get your little finger between the rubber-tire lips of a large bluegill. Instead of aggressively attacking their food, sunfish nibble and slurp. By comparison, perch and crappie slash their prey just like bass. Sunfish also eat bottom organisms such as snails and mollusks as well as large amounts of vegetation, but only rarely will you find evidence of minnows in their stomachs. Inherently the bluegill is a selective feeder. I have seen more than one experienced fly fisherman slowly lose his buttons on a school of feeding bream.

Like the fellow who stopped at our camp below Indian Town one afternoon and asked if he could fish the pool where we were eating lunch. Booga Johns[1] told him he couldn't hurt it none because there were a few hundred hungry bream popping at the surface. We had caught and released dozens of them, except for the ones Willie was frying. Obviously the man was excited because the fish were working furiously on a hatch of bugs coming off the bonnets. He put on a mighty fancy casting demonstration for about twenty minutes and the only fish he caught for all his trouble was a small gar.

Actually, gar were following every single cast. That should have been the tip-off, but he kept on casting and jiggling a pair of wet flies back the way you would for trout. Finally Booga felt sorry for him and, with bits of bream on his chin, he explained how the fly must sit motionless in the water and be just barely twitched about every ten seconds. As a rule, big bluegills will take flies only this way, and gar will hit them only when retrieved fast and steady. Bream won't bother even live insects if they run too fast on the water. They like ants, small grasshoppers, and bugs that sit in one place. The man thanked Booga, and in twenty minutes he caught five or six bream.

Of all sunfish, the bluegill, which can be recognized by the dusky blotch on the base of the soft dorsal fin, is the most important member of the group loosely termed as bream. We never had bluegill fishing that amounted to anything in New York, for instance, except in the bays of Lake Ontario. We did have big pumpkinseeds, or common sunfish, in the St. Lawrence drainage area and Lake Champlain. And once in a while, Dan Todd and I would catch big red-bellied sunfish in the Delaware while fly fishing for trout. The red-bellied and the pumpkinseed are probably the most common eastern sunfish. They differ from the bluegill in that they do not usually grow as large, but they are fun to catch nevertheless. There are several more species and numerous hybrids, but the only other one that has any angling importance is the redear, especially in the sunfish strip from Alabama to Texas.

Back around 1890, both the bluegill and green sunfish were introduced to the Pacific coast, and they have since become well-established in various

---

[1] Booga Johns, now deceased, was a guide on the St. Johns River, Florida.

parts of the West. Generally speaking, large sunfish of any kind are found in lowland areas, while in mountain regions they tend to be small. Bream must have optimum growing conditions to attain an important size, and this is the case in only a small fraction of their habitats across the nation.

The growth rate of each year's brood fluctuates, depending on its abundance and even the weather. Since fish are cold-blooded animals, their metabolism is slowed down by cold weather and accelerated by hot weather (within limits). A researcher by the name of Hathaway demonstrated some years ago that bluegills consume about one-third as much food at 50 degrees F. as they do at 68 degrees F. Thus they have a longer growing season when the winters are comparatively mild or short in duration. Too, the breams' relationship to carnivorous species such as the black bass and pike is a critical factor in growth. In waters where crayfish and minnows are abundant, the black bass probably ignore the sunfish almost completely, and if the angling harvest isn't sufficient to keep the bluegill cropped off, they tend to be stunted.

Willie McKoosh's favorite method of catching bream, and mine also, is with the artificial bug. Panfish will hit an ordinary bass-size bug now and then, and much has been written concerning the use of very small bugs in sizes from No. 10 down. But there are only two hook sizes that really count according to Willie, and they are No. 6 and No. 8. Of course, the dressing must be in proportion to the hook used. You could tie a very small bug on a No. 6 hook, much smaller than would be effective. And by the same token the hook could be overdressed. As a rule of thumb, the entire bug shouldn't be more than 1½ inches long and no more than ¾ of an inch wide. Willie claims that bugs smaller than No. 8 take nothing but baby bream. Bugs larger than No. 6 are too much for a bluegill to get in his mouth, so he tries to nibble on them and feels the barb.

Neither Willie nor Booga casts popping bugs except when the water is running muddy, and then only with the most stringent use of pops. Large bream do not like noisy bugs, but they do like them with rubber legs or feather wings that hang down in the water and wiggle. As an experiment one day I fished solely with poppers, while Willie used his favorite rubber-bodied cricket with rubber legs. I caught seven bluegills in the period he caught thirty-four.

I like to check the McKoosh bug theory once in a while, so when Woody Upthegrove[2] and I were fishing the Limestone Canal one bright morning,

---

[2] The Upthegrove family traces itself back through many generations of Florida crackers. Woody was a guide and airboat operator in the Palm Beach area, who has since retired to Lake Okeechobee.

and the bream were popping and the crappies were cracking, I talked him into helping me. It took some talking.

The bream were feeding along the bank grass and bridling the boat at the head of the pool; we cakewalked out No. 10 bugs past dozens of them. A few fish made halfhearted passes, but only one small bream took Woody's bug solidly. Then we tried No. 12 bugs and caught three or four infant bluegills. Next I tied on a popping bug, and Woody fished a No. 4 bug. All I caught was a bass. Woody raised several bream but didn't hook them. Finally we used Willie's No. 6 and No. 8 dressings. Although the fish were getting spooky from so much commotion, I caught six large bream and clipped them on my stringer with the bass. Woody released another half dozen.

Now all the bugs, with exception of the popper, were exactly the same pattern tied in different sizes; a gray-and-white bug made by Ralph Faulkner, in Frederick, Oklahoma. It is a well-built lure; it sails through the air without catching or holding a wind, lands gently on the water, and it just whispers an invitation to bream when you pass the word down the line. But the experiment was clearly a score for McKoosh.

Willie is just as methodical about live-bait fishing as he is with artificials, and at the head of his list of equipment is a garden rake. The first time I saw him use the rake was on Istokpoga Creek. Willie dumped all kinds of tools in the back of my car because we were tenting at the creek mouth, and I figured the rake was for clearing a site. We caught and released plenty of bass that morning, but I could see that Willie's stomach wasn't in our work. Every time a school of bream swam under the boat, his conversation became more protracted than usual and he'd casually ask what we were going to eat that night. While I was hacking a clearing later in the afternoon, he went down to examine the creek. The best place was too far from camp for Willie to make a show of working. A bream specialist looks for a deep hole between brush-covered banks. This shoring must not be bare on one side and wooded on the other, but preferably with bushes right down to the water on both sides. There must also be a slight current, just enough to bring food along at a speed where the fish can eat with no effort.

Willie didn't find these conditions on the oxbow around camp, so he took his rake and dug up the creek bottom for an area of about five square feet until he had a good flow of sediment fanning out in the water. Then he set up his spinning rod with a vane bobber, two or three split shot, and a wiggly worm that he snicked lightly on a No. 10 hook. After the cast he set the anti-reverse on his reel, leaned the rod over a forked stick, and began hacking palmettos with me. He didn't hack too many. Every five minutes the reel would whine and Willie would run for the rod. Before I had the first tent peg down, there was a dozen nice bream and catfish waiting for the pan.

Spinners are a subject I studied thoroughly long before meeting Willie McKoosh, and it isn't surprising that we agree on how to use them for bluegills. While bugs and flies lose their appeal for bream when a creek gets muddy, underwater lures can be very effective at such times. I don't think this is wholly a question of visibility; bluegills prefer to feed on foods washed out of the banks, especially in the plant growths that develop at water line where the level is low.

Small angleworms, jigs, bucktails, and spinners are all good in roily water. The jig can be fished with a fly rod or spinning rod; and in either case retrieved very slowly so that it hops and dives a foot or so each time you pull. I don't know whether this imitates a minnow so much as a shrimp. The shrimp is a choice item of bluegill diet. When fishing from a boat, most bream specialists simply cast the jig out and let it sink near the bottom, stroking straight up and down while the boat drifts slowly with the wind or current. This, incidentally, is a deadly method of taking crappies in southern reservoirs. A regular bucktail can be fished in much the same fashion, provided the water is shallow. But a bucktail isn't nearly as good as the jig. The tiny lead head provides a real touch of life that unweighted flies don't have.

The spinner, however, is oftentimes more effective than the jig, but you don't want to use a blade more than one inch long. Regardless of the shape of the blade, it must be thin enough to spin at the slightest pull. It should be cast out and let sink among the weeds, then free it very gently and retrieve in slow, short hops. My favorite, which I use with extra-light spinning tackle, weighs $\frac{1}{10}$ ounce. I reel it just fast enough to keep the blade fluttering, and because the hooks are so small, it very rarely gets snagged.

If you venture from the soil into places of urban carnality there is the prospect of dining sumptuously on caviar, sole, and trout laden with almonds, but take pause before those silver platters begin their rattling careers around your table. A king might fare no better than on a feast of swamp cabbage, hushpuppies, and deep-fried bream. There is a magic in these victuals which has caused high priests of anglingdom to exchange their white silk robes for sackcloth. It may be that panfish are strikingly similar in dimensions, coloring, and morality, but as the meek inherit the earth, so the bream has inherited the water. He is the most sought, caught, prolific fish in our land.

22

SAILFISH OF THE NORTH

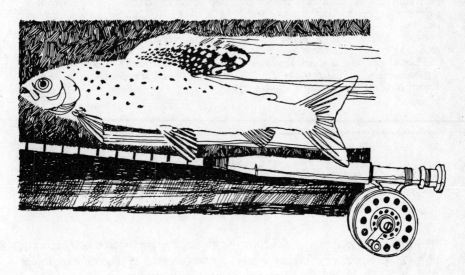

've never caught a grayling. In fact, until I read the following story by A. J. McClane, I was quite convinced they were a mythical genus—a kind of piscatorial unicorn[1]—fantasized by a handful of sentimental anglers who dreamed of a time when all rivers ran pure and trout were wild and plentiful. The myth even claimed that grayling once inhabited Michigan, and a town in this state went so far as to name itself in honor of the elusive creature. In the sub-Arctic, so goes the story, there are streams where grayling are so abundant they compete for your lure, and anything short of canned corn can catch one.

I once fished a French stream reputed to have grayling—but caught only brown trout. I even sought the Golden Fleece in faraway Reindeer Lake, Saskatchewan, but returned with only lake trout and northern pike to my credit. Paul Johnson, one of our party, did catch something resembling the fabled fish on a KB-4 spoon, and Keith Gardner caught a tiny deformed fish with a sail fin while fly casting which he insisted was a grayling. Even the guides went along with the game—but then guides generally do. I returned east, amused and touched by the tremendous effort made by so many anglers to keep the wonderful myth alive. After all, who could seriously imagine one of these delicate and dignified creatures gobbling a KB-4 spoon nearly one-half its size? And as for the misshapen whitefish caught by Keith, I simply refuse to believe myths ever come so small!

Thus it was with a shock that I read the following article. McClane's apparently well-documented claim that the fish is alive and well and actually living in Reindeer Lake has badly shaken my complacency.

GWR

SAILFISH OF THE NORTH

When I started to write for *Field & Stream* twenty-five years ago, the prospect of catching a grayling was so remote that nobody in the trade would do a column on it. True, token populations of freshwater "sailfish" existed in Montana, Wyoming, and Utah, and still do, but the era of jet travel which made the wilderness regions of Canada and Alaska available to the average man was the Renaissance period in grayling angling. For all practical purposes this colorful gamefish became extinct shortly after the turn of the century. Until that time one could easily pursue grayling on the Jackson, Lansing, and Saginaw Railroad. In the halcyon years when our progenitor *Forest and Stream* was the fly fisherman's Baedeker, articles

[1] As the fabled unicorn has a long spiral horn projecting from its brow, the grayling is reputed to have a beautiful sail-like dorsal fin.

[178]

about the Manistee and Au Sable Rivers attracted anglers from all over the U. S. to Michigan. Then suddenly the fish disappeared. The devastating loss of forest cover through lumbering which greatly diminished the water quality of lower peninsula streams is certainly one reason for its demise, but the unprecedented slaughter that took place between 1870 and 1890 when the fish were stacked like cordwood along the riverbanks and hauled out by the wagonload to be sold in Detroit and Chicago restaurants was no less a factor. Thousands of grayling were left to rot when no transportation appeared—which was all too frequent.

From what little we know about the Michigan grayling (*Thymallus tricolor*) first described by Cope in 1865, this species did not reach a large size. An average catch was between 6 and 10 ounces and the exceptional fish weighed 1½ pounds. Nevertheless, its willingness to take the fly and its singular beauty caused the citizens of Crawford to change the name of their town to Grayling—a distinction which few fish achieve.

I caught my first grayling a few days after the war ended on the Mangfall in Bavaria. The stream had been unfished for several years at least, and it was more difficult not to get strikes than to hook a hundred or so in a matter of hours. On my first attempt I landed a 4¾-pound grayling, followed shortly thereafter by one weighing a shade less than 5 pounds. I have never caught a grayling as big as these since. In subsequent years, I visited the Traun River in Austria and had my illusions shattered in finding that the game could be very difficult indeed. The elegant fish that inhabit the Tyrol come equipped with micrometers, and any fly larger than a No. 18 or a trippet coarser than 6X is viewed with paralyzing skepticism. Yet, and perhaps there is a moral here, I finally managed to hook a colorful 3-pounder on an outsized Muddler Minnow while dredging the bottom for brown trout.

No freshwater fish holds a more timorous position than the grayling. Balanced on delicate fins in a quick, clear current, the grayling soars and dips like a kite on a string. The fish is so easy to catch in subarctic waters that otherwise passionate anglers ignore him, yet he is so difficult to deceive in Alpine rivers that his followers hold *Thymallus* in an esteem that transcends trout snobbery. Who but a dedicated grayling fisherman would conceive of a No. 20 double-hook dry fly? In appearance grayling differ widely, not only within a region but within a single watershed; the fish may be gray, brown, blue, purple, or olive on the back with X- or V-shaped spots on the forepart of the body with zigzag horizontal lines between the rows of scales, which, like the spots, may be vivid or indistinct. But when seen at certain angles of light the grayling reflects lilac or gold, and at times the entire fish has a silvery or brassy sheen, as though wearing an ancient suit of mail.

The tail, pectoral, and anal fins are usually a dusky yellowish-green color,

[179]

but the pelvic fins commonly have lengthwise stripes of pink and black, which again can be more or less obscure. However, it's the high dorsal fin of the grayling that is unique. The dorsal of the male is the larger; the female's dorsal is not only shorter, but it is high in front and low in the back. The male's dorsal is reversed, starting low and sweeping high in the rear. This disproportionate fin has irregular but distinct rows of dark spots; it is often tinged with pink or white on the upper edge.

Technically, graylings consist of a single genus composed of at least four species and several subspecies. On the basis of diversity of forms it has been postulated that the origin of this group of fishes was in the mountains of southern Siberia and northern Mongolia and from here the fish migrated through the foothill lakes and rivers to Europe and across the Bering Sea land-mass to North America. Its postglacial distribution to the west which extended its range to Britain (still part of the mainland of Europe) was via a river that flowed through what is now the North Sea and its two major tributaries, the Rhine and the Thames. Today, the European grayling (*Thymallus thymallus*) is found throughout the continent except in southern France, Portugal, Spain, southern Italy, and Ireland. It also inhabits the basin of the Arctic Ocean. It is distributed in the east as far as the Ural Range (USSR), and may be encountered in the upper reaches of the Volga and Ural Rivers. This wide distribution is somewhat deceptive, because the grayling's habitat preferences within its range are narrow. It is a fish of fast-flowing, cold, clear streams. Although trout can thrive in any grayling river, grayling will not thrive in *all* trout rivers. Generally speaking, trout can exist where conditions are less than perfect, but not so the grayling.

Beyond the Ural Range two distinct species occur in Mongolia—the Kosogol grayling (*Thymallus nigrescens*) which differs from the Arctic grayling in having more gill rakers (twenty-six to thirty-three as compared to fourteen to twenty-two) and the Mongolian grayling (*Thymallus brevirostris*) which is the "largemouth" of its tribe, as the lower jaw extends beyond the posterior margin of its eye. Arctic grayling by comparison have a very small mouth with the maxilla ending at the anterior margin of the eye. Soviet ichthyologists recognize a number of subspecies and racial stocks such as the Baikal white grayling, Angara black grayling, and West Siberian grayling, which are more or less isolated to single watersheds, but from Siberia across northern Asia and into North America, the Arctic grayling[2] (*Thymallus arcticus*) has the widest range of any member of the family.

Apparently the postglacial distribution in North America was south to

[2] Now called the American Grayling (1970), revision American Fisheries Society.

what is now the Great Lakes and to the vast sea that once extended over the Rocky Mountains which isolated several geographic stocks not only in Michigan but in the Big Hole and Green River watersheds of Montana and Wyoming. It was later introduced (1899) to the Uinta Mountain district of Utah where it still exists today. There may have been yet another species which Jordan and Evermann recognized as the Ontario grayling (*Thymallus ontarionsis*) but the only clue left is two old museum specimens. Whether the American graylings are sufficiently distinct to warrant separation into more than one species is, I suppose, no longer important, since there are so few of them left.

Large grayling, fish in excess of 10 pounds, are occasionally reported from Finnish Lapland. However, we've never been able to authenticate any of these catches, and from personal experience in that area I would be inclined to doubt their existence. In July of 1970, Mr. Knut W. Swensen of Oslo, Norway, caught a 7-pound 7-ounce grayling on the Swedish side of the border at Rastojaure, which is about 300 miles north of the Arctic Circle. This is a record for the European species and it will probably stand for many years to come.

Grayling fishing in Lapland is phenomenal in the sense of great quantity, although a 5-pounder is still trophy size and the odd ten-year-old fish that exceeds 5 pounds is not an everyday event. Still, the only creature more numerous than grayling in Lapland is the mosquito, and at times it requires real fortitude to stay on the water. Several years ago on a rather ambitious trip through Lapland we hired a taxi in a northern mining town to visit a stream at the Russian border, which our driver promised was full of trout. It required hiking over several miles of reindeer moss and through scrub willows to reach the water, and throughout our journey we collected every mosquito in the Arctic. Each man had his own personal hovering black shroud; at times we walked into each other for the lack of visual orientation. Carl Tillmanns[3] and I fished for about two hours and literally caught a grayling on every other cast. Not a single trout was in evidence and the sport paled rather quickly. My largest grayling weighed 2½ pounds—a respectable catch which the driver enthusiastically converted into 2½ kilos when we returned to the hotel. This made me the captor of a 5.5-pound grayling, which caused the aquavit to flow like Niagara.

The only Arctic-grayling fishing in the United States exists in Alaska. The Holtina, Stony, Aniak, Kandik, Birch, Forty-mile, Tatonduk, and Nation Rivers are some of our more important streams. But the Ugashik Lakes in

[3] Vice-president of CBS Television.

the Bristol Bay area are probably more productive of large fish. I have not visited there in some years now, but apparently the quality of the angling is still unique. Ugashik grayling average about 18 inches in length, and to prevent their depletion the Alaska Board of Fish and Game established a creel limit of two fish per day in that watershed, which is enough for the hungriest angler. The Alaskan record for Arctic grayling is just 4 pounds; the species doesn't grow fast here. Anything over 3 pounds is at least a seven-year-old, and the chances of finding any that qualify for medicare is pretty remote. Nevertheless, Ugashik produces consistently large grayling to the fly.

The Northwest Territories of Canada have the distinction of providing the heaviest Arctic grayling in North America, with a 5-pound 15-ounce specimen from the Katseyedie River holding the present record. A number of fish in the 5-pound class have been caught both in the Great Bear Lake and Great Slave Lake areas. In common with other grayling water the world over, these lakes have an abundance of invertebrate food in the form of amphipods and copepods. The so-called opossum shrimp (*Mysis relicta*) thrive at depths to over 1,000 feet, while two species of scuds (both *Gammarus* and *Pontoporeia*) are abundant along the shore areas. These marine glacial relics are circumpolar in distribution and are more important in the Arctic grayling's diet than insects.

The value of amphipods as a forage for all salmonoids has only recently received the attention it deserves. Oregon, Missouri, Maine, and several other states have been stocking amphipods in trout waters with great success. The fat, pink-fleshed rainbows now being caught in Lake Taneycomo, for example, are gorging on these small crustaceans. Although stone flies and mayflies emerge in Great Bear and are consumed by the grayling, shrimplike animals are their basic food. The abundance of grayling in the Baltic Sea (which was once so great that they were fished commercially by Sweden and Finland) is correlated to an amphipod diet. Nevertheless, like all Arctic fauna, grayling grow slowly in lakes such as Great Bear. A 2-pound fish is about nine years old. Even their population is numerically limited, as they are unable to maintain an annual breeding cycle; although some proportion of the population does spawn each year, reproduction of any individual fish occurs at two- or three-year intervals. The trophy lake trout which earned Great Bear its reputation are thirty to forty years old when they reach the 30-pound class, so it would be relatively simple to "fish out" this fourth largest lake on the North American continent.

Elsewhere in Canada, Arctic grayling are found in the Yukon Territory, where they can literally be caught by the motorist along the Alaska Highway. This road follows mile after mile of grayling streams as it crosses the lake district. In northern Alberta, popular waters are the Swan River, Freeman River, Wapiti River, Kakwa River, Cutbank River, certain portions of the McLeod River, Berland River, Marten River, Christina River, Christmas Creek, Two Creek, Marsh Head Creek, Pinto Creek, Pembina River, Trout Creek, Sunday Creek, and Kinky Lake. In Saskatchewan, grayling fishing is available in Athabaska Lake, Black Lake, Careen Lake, Cree Lake, Cree River, Fond du Lac River, Geikie River, Hatchet Lake, Reindeer Lake, Tazin Lake, Wapata Lake, Waterbury Lake, and Wallaston Lake. Generally speaking, nearly all the large oligotrophic lakes and their tributaries in this northern region contain grayling.

All the record fish taken over the years, including the 7-pound 7-ounce grayling from Lapland, succumbed to hardware. Grayling are easily caught on a large variety of spinning lures and ⅛- to ¼-ounce wobbling spoons. The most popular baits are ¹⁄₁₆- to ¼-ounce spinners in brass, gold, silver, and red-and-white finishes. The angling techniques are substantially the same as those used for trout. However, the success of spinning tackle is probably explained by the predilection of large grayling for subsurface feeding. As the fish get older, they are much more inclined to gorge on bottom organisms or at least food forms such as amphipods and decapods which live *near* the bottom. Wet flies, nymphs, and small streamers are my choice in that order if there is any prospect of hooking a big fish. The ideal tackle would be a 7- to 8-foot fly rod matched with a No. 4 or 5 floating line for dry-fly work and a sinking-tip line for subsurface fishing. Leaders tapered from 3X to 7X cover most situations. There is seldom any need for long casts in grayling waters. The fish can be approached quite closely, and in their season in most locations winds do not pose any real threat.

As a rule grayling prefer dark flies in black, gray, or brown. Some good patterns are the Black Gnat, March Brown, Black Ant, Gray Hackle, Brown Hackle, Stone Fly, Quill Gordon, and Dark Cahill on Nos. 10, 12, and 14 hooks. It is also advisable to bring along some tiny black patterns such as ant, midge, or gnat imitation on Nos. 18 and 20 hooks, as grayling often show a definite preference for the minutiae.

From an angling point of view, grayling differ from trout in a number of ways. For one thing, they congregate in loose schools, or shoals, usually at the tails of pools or riffles where they lie close to the bottom, even when surface feeding. Trout hold their feeding position high in the water. When an insect floats over a grayling, the fish rises from the bottom to the top and down again. Depending on the depth at which it is resting and the speed of the surface current, the fish may dart upward and take the fly with a splash or, more typically, the rise will be seen as a small dimple. Arctic grayling

[183]

often leap over the surface and hit a floating pattern on the way down. As a rule, the strike occurs *behind* the fish's position; grayling tend to take a fly several feet to the rear, rather than go forward or to either side of the feeding lane. European grayling are perhaps more precise insofar as the drift is concerned and will frequently ignore a neatly cast artificial which is a foot or two off. Although they are more critical than trout with respect to presentation, grayling have an insatiable curiosity and may rise again and again to examine an offering and finally accept it. As a rule, they are less wary than trout with respect to the angler's presence, but the mere hint of a coarse leader tippet can put the fish down completely. You may come face to face with a grayling and be ignored; yet it will study every fly as though trying to help you find the right one.

A fallacy about the grayling which probably began with Walton when he wrote that "he [the grayling] has so tender a mouth, that he is oftener lost after an angler has hooked him, than any other fish," has been endorsed in angling literature for centuries. Actually, the grayling has a *small*, somewhat oblique mouth, making it difficult to get a hook attached. But once the barb is sunk, there's little chance of losing the fish. There is a tendency not to strike forcefully enough, simply because of the peculiar way a grayling takes the fly in a half-roll, which requires an almost perceptible pause before it actually has the fly inside. When a fish is lost, it's usually because only the tip of the point was stuck in its mouth. For this reason, grayling addicts in Bavaria and Austria use small double-hook dry flies to get better penetration. Tied by an expert, these little gems not only float like a cork but do result in a higher ratio of barbed fish.

The table quality of grayling is no less controversial than its presence in a trout stream. Last autumn, while fishing the Test River in England with Dermot Wilson,[4] I had a wonderful afternoon taking grayling along with brown trout. Although grayling in northern England and Scotland do not get very large—a 2-pounder would be a trophy—those on the southern chalkstreams are plump and active fish. However, many river keepers consider them "vermin," as they compete with trout for food, a rather dubious distinction in these lush pastures. I released a number of nice fish and was about to quit when a grayling somehow got the tiny fly embedded in its gill. Rather than waste it, I handed my victim to the river keeper who reacted as though I had given him a karate kick. "Me eat *that*, sir?" Courtesy finally overcame conviction and he said he would save it for his dog.

[4] Well-known British angler and outdoor writer who owns one of England's most distinguished tackle shops at Nether Wallop, Hampshire, on the Test River.

A week later I went to Paris to visit Charles Ritz, and after a casting session at the club, he suggested that we return to his hotel for dinner, an event to be treasured from a kitchen once ruled by Escoffier. Our first course was a pair of grayling smoked by his friend Kustermann on the Ammer River in Bavaria. It was so delicious that in other settings I would have licked my plate clean. The flesh of a grayling is firm and white, and the flavor is best described as nutlike. I have eaten many grayling cooked in various ways and can't ever recall one that wasn't equal—if not superior—to a trout. Even in Michigan lumbering days the grayling sold for twenty-five cents per fish. It was a fancy price to pay (caviar was on the free-lunch bar) for a very fancy fish. But that's a meal few people now remember.

23

KING PERMIT

Many members of South Florida's angling society regard the taking of a permit on a fly as the ultra-ultra experience in saltwater angling. After more than a decade of effort, flats guide Stu Apte caught his first fly-hooked permit in 1974. Al Pflueger, Jr., has reason to be proud of a pair of 20-pounders caught over a wreck, even though some purists insist permit are more easily duped in deep water than on the flats. When Lefty Kreh, former director of the Metropolitan Miami Fishing Tournament, got his first (and to date only) permit on a fly, he lifted it from the water and reverently kissed it. This 5-pounder, along with a 108-pound fly-caught tarpon, are the only mounted fish adorning the home walls of this wide-traveling angler. In the entire outdoor writing fraternity, there are only two men ever to catch six or more permit on flies: Joe Brooks, the late, great fishing editor of *Outdoor Life*—and A. J. McClane.

GWR

KING PERMIT

I caught my first permit back in the pre-Castro era off the Isle of Pines. It was not wholly intentional on my part. For about twenty minutes I had been watching the tide flood between two mangrove islands. Esteban Dio leaned on his push-pole and made small talk while the rays came up with their wing tips creasing the surface. Big and flat as doormats, they need very little water to hunt for crabs. As the level inched higher, small wobbly-tailed ground sharks followed the rays, and here and there a slender barracuda drifted under the surface with his tail fluttering slowly. The bank was coming to life in the intricate pattern of a tide cycle with the most fearless and best-adapted creatures rooting first in the marl like hogs in a bucket of slops. A school of bonefish roamed in aimless circles just at the drop-off, feeling the current and waiting for that extra inch of water that would float them safely over the grass. They would come as a school, then break into little pods as they started to tail and work along with the deepening water. I don't recall now what happened to that school. Suddenly a lone permit tailed boldly in from the drop-off. A gleaming caudal lobe stood erect in the sunlight, flickered over the surface for an instant, then disappeared as the fish pushed water and moved slowly up-tide.

I aimed my bucktail about six or eight feet ahead, enough to let the fly settle in his path and near the bottom. The bucktail was suspended below the surface for several seconds, then I lost sight of it in the glare. The next thing I knew, the water was churned milky and the rod was nearly pulled from my hand. Two hours later, and two miles from our starting point Esteban grabbed the permit by the wrist of its tail and tossed the fish aboard. It was 29½ pounds of silver muscle. First permit or last, you never forget any of them because nobody catches enough to become blasé on the subject. Even Captain John Cass,[1] who has probably taken more permit than any man alive, can recall the details of capturing his last seventy-seven.

To find Captain John Cass today you drive down the multibridge Overseas Highway to Cudjoe Key, which is twenty-three miles above Key West. At the Kemp Channel Viaduct you turn off on a sand road and go to a small dock where his launch will ferry you across the water to his houseboat anchored at Sawyer Key. John built his seventy-foot floating fishing lodge just so he could live on the permit flats. This is his dedication and profession. Cass runs a tight ship, and he knows saltwater angling inside out. He has been a fishing guide for thirty-five years, mostly in the Bahamas, during which time he attended to the capture of thirteen saltwater records. But Captain Cass was more impressed by watching a tourist catch a 39½-pound permit off the town dock. From that moment on he learned everything he could about *Trachinotus goodei*. "There's no other fish in the world as exciting to hunt and catch as the permit," he states flatly. This pronouncement coming from a man who has hunted game fish weighing up to a half-ton packs some authority. Particularly since he now pursues permit nine months of the year and counts seventy to eighty boated fish as an average season.

Personally, I have caught very few permit in all the years I've been salt-water fishing. I can total them on one hand.[2] I have lost a few on streamers and bucktail flies which leads me to believe that if I really worked at the game and studied my bonefish flats more closely, particularly at the outer edges where they deepen into cuts, and searched more banks adjacent to deep water, I would catch more permit. To find permit you have to *think* permit. Captain Cass convinced me of this by unerringly locating school after school as though the entire sea was composed of them. This game demands 20/20 vision and Polaroids that help you see through surface glare.

Picture a man who knows the habits of permit so well that he can plant you in their path. You wait ten, maybe fifteen minutes, distracted by spade-

---

[1] For John Cass's complete biography, see "Light-Tackle Convert" in *Profiles In Salt-water Angling*, Prentice-Hall, 1973.

[2] Since this article appeared in 1962, Al has caught a few more. He now needs two hands to count his fly-caught permit.

fish and grunts swimming around the skiff. Cass doesn't say a thing for a long time.

"Get ready," he whispers. Ready for what? Not a fin marks the surface. "Here they come." There's a trace of excitement in his voice. What's he looking at? With a couple of thousand bonefish under your belt you don't panic easily. But now you're staring popeyed at empty water. Then a dim shape, and another, and another ghosts along about thirty yards away. You can barely make them out against patches of grass. The lead fish might easily go at 40 pounds—the others are in the 20- to 30-pound class. Their movement stops as though poised for flight. Abruptly the boss tips down to suck at a crab hole and his forked tail seesaws up.

"Cast about three feet in front of him and one foot to the right," Cass says. So here you are with sweat in your socks, no depth perception, a quivering hand, and this nut is zeroing your sixty-foot cast with plus and minus corrections.

The pillar of Captain Cass's life is a snub-nosed middleweight that packs the wallop of a .45 and has the disposition of a neurotic monk. He's robed in bright blue along the back and his flanks are pearly silver—a providential design which makes him strangely handsome. The permit closely resembles a pompano. There are small technical differences between these fish but the main difference is size. Where the pompano reaches 7 or 8 pounds and averages closer to 2 pounds, the permit exceeds 50 pounds and will often average 20 pounds. Cass's clients occasionally hook fish in the 30-pound class and there's every likelihood that John will be at the push-pole when somebody breaks the present record of 47 pounds 12 ounces.[3]

"The big ones are there," he said, pointing in the general direction of Content Key. "We see some monsters from time to time, but let's face it, permit are real tackle busters and it takes a good angler with a lot of luck to hold 30 or 40 pounds of fish on 8-pound-test spinning tackle for two hours or more."

The range of the permit is loosely defined as various parts of the tropical Atlantic but nowhere does the species appear to be abundant. To a large degree it's a fish that is present but seldom seen, and more often seen than caught. Captain Cass believes that there are more permit in southern Florida and the Bahamas than most people realize.

"Permit tend to stay in channels and holes, but they come up on the flats like bonefish when the tide floods. The difference is that they usually wait a bit longer than bonefish because permit are deep-bodied and twice their

[3] The current record is 50 pounds 8 ounces, caught near Key West, Florida.

[190]

size so they need more water to get over the banks. They rarely make a mud like the bonefish. Occasionally you might see a little puff of sand or marl as an individual fish roots in the bottom, but I can't ever recall seeing permit cloud the water in their feeding. I look for the movements of schools disturbing the surface and, of course, their tails and dorsals when actively feeding."

Permit usually travel in schools of ten or more. Captain Cass has seen schools estimated at 500 on several occasions during his years in the Content Key area. During the two best months of February and March he has sighted 1,000 to 2,000 permit in a single day. But for all the fish sighted, John's best day consisted of six fish caught. The fish doesn't quit easily. The permit continues running long after the bonefish would quit. He will pause to twist his body or bang his head on the bottom to see if he can get the hook loose, then take off again. One of Cass's clients recently lost a jumbo after three hours of play, almost three miles from the spot where it was hooked. The line broke in the sargassum weed. John had previously jumped overboard in six feet of water to get the monofil free from a loggerhead sponge.

"It's a real heartbreaker for a man to lose his fish after playing him an hour or more over the obstacle course. You see, the first thing a permit does when he's hooked on a shallow bank is to head for deep water. Now there's a zone of transition between these grassy flats and the Gulf where the bottom is covered with sea fans, sponges, coral heads, and all sorts of vertical snags which the permit can wrap a line around. Getting over this obstacle course is tricky and it takes some luck."

To learn the ways of permit a man would have to spend at least a full season and perhaps longer studying one area. John Cass knows the Content Key region so well that he can literally predict the path a school will choose from one flat to the next as though he was following rutted game trails. This is a great advantage, more so when the wind is howling or the light is bad and the angler has no visual contact with the fish. Late one afternoon near Mud Key Bank we found a school milling around in the channel. It was a Sunday, and the family-boat traffic had made them nervous. When the permit finally came up on the flat I hooked and lost one which sent the school fleeing into deep water. There was no warning. They simply dissolved.

"Well, that's the last we'll see of them," I said. John grinned and nodded toward a mangrove island about a half-mile away. It was one of maybe ten nearby keys.

"They'll be up on the banks in a little while. Let's get over there."

We took a devious route. John poled the skiff along until we reached a channel. Then he turned the motors on to cross to another bank and poled some more. As we approached the promised land John paused and let the skiff drift. "There they are—see the tails?" The school was about 200 yards to port pushing water a bit and stopping here and there to nose the marl. No sane man could positively say that this was the same bunch of fish. Yet, there aren't so many schools skulking around the Keys that you can predict their appearance within minutes. But he repeatedly guessed the path of a school not merely from one bank to the next but over a distance of miles.

Standard permit tackle, which Captain Cass has for his clients, consists of a medium action 6½-foot spinning rod, a large capacity freshwater spinning reel with a reliable drag, and 8-pound-test monofilament line. He does not use a leader but prefers instead three feet of double line at the terminal end, which he splices very carefully. The double line is then tied to a ⅔ Eagle Claw hook—a size and pattern which Cass has found to be perfect. At least 90 percent of his fishing is done with live bait using either the finney crab or spider crab. Although one rod in his skiff is always on standby rigged with a lead-head bucktail for bonefish, he seldom suggests artificial lures for permit. Cass has two reasons for this: His average customer is not experienced enough to work with jigs or flies, and secondly, he thinks that a lure doesn't make the right noise to draw strikes consistently.

"The permit is a sight feeder. So naturally he will hit artificials. But unfortunately, when he gets his head down to look for food, and that's the way we're fishing them most of the time, he concentrates on a few square inches of bottom under his nose and ignores everything around him. I've seen people cast more than twenty times to a tailing permit and the fish paid no attention to the lure at all. It can be maddening. When a little finney crab plops on the water often as not he'll stop rooting and go for it. I don't mean *any* splash will attract permit. The sound has to be just right. Permit spook easily, and knowing what they will tolerate or accept is something a man must learn for himself. A crab of 2 or 2½ inches across the shell is perfect."

According to Captain Cass, the ideal situation for a permit to take an artificial lure is in a competitive position.

"A lone tailing permit is a lot tougher to interest than a fish who is feeding with a school. It's been my observation that when an artificial drops among a number of fish his competitive instincts get the best of him. He grabs it out of sheer gluttony whether the lure looks right or not."

Permit have a mouth with the texture of an automobile tire. It is difficult to set the hook properly and for that reason Captain Cass tells his clients to strike hard (within the limits of the tackle) and keep on striking six, seven, eight times. He also emphasizes the importance of keeping a tight line.

"Often the hook will drop out after I boat a fish. The only reason the

[192]

point stays in a permit's mouth is because the angler has kept his line tight. The instant you give him slack he'll get the point free. Permit have a nasty habit of running a long distance then diving for the bottom where they bury and rub their mouths in the sand to get rid of the hook."

Captain Cass releases all the permit he catches and he encourages his clients to do the same. Of course this beneficent act probably doesn't contribute one iota to the conservation of a fish which is hardly ever caught. But John respects his quarry. Once he has hoisted the permit aloft to be photographed or weighed, his knowing and trained hands slip the fish back into the water.

24

THE GREAT TUNA HUNT

In the fifteen years since the following story first appeared in *Field & Stream*, only a few more pieces to the puzzle of bluefin tuna migrations have been found. Many more fish tagged on one side of the Atlantic have been recovered on the other, and in 1962 one tuna made the 5,000 mile journey from Cat Cay in the Bahamas to Norway in just fifty days. Even more impressive, a 375-pound fish tagged by Mrs. Ann Kunkel in the Bahamas in June 1969 was recaptured by a commercial fisherman off Uruguay in February 1973. The fish then weighed over 550 pounds and had traveled at least 6,600 miles merely to keep its appointment with destiny. Who can calculate the true distance and to what murky destinations this fish traveled in the interim?

However, just as scientists are beginning to gain some insight into the marvelous life of the bluefin tuna, the very object of their research is disappearing. The enthusiasm with which Frank Mather and his associates at Woods Hole once worked on the project has turned to ashes in their mouths, for their meticulous research has been used by the commercial fishermen of many lands, including our own, to decimate tuna stocks everywhere in the Atlantic. Where Frank once used an 828-foot long line with ten hooks to catch a sampling of tuna for study, today the Japanese use hundreds of lines ten miles long or longer with *tens of thousands* of hooks to bite deeply into the remnant tuna population. In 1963 alone, the Japanese took 66,838 bluefin tuna from the northwest Atlantic, and today their long-line fleet has been joined by ships from Cuba, Nationalist China, South Korea, the Soviet Union, and Venezuela. While as recently as 1972 tuna could be bought dockside in Gloucester, Massachusetts, for five cents a pound, in June 1974 a single fish brought $1,400 for an average of $3.85 per pound. The situation has become so critical there is serious debate over whether the Atlantic bluefin tuna should be declared "threatened" under the law defining U. S. endangered species. If so, it will have the dubious honor of being the first pelagic species so named. Thus, read the following story with the knowledge that it has taken little more than a decade to bring a once-mighty ocean wanderer to the point of no return. Read with wonder, but at the same time pledge that so long as you have the capacity to write, speak out, and vote, you will not let this happen again to the sea resources of our nation.

GWR

THE GREAT TUNA HUNT

Last August two bluefin tuna bearing tags of the Woods Hole Oceanographic Institution were netted by commercial fishermen in the Bay of Biscay, between France and Spain. Their capture is historic: For the first time, man has absolute evidence that some tuna cross the Atlantic Ocean. The fish had been tagged at No Man's Land, near Cape Cod, Massachusetts, as yearlings weighing about 18 pounds. After being at large five years, they weighed 150 pounds when recaptured.

The bluefin research program is directed by Frank Mather III, an ex-marine engineer turned career biologist. He, like the fish he pursues, ranges back and forth from the Caribbean to Europe. I called on him last winter at the institute's headquarters and found him a quietly efficient young scientist who has been pursuing the bluefin for ten years, logging 25,000 nautical miles and uncounted hours of flying time. His is a classic search that would leave Sherlock Holmes mumbling in his tea. At the institute, oceanographers, meteorologists, and statisticians work with texts, test tubes, microscopes, and liver cross sections. No whodunit offers more mystery, chill, and chase than the Great Tuna Hunt—or more promise for anglers.

If you have fished for tuna, you will remember the long line of draggers creeping back from the Mud Hole like red ants crossing a slick red road, and when you gunned the engine your bow threw a brilliant gold spray over the cockpit. And there were the slate-colored gulls that stepped like ghosts from a slate-colored sky over Rosie's Ledge. There were all the bad turns you made off Wedgeport, the lines that got fouled on keels, and the tuna that kept right on going. And the day off Cat Cay when the sea was like a furnace. That was a ball. You hung five tuna and lost them all.

If you're a saltwater man you'll know that in every port somebody has a different theory about where tuna come from and where they go to. And how some captains figure that if more facts were known about tuna, more of them could be caught. Not until 1930 was it discovered that bluefin tuna could be taken in the Bahamas. The fish would be there in the spring, off New Jersey and Montauk by early summer, and at Wedgeport before fall.

After Wedgeport? Well, most people guessed that tuna crossed the Atlantic and lived off the coast of Europe for at least part of the year. But Baron Bluefin is a sly one, with a record that goes back to the days of Aristotle, Herodotus, and Pliny; the facts eluded these venerable sleuths, and they decided that a tuna lives but two years. So men have muddled along for centuries with no real knowledge of one of the largest fish in the ocean.

Perhaps the slickest trick Baron Bluefin has demonstrated in recent years is his ability to elude tournaments. He has been an aquatic nightmare to public-relations men. In 1958 the annual International Tuna Cup Match, held at Wedgeport, Nova Scotia, went fishless. In 1959 the tournament was called off for lack of fish. Wedgeport had previously been a tuna trap where sportsmen had the herring-snatching caper stopped cold. They remembered the halcyon summer of 1949, when 1,774 bluefins were boated in those waters. But since then the tally has dropped alarmingly. Now it requires a board-of-directors meeting to decide whether the great tuna classic should be held at all.

"Giant bluefins are more consistently numerous in the summer along the coast of Nova Scotia than anywhere else," Mather told me. "I can't say *why* they aren't being caught at Wedgeport, but I do think other potentially good grounds have been neglected in the same general region. You know, sportsmen could help shed some light on the problem by regularly tagging more tuna. Our new dart-type tag, which is harpooned into the back of large game fish, is really efficient. And needless to say, I want to get tags in bluefins of all sizes—not just the giants.

"You might say," he went on, "that it's not a case of what science can do for sportsmen, but of what the angler can do for science. The tuna at Wedgeport are twelve to fourteen years old, and where they go from there is anybody's guess. Fish of that size—700 to 1,000 pounds—don't appear anywhere else. It may well be that they're at the end of their life cycle."

Putting the finger on Baron Bluefin is decidedly not a one-man job. The names Scattergood, Schuck, Rivas, de Beun, and Bullis appear regularly in technical literature about the Atlantic *Thunnus*. Marine-fisheries investigators often work on one phase or one small area of a problem, exchanging information with one another. Woods Hole Oceanographic Institution alone operates six research vessels. One, the 142-foot steel-hulled ketch *Atlantis*, is at sea an average of 250 days a year and has logged over 1,200,000 fact-finding miles. From the *Atlantis* long-line fishing is carried on. The bulk of tuna are collected with nylon lines 138 fathoms long and carrying ten baited hooks.

Mather periodically spends up to three months at sea actually fishing for tuna, and his captures are backed up by data from specialists in all the branches of marine biology—men who can tell him the velocity and the direction of the ocean's currents at any point, how much salt is in the Gulf Stream on a particular day, or the vitamin content of the tuna's liver when he ducked out of Cat Cay. But when Woods Hole began investigating the bluefin, there was nothing in its files except a muddle of aliases and descriptions that didn't give Mather a solid lead. In fact, his first job was to check out rumors on where the Baron operated at various times of the year; to the untrained eye, yellowfin, blackfin, albacore, and big-eyed tuna all bear a strong resemblance to the bluefin. Helpful citizens had the suspect spotted everywhere—simultaneously.

Falling back on intuition, Mather first examined the probable southern extremity of the bluefin's range—an area between the Virgin Islands and the Windward Passage. In April 1955 the research vessels *Oregon* and *Hermes II* began long-lining bluefins south of Cuba on a broad trail from the northern Yucatan Peninsula to the Windward Passage.

"The fish were apparently most abundant at the passage, and moderately abundant west of the Cayman Islands," Mather recalled. "There's no evidence of their presence at this time of the year south of western Hispaniola or south of Puerto Rico and St. Croix. In all probability, giant bluefins are scattered in the Gulf and the Caribbean during the winter months, but tend to concentrate in certain places by spring—places like the passes between islands. We believe the big concentration at the Windward Passage is the major one, and that bluefins spawn in this area."

So the first real lead on the Baron was his love life. A careful investigation of his reproductive organs revealed that he was ripe, or recently spent, when he moved into the islands. The great schools coming into the Bahama Banks in mid-May—running close to shore and making erratic turns in their course, sometimes reversing direction and running off into blue water where their movements settle down—are presumably the main body of fish that came through the Windward Passage.

Just to make certain that he was not being misled by stray fish, Mather boarded a Coast Guard plane and roared aloft with Professor Luis Rivas of the University of Miami Marine Laboratory. Under the glare of a winter sun, the silhouettes of northbound tuna were clearly visible just inside the drop-off of the Bahama Banks. Rivas later lowered hydrophones into the schools to listen to the tunas' conversations (a technique that is proving valuable in the study of whales and porpoises). But instead of emitting a Niagara of sound, the tuna were as quiet as clams.

Both investigators agreed that most giant bluefins continue their northward migration east of the axis of the Gulf Stream until they have passed Cape Hatteras. There are sport fisheries from Miami north to the Chesapeake, but the only region where tuna are known to occur frequently is at Cape Hatteras, North Carolina. Here the fish are of various sizes and appear in different seasons. There is no evidence that tuna on these outer banks are part of the northbound migration of bluefins.

"It's fairly certain," Mather said, "that the migratory pattern of tuna changes at certain stages of its life. Of course, there are little overlaps in the age and geographical distribution of various groups, but for all practical purposes we can think of tuna in four classes. There are the very small ones less than one year old and under 5 pounds in weight. Next, there are the small tuna, one to four years old, weighing from 5 to 69 pounds. The medium tuna, five to nine years old, weigh from 70 to 269 pounds. Finally, there are the giants of nine years or more, and they weigh over 270 pounds.

"These four classes are independent insofar as abundance and seasonal distribution are concerned. In Cape Cod Bay, for instance, the first tuna taken each year are giants. They arrive in June and become abundant in July and August, tapering off thereafter. On the other hand, the largest run of medium tuna doesn't start until August or later, and these fish remain until October, when the other age classes disappear."

Mather took a hydrographic chart of the Atlantic coast and made a long sweep with his finger from north to south. "I would say that the overall distribution of bluefin tuna in the western Atlantic ranges from northernmost South America to Newfoundland," he said. "The fish seem to stay fairly close to the 100-fathom curve. Broadly speaking, tuna frequent northern waters from late spring to fall, while southern waters hold the fish from late fall to spring.

"But, as I explained, size plays a determining role. The very small fish of less than 5 pounds appear in three widely separated regions—the Gulf of Mexico, the Straits of Florida, and the area from Cape Hatteras to Cape Cod. Small tuna, on the other hand, are only found in numbers north from Cape Charles to Cape Cod, but well offshore they range even farther north and east to Browns and La Have Banks.

"It appears that bluefins tend to summer in colder water as they grow older. You may recall that before World War II great concentrations of small tuna were found off Long Island and up to Martha's Vineyard. Well recently they have become less common in the New York Bight, but they've moved in great numbers east of Cape Cod and Cape Cod Bay. Pound-net records indicate that large runs of small bluefins only *began* in the ʿfallʾ of 1950."

The researchers suspect that this shift in habitat is due to the general increase in water temperature that has occurred in recent years. The mediums appear in the same region as the small ones, but also in the Gulf of Maine and along the coast of Nova Scotia. The annual catch of mediums varies greatly from year to year, maybe a few hundred some years, perhaps 10,000 in others. Mather thinks that this variation may be due to the tendency of that year's class to remain far offshore much of the time.

The giant tuna cover a much wider geographic area than the other sizes. Their summer distribution also seems to have been modified by climatic changes. The number of giants taken off the Rhode Island coast, for instance, declined greatly until the cold winter of 1955-56, which was followed by excellent fishing.

Mather slumped in his chair and gazed at the gray New England landscape. A thirty-knot wind was whipping across the bay. "Of course, until last year we had a convenient theory—and I might say a sound one—that tuna are divided into two races, one in the eastern Atlantic and one in the western. Those two tagged fish upset the applecart. But the theory could *still* be right. It might be that these fish were just strays."

He reached up to the bulletin board facing his desk and pulled out two tags, barbed streamers of yellow plastic. "If only we had more of these to work with. What I can't understand," he said in puzzlement, "is that Luis Rivas took measurements of European tuna and so did I. We worked independently and we both found differentials in proportions and counts. Enough to assume that there are separate races of bluefin tuna. Yet these tags lead us right back to the old theory of transoceanic migration."

As we left Mather's office for hamburgers at the Jolly Whaler, I recalled how Rivas had turned up the hottest clue yet. One of the tools of modern fish detection is a routine check called biometric analysis. The field agent measures a species over and over again, getting the fork length, head length, girth, and literally dozens of other measurements at certain reference points until so many figures have been compiled that he knows the relative sizes of all parts of the fish's body—proportions that remain constant. In sizing up his suspect, Professor Rivas decided that if a single bluefin-tuna race frequents *both* sides of the Atlantic, its bodily proportions would be constant even if they were disguised behind a bellyful of herring.

So, armed with measurements he had made on Bahama tuna in the spring of 1952, Rivas tailed Baron Bluefin from Spain to Sweden the summer following. There were monotonous dawn-to-dark days in the North Sea, a sandwich and a wine bottle in one hand and calipers and tape in the other. But research is expensive. The commercial men wouldn't let him leisurely probe into a fish's plumbing without first buying it, and tuna cost about $60 each. Rivas resorted to measuring fish in the auction places, and sometimes they were sold before he could finish. But the American professor picked over his clues. When the trail got hot, he bought three tuna—and there was the lead he needed. European bluefins have smaller heads than the American fish!

Now Rivas knew that fish with consistently larger heads within a species grow in thermal water. He remembered the big-headed mosquito fish that were reared in cooler water. And he knew that western Atlantic bluefins spawned in the warm water of the Caribbean. So presumably the bluefins of Europe were the same species but a different race. They couldn't possibly cross the ocean and shrink their heads, too, he concluded.

When the sport fishermen left Wedgeport to the winds and the press agents in the fall of 1953, Rivas stuck to the fish sheds like a remora on a shark.

There were still a few big tuna being taken by the commercial men, and the nimble-fingered taxonomist cut and probed, measured and preserved. But the only thing he learned was that tuna fish have a big chunk of meat in the back of their skulls that nobody ever bothered to butcher when the fish were being dressed for market. Rivas pointed this out to some commercial fishermen and demonstrated how the tuna should be cut. He deftly slipped his scalpel under a cadaver's skin behind the head and pulled the skin over the skull. It shucked off like a rabbit's hide, and as Rivas lifted it up for all to see he found himself staring at the skin against the setting sun.

And there in the middle of the skin was a round patch of transparent tissue that fitted perfectly over a hole in the tuna's skull. In the hole was a tube that ran directly into the fish's brain. So Baron Bluefin's head apparently held a secret pineal apparatus, which would mean an ability to pick up sunlight through the top of his head!

A jury would be hung on this one, but the evidence indicates that tuna may be getting around by measuring or absorbing the rays of the sun. Recent discoveries on the light sensitivity of other fish indicate that orientation during migrations may be controlled by the seasonal variations of sunlight. There is considerable reason to believe that school behavior is affected by illumination, dispersal taking place when the light is dim and grouping occurring when the light is bright.

The fact that schools are of uniform size is thought to be a matter of speed; each fish within a school must respond to the direction and pace of its fellows. Big tuna probably travel faster than small ones; Mather estimates that giants cover 200 miles per week along their main path of migration. But it's all supposition, and the Baron cannot be tried on circumstantial evidence alone.

As we awaited our hamburgers Mather introduced me to a bearded young man by the name of Bill Chevill. "He's an authority on whales. His real interest is cataphonics—you know, what whales talk about. That's a project of the Office of Naval Research. But getting back to what I was saying, it's difficult to ignore the fact that large ripe and maturing bluefins arrive off the Atlantic coasts of Spain and Portugal in May. They spawn there in June and July. These *cannot* be the same group that passes Bimini in May; not only is the distance too great but the Bimini fish are spent.

"Now, we know that giant bluefins summer in the North Sea and in Scandinavian waters, which indicates a migration from Norway to Spain along the European coast. It's probably comparable to our run from Cat Cay to New England. So we *must* be dealing with two distinct populations. The only thing we can conclude on the basis of two tag returns is that there's some interchange between east and west. Why, I don't know. It would be comfortable to think that those two fish were strays, but eight other tuna wearing our tag have been reported in the Bay of Biscay. Unfortunately we didn't get them back. I say *our* tag because the French and Norwegian biologists have a program of their own. They've had some results also, and since the No Man's Land episode their work is being accelerated."

25

WANTED! MORE SALMON FISHERMEN

This past decade has been a period of terrible exploitation for many sea resources. Among them was the Atlantic salmon. While Japanese long-liners and American purse seiners were making devastating inroads on the bluefin tuna, Danish drift netters were wreaking havoc with the salmon. A hue and cry by salmon anglers has recently given the species some respite. Stricter quotas for fish caught on the high seas have been established, and the short-term threat has been overcome.

But what about the long term? What is the future for this king of anadromous fishes? On the surface, things are looking up. The Canadian maritime governments are trying to hold the line on water quality, and New England state governments are actually improving many of their rivers. Maine particularly has made an enormous effort to restore Atlantic salmon to a number of coastal streams, and in 1974 the last major obstacle on the once-famed Penobscot was made passable to fish.

Yet where are the anglers? By July 16 last year, state biologists had caught 456 salmon in Penobscot traps, but sport fishermen had landed only 16. Up on the Machias, the rod catch by that date was just 10. State officials won't say it, but many are discouraged that after they have spent so much time and money to restore the salmon, the society of traditional salmon fishers still won't unbend its allegiance to Canadian or British waters and fish Maine.

"We need some of the Miramichi crowd to get the ball rolling," a representative of Maine's Fishery Research and Management Division told me. "But we're afraid they're so accustomed to bypassing New England on their pilgrimage north, we may never develop the angling statistics we need, not only to keep the present program healthy, but to see it expand."

Thus we have what to nonfishermen may seem a paradox—that in order to build a solid conservation foundation for Atlantic salmon, we desperately need more sport fishermen to catch them. Go north, young angler, go north—but stop short of the Canadian border.

GWR

WANTED! MORE SALMON FISHERMEN

A man whose working day consists of heaving Atlantic salmon into the Machias River, then driving around the countryside encouraging people to catch them, may seem to the casual observer to be somewhat eccentric. He isn't. Although James S. Fletcher may be likened to Johnny Appleseed, he is an expert biologist and a member of the Atlantic Sea Run Salmon Commission. His sole duty is to manage and restore *Salmo salar* in waters from the Aroostook River in the north of Maine to the Sheepscot in the south.

Within these narrow limits, comprising eight different watersheds, rests the fate of public Atlantic salmon fishing in America. The dream of bringing salmon back to Maine waters in quantity is so close to reality today that Fletcher has had to face another problem: anglers have forgotten how to fish for Salar!

Last July I drove to the town of Machias to learn what was happening in the largest of the restored salmon streams. Word had spread all over the state that a 40-pound Atlantic salmon had entered the river, and I wanted to meet the optimist who'd said: "The only trouble with our fishing is that we don't have enough fishermen." This was too much to swallow; I figured this bird couldn't locate his nose with both hands.

I found Fletcher patching his waders in the backyard of his home. He is a spare, 170-pound, graying man who speaks softly but with the diamond clarity of the scientist. Except for a hitch in the Air Force during World War II, he has worked and lived in Maine for the greater part of his forty-two years.

"I'm going down to the counting station now. You can come along if you'd like," Fletcher said. As we drove through the busy village he recalled how dam building and pollution had brought about the decline of our Atlantic salmon fishery. The Machias River was completely blocked five years after the town was settled in 1763. Soon the runs declined so badly that a feeble attempt was made to ensure the passage of migrating fish, but dam building continued, and by 1874 only a remnant population remained. The situation didn't improve until the early 1940s. Today, though there is still an argument about installing a control dam on the famed Narraguagus, Maine salmon rivers haven't looked as promising since Hector was a pup.

Fletcher parked behind an old warehouse and went inside to get his dip net. Then we proceeded to his trap, at the top of the gorge, opposite a laundromat and a five-and-ten. I couldn't imagine a more unlikely place to find the noble Salar. He walked out on a board platform and looked down into the churning water.

"Some fish came in last night. Let's see what we have here," he said, slipping the mesh bag into the flume and feeling carefully for the salmon.

He made a sudden, powerful sweep and lifted two kicking fish from the trap. He said they'd run 8 and 10 pounds. From long familiarity, he can estimate the weight of a salmon to within a pound. With hardly a pause the biologist stepped to the end of the platform, rotating the net and looking for tags or clipped fins. Then he heaved the fish into the Machias. Both sped upstream.

Fletcher netted four more fish, including one of about 20 pounds, and sent them on their way. "I hope somebody catches that big one," he said. "Probably won't, though—people just don't have any idea of what we have in this river. Let's go to Whitneyville Dam, and I'll show you what I mean."

We stopped in the village long enough for him to chalk on a scoreboard in front of the post office the total number of salmon that had entered the Machias. The tally stimulated some interest, he said, but not enough.

On the way north, Fletcher touched on this lack of interest. "Do you realize," he asked, "that fishermen are confining themselves to two and a half miles of a sixty-mile river? Right now everybody fishes from the tidewater pool—which is just below that counting station—to the dam. And over 90 percent of the fishing pressure is at the dam itself. People can see salmon there, so naturally it's fished constantly.

"There are a number of other pools that are hardly touched at all, starting at the end of Water Street. Lord only knows how many good spots exist upriver above the dam. We actually don't get enough fishermen to find out what the potential of the Machias is. Right now, with the season just 118 days old, 418 salmon have been caught. There aren't many two and a half-mile stretches *anywhere* with a four-fish daily average."

Fletcher paused to let his words sink in. It's hard to believe that public water is left unfished these days, but I discovered later that of Machias's 2,600 residents, not more than forty fish regularly for salmon. To some anglers, such as real estate man Bruce Woodman, the world begins and ends with squaretail trout.

"Salmon? Why, I wouldn't waste my time," he told me. "They don't mean to take a fly, and I don't mean to give 'em one. Now, I know the prettiest trout stream about forty miles north of here . . ."

Fletcher listened glumly. It is the brook trout that has typified Maine for recent generations. "Fortunately we're getting more tourists, but not the serious ones who understand salmon technique," he said. "Most people fish them the way they'd fish trout."

One drawback is the fact that the Atlantic salmon is not easy to catch. Once it enters a river it ceases to feed. It may come to the Machias as early as April, and it will be there until after the spawning period in October; meantime it will eat nothing. Naturally, it deteriorates in flesh and spirit. The male, or cock, fish becomes suffused with red and its lower jaw develops a pronounced hook. The hen becomes dull and gray. Salmon of the Machias turn dark very quickly, and may even enter the river with a brownish cast if they have held in the bark-stained waters of the tide pool for more than a couple of days.

Some anglers maintain that salmon *do* feed while in fresh water, and they

[208]

cite individual autopsies showing that salmon have swallowed food.[1] It's true, too, that salmon are caught on night crawlers, prawns, and herring in countries where such fishing is legal (in Maine it is not). Yet the exception is not the rule, nor can the acceptance of a bait always be described as a response to hunger. In fact, it appears that strikes are caused by anger, irritation, curiosity, or recent memories of feeding in the sea.

Whatever the cause, the salmon is unpredictable, and the fly-fisher will run into periods of success and of failure. Familiarity with a salmon river is most important. Salmon do not lie in the type of water favored by trout. Some holds will fish well, whereas others—inexplicably—will fish poorly. Instead of a beautiful calendar-picture pool, the salmon may select some homely depression in the stream bottom within spitting distance of a highway. There is one such inconspicuous lie just below the Whitneyville Bridge. It is a popular spot, and through the season it produces many fish.

"I saw a fellow under the bridge work over five salmon one day," Fletcher said. "There was a mob of people on the bridge giving him advice, including his bride. She said they were Jerseyites on their honeymoon, and had just happened to be driving by when her husband spotted the fish. She said he was a nut. He was still in his pin-striped suit.

"Anyway, he cast for at least an hour. Once in a while a fish would stir and everybody would start shouting at him because he couldn't see it against the sunlight. He had never caught a salmon before, and you could tell he was excited. Finally one came up and grabbed the fly. The poor guy struck too fast, and the fly popped out of the salmon's teeth. People on the bridge were so quiet that you could hear the water slapping the abutments. Too bad. It would have been a nice wedding present."

Fletcher wheeled the station wagon into a parking lot next to the river. "Well, here it is—the Whitneyville Dam."

Surprisingly, the river wasn't crowded. There were five or six casters working over many hundreds of yards of water. But a great many people had come to sit and watch. One rock was especially popular with anglers because it faced a taking lie that invariably produces a salmon. Fletcher said people even come to sleep on the rock in order to be there at first light.

I noticed quite a few out-of-state license plates and met a Mr. and Mrs. McCormick from Delaware. They had pitched a tent on a knoll overlooking the river. McCormick said he'd taken three salmon in the past week and

---

[1] "I have watched salmon repeatedly rise to naturals on several occasions in the Miramichi River," says A. J., "and in fall have caught them literally gorged with spruce budworms—or as the New Brunswick guides call them, 'bloodworm moths.'"

hooked five others. A small crowd of anglers on the bridge held fly rods and were teasing their feathers over the heads of a half dozen salmon that were lying some forty feet below street level. "See what I mean? Nobody *in* the stream." said Fletcher. "I don't know what would happen if one of those fish came up and hit a fly."

As we walked up to the dam everybody had a big hello for Jim Fletcher. Even in the friendly town of Machias he would win a popularity contest. Aside from being the local scoutmaster, he is also general factotum of the Little League and devotes most of his spare time to youth activities. "All Jim needs is a baton, and we'd give him a brass band," said one man.

Like most competent biologists, Fletcher devotes fully half of his efforts to public relations—preaching the gospel of conservation and helping anglers to learn where, when, and how to catch more salmon. A freckle-faced kid, dragging a huge eel, came out of the bushes.

"Isn't it true, Jim, that you put a 40-pounder over?" he asked. "Isn't it true?"

"Yes, Georgie," Fletcher said. "I did."

The boy turned around and shouted at some unseen audience in the willows. "I *told* ya he did!"

We scuttled out on the slippery wet boards of the dam, where Fletcher's assistant, Frank Gramlich, was waiting for another count. By auditing the number of salmon passing over the Whitneyville fishway, Fletcher knows how many salmon make the complete journey to their spawning grounds. Although some fish do build their redds in the lower river, most of the good breeding area is far upstream.

The quality of Machias fishing four years hence will be reflected in the count Fletcher was making. For example, the year 1960 was a predictably bad one on the Machias. For that matter, it was a washout on many of the famed Canadian streams. In the cyclic cause and effect of salmon runs, the low-water winter of 1955-56 was detrimental to the eggs. Parr survival was low, and as a result few salmon entered the rivers in 1960. By the same reasoning 1962 should be a good year, even better than last season, because of the above average conditions in 1959.

Where proper habitat exists, almost any species of fish or game has the resilience to survive. No predator other than man has the capacity to knock it out. With all the salmon stocking done in Maine water (and it's still necessary to reinforce the runs) the largest returns are from native fish. To reproduce successfully, the nest-building female salmon needs gravel that can be moved by her tail. Enough water must flow through the gravel to provide oxygen for the incubating eggs.

[210]

The Machias and its tributaries offer 859,367 square yards of suitable bottom. What does that imply for future populations? According to Fletcher, the production of salmon smolts per 100-square-yard unit should be three fish, or a conservative potential of about 25,500 young salmon. If only 15 percent of these return to fresh water, the Machias would draw 3,825 adult salmon. And if only 15 percent of that run is caught by anglers, their harvest would be 575 fish averaging $9\frac{3}{10}$ pounds in weight. However, the three smolt figure might easily run to six as the river is developed. Small sections of it are already producing 10 to 12 smolts per 100-square-yard units.

While Fletcher emptied his trap (eight fish including a 30-pounder) I watched two anglers working the Line Pool a short distance below the dam. These were experts—Charlie and Henry Dowling. Charlie had taken a 15-pound 4-ounce salmon that morning on a dry fly, and later Henry scored also. Generally speaking, salmon are most susceptible to the dry fly when stream temperatures run over 60 degrees. Until that point wet flies are superior.

Maine rivers invariably have drought conditions during the summer months, and thus the purist will often do as well as, if not better than, the wet-fly artist. From August 1 to 20, when the river was stale at 72 to 74 degrees day after day, thirty salmon were caught in the stretch below Whitneyville, mostly on floating flies.

The Dowling boys, who undeniably take the lion's share of Machias fish, use Nos. 6, 8, and 10 hair-wings of their own design. Charlie showed me one that looked something like a hair-wing Ginger Quill; it's his favorite. Traditional wet-fly patterns, such as the Silver Wilkinson, Black Dose, and Durham Ranger, are used only occasionally; everybody is Cosseboom-happy. Orange, Black, Green, and Red Cossebooms account for the greatest number of salmon.

The main thing is, of course, to fish any fly properly. A dry pattern for salmon must float high on its hackles, and a long, fine leader is a tremendous asset. For the most part, the floater is fished straight across or quartering downstream. A wet pattern must be gauged to drift at a precise speed and near the surface. It's best displayed broadside to the salmon without drag or any other movement except that imparted by the play of the currents.

With either method the salmon is a heavy-mouthed fish; as they once said on our ancestral rivers, there is plenty of time to mumble "God save the king" between rise and strike. Unlike trout, salmon will hold a fly in their jaws for a long instant before ejecting it. The strike should be firm, but be mindful of the fish's weight against a light tippet.

As we were walking back to the car a fifteen-year-old boy hooked his first salmon. Fletcher knew the lad, so we joined the Monday-morning quarterbacks who came galloping over the rocky landscape with their steel-tipped gaffs at port, looking like extras in a Cecil B. De Mille movie. The fish had jumped once in the beginning, but now it seesawed back and forth across the pool until the boy's green line was cutting farther and farther away.

Everybody gathered in a respectful circle around the young angler. His fleeting thoughts were reflected in their faces. For twenty minutes by my watch he stood there, his rod bent and vibrant, while the salmon circled with a heavy, almost dead, pull, as though trying to rub out the hook on the bottom.

"Hang on," the man next to me whispered.

"You're doing great, boy," Fletcher said.

Abruptly the line stopped and the lad said he thought the fish was hung in a log; the Machias is full of old timber. Two men ran over the boulders and all the way back to the parking lot to fetch their auto-top boat. It was an amazing display of sportsmanship. Returning, they staggered under their load and other men rushed to help them, taking the weight and the scraped shins in relays. By the time they launched the craft the boy was almost in tears.

The men worked skillfully, following the line with a paddle edge and working it with their hands. A grizzled old character who looked familiar with a peavey pole nearly fell out of the bow in attempting to feel for the salmon below. But it was too late. They finally raised a grotesque black branch. The fly was stuck in it, but the salmon was long since gone.

"You handled him beautifully, boy!" the man next to me shouted.

"Better luck next time, kid," another man said.

The angler brushed an eye with the back of his hand and reeled up. For a moment he actually looked happy. I remembered feeling like that once, a long time ago.

On the way home we stopped at a restaurant in Machias for a cup of coffee. We sat in the back, where the booths overlooked the tide pool. Alewives were rising steadily to a midge hatch, and the river was strangely pretty in the purply light. A busload of Portland-bound tourists came in, and for a while we couldn't hear each other over the noise.

Suddenly a woman jumped from her seat and screamed, "Good heavens!" Her coffee went all over the deck. Some people turned and stared, but the local folk just smiled. They have become accustomed to it. Out over the darkening stream a great salmon had vaulted high into the air and fallen back into the creaming water.

Fletcher studied the widening rings thoughtfully. "Looks like I'm going to have more customers in the morning," he said. "How about another cup?"

PART VI

HOW IT ALL BEGAN

26

FISHING WITH THE COMPLEAT ANGLER

Like the Bible, copies of *The Compleat Angler* are owned by many fishermen but read by few. One acquaintance is so busy collecting different editions he doesn't have time to get straight the personalities of Izaak Walton (1593–1683) and Charles Cotton (1630–1687): "Was Walton the one who used live bait and Cotton the expert on artificials? Or am I confusing them with Rosencrantz and Guildenstern?" Walton is reverently invoked as the Father of Angling by bank presidents, newspaper editors, and elected officials of every sort, but the truth is few of them know what they're talking about.

Apalled by the plethora of misinformation on seventeenth-century angling, Al McClane set out to write a primer on the subject for those readers who, like himself, yearned for an enlightened guide through the gloom of supposition and the murk of nonsense. However, A. J. is not your ordinary researcher. No paraphrasing of encyclopedias for him. With the curiosity of a scientist and the devotion to accuracy of a historian, Al set out to make and test horsehair lines and needle hooks. He meticulously read Walton's precursors and his contemporaries (at least one of whom was a fierce adversary of Walton.) He toured Walton's English countryside and tracked down local legends and angling customs. He visited and photographed Walton's home and tomb, only to discover that Izaak is "Isaac," a small detail that made every wire service in the United States. While the results read as easily as a primer, within McClane's gracious prose stands the structure of a master's thesis on the venerable Piscator of Stafford.

GWR

FISHING WITH THE COMPLEAT ANGLER

And before you begin to angle, cast to have the wind on your back, and the sun, if it shines, to be before you, and to fish down the stream; and carry the point or top of your rod downward, by which means the shadow of yourself, and rod too, will be the least offensive to the fish; for the sight of any shade amazes the fish, and spoils your sport, of which you must take a great care.

This quaint, yet entirely modern, advice is one of the many practical observations made by Izaak Walton. Even though he breathed in an atmosphere of troubled times, his cut-crystal words have been ringing through the dimness of time for three centuries. Now, at an age when everything that is about to take place tomorrow obscures all that has passed since the world was created, I humbly submit that the art of angling has changed

[216]

very little and that perhaps the great wheel of history will wobble on its shaky path without a halt. Having come thus far in this scholarly issue, let's abandon our moral tale to sift Walton's nuggets of native wisdom from the River Lea.

Most of the world still thought it was standing on a flat, immovable platform when the serious business of fly fishing began. This first text, *A Treatyse of Fysshynge wyth an Angle*, was written by a woman in the year 1496. Dame Juliana Berners not only preceded Walton, but her technically detailed work stood the test of time and shaped much of Izaak's early learning. The good prioress was so convinced of the perfection of her own methods that she purposely incorporated them in the great *Boke of St. Albans*, "so that idlers shall take little interest in the sport of fishing which they might destroy utterly by virtue of the skill acquired from this treatise, which has been put beyond their reach." The astute reader will perceive with no further instruction that there is a familiar irony in the lady's secret, for idlers have kept it these 457 years.

Heat treating and hollow-built rod construction were well-known to Berners, and she set down very precise instructions for both. The hollow-built rod, however, had none of the serious implications of greater power for less weight, but existed solely as a means of disguising the rod, "so that no man will know the errand on which you are going." Angling was in her day a game of questionable amusement, and by hiding the rod sections inside a crop or walking stick one could look like anything but an angler in the received sense of the word. This explains our heroine's protracted maundering to herself over the sports of hunting, hawking, and fowling—the hunter must blow his lips to a blister, while the hawker's hawk pays no attention to him, and the fowler must be out in the coldest and most inclement weather. Even Walton had to reaffirm the virtues of being an angler by starting off his book with a few quick jabs at the three manly amusements. The difference between Berners and Walton, however, is that Izaak created a popular habit.

I suppose that on any Saturday in the year 1653, holiday seekers funneled out of the city's maw to breathe in the hills and plains and the dying sunsets. Izaak Walton was, of course, one of the country-goers and he went from Fleet Street to the rivers around London, usually in partnership with a pastry cook by the name of Thomas Barker. The tackle they carried was far from crude. Their hazel and ash fly rods were long, carefully tapered, and light enough to be fished with one hand. Tom bought his rod at Charles Brandon's tackle shop and Izaak used one made by John Margrave, whose store was at the sign of the three trout in St. Paul's churchyard. They were earthbound among a mass of quiet folk, and in the warm sun their faces shone with perspiration. It was twenty miles to the River Lea at Wareham. But the "May butter" was on the water—that great hatch of green drakes which fattens a trout to bursting. As the sun rose above the trees, Walton's rod threw a long shadow across the green paths ahead.

New readers to *The Compleat Angler* are usually bewildered by the fact that his book is written in dialogue form. We have grown to expect a direct monologue in our angling works, but in Walton's day there was time to wet now-dried Elizabethan prose, and it is a pity really that words are perishable. As the two men walked to their river, the tremendous secret of an honest life was unfolded. Izaak's literary harvest was merely the shreds of these conversations, for he was by nature a profoundly inquisitive man. Even in reading him as the practical fisherman we find none of the dull stuff chronicled by scholars in the years following. To this day, nobody has written a more finely detailed study in the art of using live baits. Walton's eloquence lagged only when the subject of fly fishing became too pressing, and here he turned to his friend, Charles Cotton.

Cotton would be on the River Dove that day, fishing with Captain Henry Jackson. Their fly rods came from Yorkshire and were made of eight sections of seasoned fir and willow. The fir was used in the first three butt pieces, and, lacking ferrules, the end of each section was beveled to fit the other and then wrapped around with silk thread. In winters when they didn't go grayling fishing, the windings could be removed and the pieces stored in a dry place. But Cotton seldom put his rods away—he was casually lethal in his approach, a practiced hand of great skill. His companion would be sitting in the meadow grass with a bag of feathers and hairs building copies of insects on hooks that he had armed the night before. Jackson was a keen fly tyer and he worked his miracles with blunt, seamy hands—camel's hair, bright bear hair, and the beard of a black cat were spun ever so carefully.

Their play has been told against a thousand backdrops and will be told against a thousand new ones before the curtain finally falls. A Green Drake settling to the water, a flash of gold, and then a trout dashing toward his shelter of weed before threshing against the pliant rod. Cotton knew how to keep a fish from this dangerous retreat, and even though he may have angled for reasons different from Walton's, his talents helped lubricate the machinery of Izaak's philosophy. So, good friend, you will be left to bob impotently on a river of words if you look to *The Compleat Angler* for supernatural aid in the capture of fishes. Are you disappointed? Would you have the man Walton dispensing universal prescriptions for the mending of broken rods without debating first the proposition, to wit: that all of angling is not catching the fish?

Lest you imagine that I belittle the master's skill, let me put together his tackle, which can be fished with even tomorrow. You could profit much in making and using these delicate instruments, for they breed the unconscious contentment of self-knowledge. In a more practical sense, such tools are productive of amazing results. The fly line of 1653 was made of horsehair and it was tapered. A horse's tail isn't long enough to make twelve or fifteen feet of line, so equal lengths of hair were twisted and then knotted together by using a water knot. Each one of these line sections was known as a link. Walton used a somewhat heavier line than Cotton because he angled differently. Cotton built a light front taper of two hairs for two links next to the hook, three hairs for the next three links, four hairs for the next three links, and so on up the line. He concluded that such a taper would fall much better and straighter and with greater accuracy. The horsehair line was so light that the angler was forced to sink part of it in order to keep the fly in the water when a strong wind blew. Cotton's taper shows us that fly fishing had become a great deal more sporty since Dame Berners twisted her links at the nunnery of Sopewell. She advised the two-hair taper for perch and twelve hairs for trout. Walton's disciple was not given to idle boasting when he set down his mark of ability: "He that cannot kill a trout of twenty inches with two, deserves not the name of angler." A 20-inch trout is, of course, a good 3 pounds, and it would be no mean feat to subdue a brown trout of this size on two hairs.

The average tensile strength of horsehair is less than that of raw nylon monofilament. It is somewhat stiffer and has a greater elongation than nylon —stretching about 30 percent. I recently obtained locks of hair from a horse who worked in a British brewery and from a contemporary animal who grazes in South Otselic, New York. The Gladding Line Company provided their laboratories, and from these samples we learned that hair diameters range from .010 to .006 or 1X to 4X, with a tensile strength of 1.7 to 0.9 pounds. White, or "glass-colored," hair proved consistently stronger than dark-colored hair assuming that horses' tails haven't changed too much in the past 300 years. Charles Cotton probably fished with a tippet testing about 2.5 pounds. Remember, the angler couldn't let his fish run, so a two-hair trout was no easy mark.

The real problem in line building was finding the right horse. Walton's ideal was a lock of round, clear, glass-colored hair without scabs or galls. The hairs had to be of equal diameter so that they would stretch at the same ratio and have an equal breaking strain. This parallels the problem of our modern line builder in getting a finish that stretches at the same ratio as the raw line inside. Unless the elongation is identical, the line simply stretches away from its outside protective cover and the whole business cracks apart.

But oil and plastic finishes weren't used in those days; finishing usually consisted of dyeing the line some color for purposes of camouflage. Berners, in a truly feminine fashion, believed there was a color for every situation and gave instructions for dyeing lines red, green, yellow, blue, brown, and whatnot. Walton decided that most of this was unnecessary and advised a nearly transparent line with just a slight greenish tinge. "And for dying your hairs, do it thus: Take a pint of strong ale, half a pound of soot, and a little quantity of the juice of Walnut-tree leaves, and an equal quantity of allum; put these together in a pot, pan, or pipkin, and boil them half an hour; and having so done, let it cool; and being cold, put your hair into it, and there let it lie; it will turn your hair to a kind of water or glass colour, or greenish, and the longer you let it lie, the deeper coloured it will be: you might be taught to make many other colours, but it is to little purpose; for doubtless the water colour, or glass coloured hair, is the most choice and most useful for an Angler; but let it not be too green." This agrees with the choice of many experts today.

Walton went through an evolution of rods, starting with simple, painted, two-piece sticks—many of which he made himself—to eight- and ten-piece rods built by more clever hands. As his friendship with Cotton sprung to mushroom intimacy—the young disciple providing a temple for his prophet in the Dove fishing cottage—Izaak became steeped in fly-fishing lore. In his first edition Walton recommends Charles Brandon, Mr. Fletcher, or Dr. Nowel as suppliers; he next made a marginal note on the value of tackle in his second edition; and finally there appears, on the reverse leaf of Cotton's part of the fifth edition in 1676, a memorandum to the effect that one may be fitted with the best fishing tackle by John Margrave. Before you suspect Walton of whimsy, realize that this change kept pace with his new interest.

Actually, the length of a fly rod was determined by the width of the river one fished. It had to be long enough to make a cast near midstream. The standard length for trout fishing was fifteen to eighteen feet, and if no wind was blowing, the angler would employ about half that length of line. When the wind blew, Walton and Cotton fished the quick fly, which required using a line as long as the rod, "wherein you are always to have your line flying before you up or down the river as the wind serves." One evening after a rain, Charles Cotton stood in a whistling wind and played his Green Drake over the surface, catching thirty-five very great trout. Five or six large fish broke off, even though he tried them on three hairs.

This same method of fly fishing occurs to almost every generation of anglers as a novel departure from orthodox casting, but actually it is the oldest way of getting a natural or artificial fly to feeding fish. Using a long fly rod, a short but light line, and a long leader, the modern angler turns his back to the wind, and lets his bivisible flap in the breeze, lowering it to the surface where he thinks the trout might be. There is absolutely no drag and the fly dances like a live insect.[1]

Cotton had a self-conscious elegance that led him directly through his narrative minus those touches of unexpected detail that marked Izaak Walton's style. Walton had never been yoked by the harness of royalty—his soul was as unmarked by artifice as the face of his milkmaid was unmarked by modern paint. Not only did they write differently, but they fished differently. Without a wind, Walton and Cotton whipped their lines back and forth, but basically they had two different styles of angling. Walton was a short-line artist—"Now you must be sure not to cumber yourself with too long a line, as most do"—and he much preferred the rustic art of dibbling. Cotton was for his day a long-line caster—"to fish fine and far off, is the first and principal rule for trout angling"—and, indeed, with a 15-foot rod he was working thirty to thirty-five feet away from his quarry.

The sometimes-wealthy Cotton could afford such luxury, because the problem with a reel-less rod and long line was in landing the fish. A gentleman angler would hire some rubber-handed fellow to take the line in for him. This is what he meant when he said in his discussion on line length, "Everyone that can afford to angle for pleasure has somebody to do it for him." It also explains why the art work of that period frequently depicted an angler taking his fish with the help of an assistant. Landing nets were used a great deal, but even a long-handled one served very poorly when the angler couldn't release the line at the critical moment.

Dibbling with both the natural and the artificial fly was probably the most common method of catching trout, and the technique is as effective today as it was then. The dibbler usually works very close to his fish by crawling or knee-walking along the bank. At a place where he knows the trout are, or ought to be, such as an undercut, the pool below a footbridge, a weed bed, or boulder, he cautiously pokes his rod out over the water and drops his fly to the surface. A minimum of rod and line will show if the angler is crafty. Perhaps he'll watch the float of his fly, but the skilled dibbler plays by sound, keeping himself well out of sight. Of course the fly will float beautifully,

[1] A. J. described a similar technique in his first outdoor story "Bouncing for Trout" using silk and dental floss for "line."

as there is no drag from the line and no more than an inch of leader will touch the river. Walton liked this method and well he should—country boys have taken billions of trout this way in the past 300 years.

You would be blessed to breathe the nights in that little stone house on the Dove, when copper mugs finished their rattling courses around the black marble table, and our two anglers waded into the bottomless pool of fly patterns. Walton described his "jury of flies likely to betray and condemn all the Trouts in the river" in his first edition, and they were almost exactly the same twelve patterns recommended by Dame Juliana Berners 157 years before. Fly fishing had changed very little in that period; less than a dozen other works on angling had been published. A feather or two had changed in some of the dressings, but the Dun, Stone, Moor, Shell, and Wasp flies, for instance, were still identical. In fact, Berners' descriptions of certain patterns give us the origin of the March Brown, Black Gnat, Alder, Stonefly, Whirling Dun, and the fly that was "discovered" in our Ozark Mountains, the Woolly Worm. Being a comparative neophyte in fly fishing, Walton allowed that there were other patterns that would kill as well, and promised to correct or add to his list in future editions. But on the Sow, the Tame, the Derwent, and the ever-glorious Lea, these twelve simple flies served him well. Cotton brought such technical embellishments to fruition in the fifth edition, with his "Instructions how to Angle for a Trout or Grayling in a Clear Stream." Here we find the Cowdung, Whirling Dun, Green Drake, Black Gnat, Stonefly, and many others which are either new patterns or versions of old ones. It is noticeable that Cotton escaped from the use of wools in his fly bodies; almost all of these patterns require dubbed underfur. In his Blue Dun, for instance, he suggests that the angler "comb the neck of a black greyhound, and the down that sticks in the teeth will be the finest blue you ever saw." His two favorite flies were the Stonefly and the Green Drake, and he observed that "the trout never feeds fat, nor comes into his perfect season, till these flies come in." This, of course, is as true today as it was then.

Although Walton's instructions on fly tying were sketchy by modern standards, he had the professional tyer's approach in stressing the right proportion between material and hook size and strongly urged that his pupil see a fly made by "an artist in kind." Furthermore, he advised that the angler study aquatic insect life and carry a bag of tying materials at the streamside so that he could make imitations of whatever flies might be hatching. Cotton elaborated on this point and also advised that the angler open the trout's stomach to learn what the fish was feeding on. The beginning fly fisher of today can profit immeasurably by this same advice.

[222]

Hooks in the fifteenth century were made from needles. The smallest ones were made from embroiderers' needles, while tailors' and shoemakers' needles were used for larger fish. Commercial hook making was established as a business in that period between Berners' and Walton's time, but many fly tyers continued to make their own hooks, as prescribed by Dame Juliana. "You must place the square headed needle in a red hot charcoal fire until it becomes the same color as the fire. Then take it out and let it cool and you'll find that it will be tempered for filing. Then raise its barb with your knife and sharpen its point. Then temper it again or else it will break in the bending. When the hook is bent, beat the hind end flat and file it smooth for the purpose of binding the line to it. Place it in the fire until it barely glows. Then quench it in water and it will become hard and strong."

When I asked Helen Shaw to tie the Shell-fly,[2] she pursued the task with her usual regard to detail, including the making of the hook. This summary of her research gives us an inkling of what ancient hook makers were up against. "After destroying several papers of embroidery needles I was forced to the conclusion that the good Dame didn't know what she was talking about, or that perhaps chrome-plated needles were not the order of her day. While I didn't exactly work my fingers to the bone, I was neatly impaled that deeply twice, while trying to remove the chrome with emery. I searched the stores for unplated needles and finally found a few packets of them. The enclosed are the fruits of my labors, crude, but having, I think, the dignity of four centuries to recommend them. In Juliana's day her knives must have been different from the ones I used. Her description sounds so simple, as though raising the barb was mere child's play. The only tool I could use with any success was a pair of bass-fly scissors, which now have an edge similar to a pair of pinking shears, except that the teeth don't mesh."

Eyed hooks were unknown in Walton's day, so when making flies the tyer used a link of one, two, or three horsehairs to serve as a snell. This was secured to the hook first, and then the fly was dressed over it; whenever more than one hair was necessary, there was always some question whether they should be twisted or left untwisted. Cotton decided that the untwisted way was better "because it makes less show in the water," but he wisely observed the twisted hairs to be stronger. Hair twisting was a semi-mechanical

[2] Helen Shaw recreated all of Dame Juliana Berners' original list of trout flies for McClane's *The Practical Fly Fisherman*, Prentice-Hall, 1953. Born in Sheboygan, Wisconsin, she was taken under the tutelage of Art Kade, artist turned fly tyer, and as Arnold Gingrich has observed, she eventually outdistanced her master and became "fly tyer turned artist." She lives in New York City with husband, Hermann Kessler, former art director of *Field & Stream*.

procedure, in that the angler used a stand having a perforated arm which held the hairs at the upper end, while a turning weight at the lower end made the necessary twists.

Although dry-fly fishing is considered by many students of angling history as a modern innovation, floating flies were used as much as sunken flies in Walton's era. Dry-fly fishing did not exist as a definitive method; the idea was to put the fly over a trout, "angling on top," and then either drift or retrieve it back, floating or wet. Although very few fly patterns other than the popular palmer-tied flies had hackles, most of them had dubbed fur bodies which were picked out, or "bearded," making the small steel needle hooks very buoyant. Walton was much more concerned with presentation, a point that is not nearly so well-exploited today: "When you fish with a fly, if it be possible, let no part of your line touch the water, but your fly only; and be still moving your fly upon the water, or casting it into the water, you yourself being always on the move downstream." Walton preferred to fish with three hairs next to his hook for this reason; there was no line left to give to a large trout after he struck, as the fly dangled on the surface directly below his rod point. Not having a reel (contrary to the art work in many later editions), he was "forced to tug for't," and a strong link of hair meant the difference between success and failure. Only a few salmon fishermen of the seventeenth century used reels, and these were crude wood cylinders that were much too heavy for trout fishing.

Walton admitted to throwing his rod in the river when he couldn't play a large fish, tactics which earned him a trout nearly one yard long and whose picture was traced and hung at Rickabie's place, the George, in Ware. Purist Cotton found this innocent directness uncomfortable in print and censured him thus: "I cannot consent to his way of throwing in his rod to an overgrown trout, and afterwards recovering his fish with his tackle. For though I am satisfied he has sometimes done it, because he says so, yet I have found it quite otherwise." Actually, fly fishers of the day fastened their lines to the rod tops with waxed silk and in Izaak's south country rivers there must have been a few large trout that demanded more than fifteen feet of line.

Walton had his opponents, both technically and morally, but nobody attacked him more vehemently than a fame-crazed egomaniac by the name of Richard Franck. In a fashion, this was the original battle of the experts. Franck referred to Walton's methods as an "uncultivated art" and to *The Compleat Angler* as "an undigested octavo, stuffed with morals from Dubravimus and others." He also predicted that nobody would ever read Izaak's efforts. Franck wrote his *Northern Memoirs* in 1658, which first flatters the old master by grossly imitating his style and then covers him with abuse.

Franck was not only a Cromwellian captain and an independent (which opposed the loyalist Walton), but he was a one- and two-hair caster, with a broad fishing background—which he wrongly considered the qualities of an angler. In the land where bright water flows eternal, and very great trout always come to the fly, Richard Franck must still walk his eager, infinitely mistaken way.

Whether Walton's book was written or not, did it really matter? Readers scanning this history three hundred years from now may wonder. Much has changed in centuries past, but little has happened to the harmless profession of angling. The day after Izaak died, the sun rose, the nymphs ate the plankton, trout ate the nymphs, men chased the trout, women chased the men, and our terrestrial globe made one more spin. These things are as permanent as *The Compleat Angler*, and should future generations be troutless, I suggest that they open their closed book in the green month of May to find our deep and entirely wholesome truth.

27

THE GOLDEN AGE OF TACKLE MAKING

Fishing is not merely to catch fish. That may be the heart of the matter, but the person who goes fishing yet remains insensitive to his cathedral surroundings must be a dolt indeed. Furthermore, angling without acquiring an interest in the history and customs of the sport is merely swallowing the wafer without ritual or blessing. In the following article written for the sixtieth anniversary issue of *Field & Stream*, A. J. McClane reveals his deep understanding and knowledge of angling traditions.

GWR

THE GOLDEN AGE OF TACKLE MAKING

In the summer of 1898, Judge William Tuttle boarded the night train for St. Louis, gateway to the Ozark Mountains. He had dined at Chicago's Union League Club that evening under a mural depicting a battle between the Crows and the Blackfeet, but the toil of the artist went for naught, since the ritual of eating at the club was veiled in a fashionable gloom that obscured painting and member alike.

After a Hennessy and a Corona, the judge had his Vandyke trimmed by the resident barber. Now, settling back in his drawing room, he watched the porter carefully arranging a pyramid of leather bags behind the door. The long hand-sewn cases held rods made by H. L. Leonard of Central Valley, New York, and C. F. Murphy of Newark, New Jersey, and the circular ones held reels from Henry Chawner of London, and Benjamin C. Milam of Frankfort, Kentucky. The Milam bait-casting reel had won first prize at the International Fisheries Exposition in Bergen, Norway, and the judge had paid $100 for his copy.

As seen in his tweeds, he was a sober man—resolved, not given to the creation of legend. His 2-pound smallmouth always remained a 2-pound smallmouth in the telling. Although he had caught bass up to 6 pounds at Muskoka Lake in northern Ontario that summer, he had been impelled into further travel by the June issue of *Field & Stream*, which announced the opening of the Ozarks to anglers by the Frisco Line, a railroad that also penetrated Indian territory. This spread of rail suggested that while Indians were not actively pursuing the tourist trade, one could find primitive fishing.

The magazine further stated that although the mosquito dwelt in the

Ozarks, "he is retiring in disposition, not avid for blood." The judge found this a reassuring detail and reminded himself to renew his subscription. The then three-year-old publication had already acquired the authoritative impact of a Supreme Court gavel, but as the train barreled through the night, neither magazine nor judge could have been aware that he was riding into the dawn of a new era. Certainly no one could have envisioned the whole new galaxy of stars that streamlined transportation was to bring within reach of the modern angler—from hibiscus-*cum*-chromium Miami, Bimini, Cat Cay, Boca Grande, Talara, and Iquique in the sunshine world of the millionaire, to the Promised Land of the TVA bass circuit, where no water—let alone roads and fishing—yet existed.

Today's fisherman thinks nothing of tooling off to Alaska or Africa just for kicks. His eyes may be red-rimmed from last night's gin rummy game or last month's bank statement. He'll invest in fishing. The nine-billion-dollar angling industry is shadowed only by the eleven-billion-dollar automotive industry. Since 1940, the fishing-tackle business alone has increased approximately 400 percent, and its total now approaches a cool 75 million dollars annually. Of the vast army of people who went afield last year, 32 million bought hunting and fishing licenses.[1] In comparison, our national pastime of organized baseball earned 18 million paid admissions, and many of these were repeat sales to bleacher *aficionados.*

Sport fishing is now a large part of the economy of many states, chiefly in the South, where mammoth recreational facilities are in the making. Judge Tuttle would have done a flip if he had been in Savannah, Tennessee, this year. There, to quote a Southern euphemism, they had a "real bust" in selecting the National Catfish Derby Queen. The guest of honor, a 102-pound blue cat, expired before the young lady was crowned. The Davy Crockett Kadets and Savannah Catfish Queens (I'm not clear on how many queens there were) sang the ballad of Davy Crockett and fired a three-gun salute before shipping the late lamented to a frozen-food locker.

But as the new century marched over the horizon, it would have taken a prophet indeed to foretell that such a brave new world was in the making. True, there were signs and portents. Benjamin F. Meek, last of the Kentucky handcraftsmen, had built a factory to mass-produce the famous Bourbon County multiplying reel. John Pflueger's tackle company had grown out of an Ohio farmhouse into a formidable three-story building. The Horton Manufacturing Company was making Bristol steel rods in eighteen sizes, and anglers had begun casting overhead in Kalamazoo style. But the lure-making

[1] This figure is closer to 52 million today.

business, far from being the roaring colossus it is now, was still a novelty trade patronized by an elite corps that swung out over the waters some really amazing creations, many of them bristling with from nine to twenty-one hooks.

James Heddon broke the quiet with a lightning flash—his Dowagiac Minnow, the first floating-and-diving plug. The excitement that greeted its debut clearly presaged greater things to come. The bandwagon had begun to roll and the passengers were eager to climb on.

William Jamison issued the challenge in *Field & Stream* that electrified bass fishermen from one end of the nation to the other: "I offer to meet any angler on earth, manufacturers of artificial baits preferred, in a three days' fishing contest on any lake within 500 miles of Chicago to prove that the sportsmanlike Coaxer, with its humane armament, will catch more fish than any other bait on the market, or than the live frog or minnow."

Before subscribers could rehinge their jaws, Ans Decker, who was promoting a top-water plug with a revolving head called the Decker Hopatcong, accepted the challenge.

The Jamison versus Decker affair was reported at great length by *Field & Stream* in 1910. The fourteen-year-old magazine had acquired among its readers an army of bass experts whose enthusiasm was reflected in such precontest missives as "If I had a million dollars . . . I would bet it on Ans Decker in his coming bass-fishing contest . . . If the Coaxer wins, the most surprised fisherman in the country will be, yours truly, Sam S. Stinson." And though Jamison or his bait clearly outpointed Decker by a score of 28 to 16, postcontest letters to the editor kept the pot boiling. Some said that Congress Lake, Ohio, scene of the duel, was too weedy for the Decker plug, and others believed that Jamison was simply a better fisherman. Still others maintained that neither bait was any good and that a Dowagiac Minnow, Cooper's Porker, or Hildebrandt Spinner would have creamed them both.

The only question the duel seemed to have settled was that a new breed in the angling order had definitely emerged and was about to multiply—rapidly. It remained only for a Tennessee stonemason by the name of E. H. Peckinpaugh to make the final, telling contribution. Cork-bodied bugs had been in use for a long time, but Peck's Night Bug struck the popular fancy, and by 1913, a scant few years after the *affaire* Decker-Jamison, the John J. Hildebrandt Company was selling them to an eager national audience through its catalog.

And while the American caster was breathing the intoxicating ozone of fast reels, short rods, and floating bugs, Alfred Illingworth, scion of the Bradford worsted trade in England, had taken out his first patent on a reel that was destined to become one of the most catalytic inventions in the history of angling. Peter Malloch of Perth, Scotland, had made a fixed-spool reel in 1884. The spool was mounted on a turntable, and in casting, one moved the spool so that its axis was in line with the direction of the cast. Line then uncoiled freely. In retrieving, one moved the spool so that its axis was at right angles to the line, and the spool could then be rotated. In effect, it was a combination fixed-spool and multiplying reel.

Illingworth was quick to see the advantages in the stationary part of the Malloch and, quicker yet, its similarity in principle to the spinning spindles used in wool making. Using a fixed wooden spindle for his spool, Illingworth built an aluminum framework of two circular plates which housed the working parts. The flier, or pickup, mechanism rotated around the spool, laying the line down and simultaneously reversing the twists made by casting. While Jamison was challenging American lure makers, Illingworth was taking first place in the light-bait event of the International Casting Tournament.

After Illingworth made his reel, conservative European firms, chiefly Hardy Brothers in England and Pezon-Michel in France, redesigned and improved the fixed spool until it resembled our modern reel, which first arrived on these shores in 1935. As agent for Pezon-Michel, the cologne-lashed gentleman-angler Bache Brown introduced the Luxor reel, but its initial reception was lukewarm. Before spinning could get off the ground floor here, France was locked in World War II and so was Brown's source of supply.

It remained for America's gargantuan technical facilities to get spinning to the masses, but it was the parallel development of nylon that turned the trick. Ever since 1884, when E. J. Martin of Rockville, Connecticut, made the first braided-silk casting line, anglers had been holding their thumbs on a material that absorbed water, flattened, rotted, weakened, and mildewed. Through slow evolution, waterproofing and hard braiding appeared in 1910 and gradually improved, but silk was in no way adequate to rotating casts and rotating lures. In 1939, the Ashaway Company put out the first nylon line, jointly developed with Du Pont.

Nylon not only solved the multiple problem of bait casting—line twist—but made the fixed-spool reel practical. Basically a derivative of coal, nylon absorbs about 3 percent moisture, with slight loss of tensile strength, and its specific gravity is about 12 percent lighter than that of silk. With a cross-section strength of 70,000 to 80,000 pounds per square inch, nylon is comparable to light steel. Without nylon lines the fixed-spool reel would have been just a gadget instead of a revolution.

But above the scrunching of the reels of progress the fly fisher has gone serenely on his sometimes lonely path. Although the eastern United States

[231]

was being inculcated with the virtues of trout fishing at the turn of the century and wet-fly fishing had long had devoted disciples, it had never fully engaged the popular interest.

There was a practical reason for public apathy. Men like Judge Tuttle were solvent enough to indulge their angling appetites, to make use of our rapidly expanding network of railroads to get where the fishing was good. When *Field & Stream* described the unexcelled trout opportunities in the Sapphire country of North Carolina or in the little-known Rogue River of Oregon, they could hop on a train and reach it quickly. But for a vast number of other men, it was a question of getting your fishing near home or not getting it at all. Thus black bass and panfish became very popular varieties.

Nevertheless, there was a large group of Americans devoted to the trout —rainbow, steelhead, brook, and brown. An early *Field & Stream* writer described a wilderness Indian's astonishment at the white man's terminal tackle—"horsehair leader and single-hair snells and artificial flies on tiny hooks." This was in 1847. The cult of the trout prospered quietly as the decades passed, but it was a wet-fly cult. Though Thad Norris had written about dry-fly fishing on the Willowemoc in New York as early as 1864, only a handful of Americans used the dry fly in the years before 1912; it has been estimated there were only a few hundred of them. But just before World War I, men like Theodore Gordon, Emlyn Gill, and George LaBranch began to preach the gospel of the top-water lure, and it took hold. The transition from enameled to vacuum-dressed lines, introduced in 1930, and from soft rods to sharply tapered ones marks the rise of trouting popularity as we know it today.

There is a noticeable trend now toward fly fishing, which will always remain the epitome of all angling. Actually, the case for coexistence is strong. Some form of plug casting must exist, whether with the fixed spool or the multiplier, but of the increased angling population created by the relative simplicity of the spinning technique, a fair percentage will develop the confidence and interest that make the fly rod a career.

Last spring, 105 members and guests of the Harrisburg Fly Fishers Club gathered at a formal dinner to examine a split-bamboo fly rod made by Solon Phillippe in the year 1862. By way of whetting their appetites for the event, the club had already established that Samuel Phillippe made the first American rent-and-glued cane rod in 1846. And that led to the erection of a state historical marker at the site of Phillippe's home in Easton, Pennsylvania. But the eleven and a half foot shaft made by his son was the first known example of a six-strip bamboo rod, which made it the progenitor of modern rods.

Dr. Donald K. Cadzow, director of the Pennsylvania Historical Museum, accepted the rod for permanent display. Whether the club has won the international Donnybrook which has raged for years about who made the first rod entirely of split bamboo remains to be seen. The British have contenders for the title, notably Lane and Aldred, and it may that—like most articles of tackle—the fly rod slowly evolved through the sharing of common experience.

When contrasted to a meeting which I attended at the New York office of the Owens-Corning Fiberglas Corporation in 1948, the Harrisburg unveiling and formal totemization of Phillippes, *père et fils*, is sharply nostalgic. The fiber-glass meeting was held in an ultrageometric showroom, and my invitation promised to clarify the role of glass in the tackle industry. I was met at the door by a young lady who held a sheaf of publicity releases in one hand and swatches of glass cloth in the other. Coffee was served, followed by martinis, which I traced to a source behind a curtain of fiber glass. As I sipped my coffee I studied the release, which informed me that rods were now being built in four ways: the convolite process, cylindrical molded, molded rectangular, and cellophane wrapped. The young lady then offered to introduce me to members of the engineering staff and led me to a spot where three young men were in earnest conversation on polyester-type resins. One of them, readily identified as a practiced lecturer by his ability to hold papers, swatches, coffee, and conversation, informed me that since fiber glass is a solution of metal oxides, the fibers can exist indefinitely, cannot absorb moistures up to 1000 degrees F. He further explained that by varying such things as amount of glass, makeup of the plastic which binds the fibers together, and taper, a manufacturer can produce rods of different strengths, weights, and actions. Having only a minimal knowledge of engineering, I turned the subject from thermal-expansion coefficients to casting, but he was not a fisherman, so I tactfully retreated.

I doubt that men in afterages will go searching for Dr. Arthur M. Howald's original heat-treated Plaskon 911-11 resin-reinforced fly rod, even though it is the most significant tool in the history of tackle making. Glass has replaced everything from steel to noibwood, but it has not entirely replaced bamboo, and it doubtless never will. Glass is impersonal. It lacks the warmth of a master's touch. Nevertheless, when the Shakespeare Tackle Company sponsored Howald's revolutionary rod in 1947, it went off like a delayed-action bomb, and without doubt it is the quantitative future of rod building.

The fish themselves have changed. While the brown trout was little more than a curiosity the year *Field & Stream* was born, this Scotch-German import is now a dominant factor in our national fishing. With generation after generation of hatchery trout being funneled into our rivers, purist anglers are concerned because the brown is no longer a "free riser." Having no memory pattern to shape his insect diet, the world's foremost surface feeder must start his career by learning to eat natural food. Well, the modern fish culturist can correct everything from anemia to basic nutritional deficiencies among trout, and presumably he will develop a race of fish with retentive mental apparatus. Indirectly, the trend has already begun with the crossbreeding of brook trout and lake trout to produce the "splake," a fish combining the weight of the laker and the insect appetite of the brookie.

And while the men of science can point with pride to minor miracle-making of this kind, the keepers of the public domain can claim a greater victory; nature, after all, can be more readily cajoled than the pressure of special interests. Stalking the West like a trio of blanket Indians are timber, irrigation, and hydroelectric power projects, and it's only because of militant conservationists that millions of steelhead have been saved. The East, long ago ravished by pollution and lumbering, is slowly healing, and progressive anglers grow stronger each day.

Realizing their share of the responsibility, the Association of Tackle Manufacturers in 1950 formed the national Sport Fishing Institute under the able aegis of the late Dr. R. W. Eschmeyer. The Institute, devoted to conservation education, is the first logical attempt to blend science with business, and is dedicated to the proposition that career biologists shall not find themselves mumbling in a void.

The rich diversity of resources, techniques, and equipment within reach of today's angler flows directly from the interest and the passion of intrepid men devoted to the fisherman's weal. Almost sixty years have passed since Judge Tuttle started out on his Ozark travels. He would scarcely recognize the modern fishing scene, and he would certainly disclaim any responsibility for its phenomenal cultivation. He was, as we have said, a sober man. But the history of angling is really the story of such as he, willing to try new techniques and equipment, to explore new grounds. Bait caster, fly fisherman, threadliner—all have some kinship with the judge and the men who followed him. Awkward and intense, old-fashioned and streamlined, these sixty years are your legacy.

28

MY OLD KENTUCKY REEL

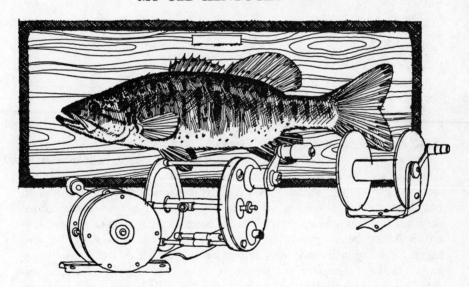

Some years ago when I was serving as *Popular Mechanics'* boating and outdoors editor, my boss—a nonfisherman—asked me to explain to him, and then to the magazine's readers, why certain old fishing reels seem to have a mystique and attraction for fishermen like old shotguns have for hunters or early engines for mechanics. I found it easier to feel mystique than explain it, and as I cast about for a precedent in this delicate task, A. J. McClane popped up everywhere I looked. In addition to his ubiquitousness as an angling historian, Al has a rare talent for evoking nostalgia without either becoming saccharine or straying from the facts. In the current revival of the cult of the black bass (the genus has survived several surges of popularity since the beginning of the century), much gibberish has been written about the origins of the tackle that first made bass angling the art and science it can be. In the following account, A. J. guides us through those early days with a clarity and precision only matched by the reels themselves. Yet in the process he enhances the mystery of their creation.

GWR

MY OLD KENTUCKY REEL

There was a group of anglers living in Kentucky at the turn of the nineteenth century who were convinced that the road to happiness lay in fishing for black bass. To be precise, this was more than a conviction, because in the same way they were convinced that it was a good idea to eat. They went down in history as the most rabid collection of technicians that ever spooked a fish. At that time, the Kentucky River was a free-flowing stream where the people of Bourbon County dipped their branch water and savored the crystal melody of a singing reel. The fact that reels could sing had its basis in fact, a feature of one reel was the "bell click," which was made on the same principle as an alarm clock. The bells were tuned in thirds, and when a fish was hooked—sweet music filled the angler's ears. We can presume that the actual music fell short of the reel's ability to make it, but this was tuned to the period in which our hero lived. Enter here the man who revolutionized the sport.

George Snyder migrated from Pennsylvania to Hopewell, Kentucky, in 1803. He was a watchmaker by profession and, like most honest anglers, seldom concerned with snaring worldly luxuries. In fact, George mended the march of time just to keep Bourbon County anglers on schedule. After trusting him with their watches, they brought reels for repair, and, having a craftsman's pride in the smooth clicking of parts, it was a simple matter to put them in shape. There were only two kinds of bait-casting reels available in that day—the English single-action reel made of brass, or the wooden kind usually made from a discarded sewing spool mounted on a frame by the local tinsmith. The rods used by these pioneer bass fishermen were native woods (bethabara, hickory, Osage orange, etc.) nearly 10 feet long, but they were extremely light—weighing from 4 to 6 ounces. With a fine raw-silk line they could cast live minnows about fifty or sixty feet, provided the wind was right. The "cast" was what we know as strip casting today. The angler would lay coils of line in the bottom of his boat or, if he was really good, hold them in his hands and propel the bait with a side-swiping motion. The inertia of a heavy single-action spool was too much for the bait to overcome.

This was nearly one hundred years before James Heddon manufactured the first bass plugs, so Snyder's customers were actually looking for a very sensitive spool with which to cast live baits. Having a watchmaker's knowledge of gearing, one thing became immediately apparent to George—the spool should revolve several times to every turn of the crank handle, not once, the way single-action reels do. That was a waste of mechanical efficiency, so he set out to make things right.

History in the making is seldom more recognizable than a horseman galloping through the park. We might both admire his skill, never realizing that the horse is a runaway and that the rider eventually broke his neck. Thus different observers come upon the episode admiring his form, or wondering how long he will stay in the saddle, or wondering at the very last where he will land. Being a bluegrass gentleman, George Snyder didn't fall off a horse. Historically speaking, he was seen at a wild gallop. In 1810, he built the Kentucky reel—the first multiplying reel in the world—and although elected president of the Bourbon County Anglers Association, he remained unknown to the angling public.

There was no such thing as mass production in those days, so even though George had won local acclaim in making the greatest reel ever, he could make very few of them. However, more watchmakers were about. You must remember that these men were watchmakers by virtue of their training, but this peculiar history of Kentucky's repairmen happened at a time when the Licking, Elkhorn, Stoner, and dozens of other streams were heavily populated with black bass and walleyes. Some of those timepiece experts would no more repair a watch than write a cycle sonnet on the subject. There was too much fishing to be done, and Snyder's clients were flipping their minnows with telling effect.

[237]

In the Snyder reel, the steel ends of the spool shaft were beveled to points, which in turn fitted in beveled recesses of pivots that screwed into the center caps of the outer disc plates of the reel. This compensating measure would take up any wear and the running of the reel could be regulated by a turn of these screw pivots. How sound George's methods were is best shown in the reel he made for the Honorable Brutus Clay in 1821. Seventy years later the same reel was being used by Clay's son! This, like all of his reels, had its pillars riveted to the back plate and projecting through the inner front plate, where they were secured with wire keys. Snyder reels were also quite narrow in spool diameter and long, in accordance with the belief that a long narrow spool runs more rapidly than a short one of greater diameter—all things being equal. On some of his reels he built an oddly shaped flat lever to operate the click spring with a pin working in a curved slot.

There are pivotal characters in any story—those who innocently contribute to the course of events—like Mrs. O'Leary's cow in Chicago or, as in our narrative, Judge Mason Brown in Frankfort, Kentucky. His Honor did nothing more than lose his reel, and finding George too busy to make him a new one, he went to another watchmaker by the name of Jonathan F. Meek. Although Jonathan has often been credited with "inventing" the bait-casting reel, let it be stated here that he had only the improving urge, and because of the rapidity of events that followed, he was often seen riding George's historical horse. Jonathan's reel was an improvement over the Snyder. His best work was probably the reel he made for a customer named Higgins. There was a collar around the crank shaft; the ends of the spool did not project, and the click-and-drag springs were operated by sliding buttons, as in the modern reel. He made the reel for Judge Brown in 1832 and continued making reels along until 1840, when he formed a partnership with his brother, Benjamin F. Meek, who was, of course, a watchmaker. Ben proved so good at building reels that for a while he made all of their production, stamping the side plates "J. F. & B. F. Meek."

I would hesitate to tell you of the gallons of mellowed branch water that passed down the throats of Walton's disciples in the year 1840. But this simple and moral diet was accompanied by platters heaped with chunks of black bass, like warm snowballs flaked with gold, and these foods were not without spiritual profit. The Kentucky rifle had sent a shiver of dread through the savage breast, and in tracking the clay feet of history, we now find our bluegrass pioneers living by the best traditions of Old Isaac. They would fish at the drop of a jug, or, as a popular ballad, "You Get a Jug and I'll Get a Pole," allowed—at the filling of one. These were unquestionably days of inspired merriment. The art of jugging for catfish had its origin in the picnic parties of their forefathers. Sport fishing was on the march, however, as there are evidences of fly fishing for black bass just six years later and a fantastic demand for Meek reels.

At about this time, still another maker of watches turned to reels, a man named J. H. Hardman of Louisville, Kentucky. His reels were a great improvement on the Snyders and the Meeks. Instead of the 3 to 1 and 3½ to 1 gear ratio popularized by Snyder, Hardman used a 4 to 1 gearing—and as a result he is often credited with making the first quadruple multiplying reel. However, George Snyder had been using the quadruple gearing in his personal reels several years before Hardman began building. Hardman did make a more modern looking reel; he shortened the spool and increased the diameter, affixed the pillars to the disc plates by screws instead of riveting, and added some ornamentation. The use of screws, incidentally, made the Hardman reel the first one having a "take-down" feature. The Hardman reel of 1845 was made of German silver with gold-plated click buttons and screws. But there's another name to contend with—a watchmaker who had visited Hopewell, Kentucky (then called Paris) to see George Snyder.

Benjamin C. Milam was most unique in that he stated flatly that he didn't like the watch repair business. On the streets of Frankfort this pronouncement was probably no more epoch-making than a comment on the weather. Milam joined forces with the Meeks as an apprentice. After the retirement of Jonathan Meek, the firm became known as Meek and Milam, which was in turn dissolved at the end of five years. The partners continued to occupy the same store, Milam devoting himself to making reels while Ben Meek reestablished his watchmaking and jewelry business. All reels made by Mr. Milam continued to be stamped "Meek and Milam" until 1878. Having trained his son to the trade, Milam took him into the business under the firm name of B. C. Milam & Son. How well they succeeded may be seen in the fact that a Milam reel won the international first prize in Chicago in 1893 at the World's Fair, at the Fisheries Exposition in Bergen, Norway, in 1898, and at the World's Exposition in Paris, France, in 1904. Grover Cleveland wrote Milam letters of appreciation for the workmanship in his reels.

The Kentucky reel prior to 1880 was entirely a handmade mechanism. Yet every one of them was made with painstaking exactness. No two screws were alike, and as a result every screw had to be put back in its proper place after the reel was taken apart. The lathe work, fitting, and filing were truly perfect. Reel handles were chopped out of sheet metal with a cold chisel and then filed to shape. The gears were usually slotted on Swiss cutting engines and then filed by hand. The main gear wheel was always made of brass casting or a section of brass rod that was hammered on an anvil, while the small wheel or pinion gear was made of the very best tempered tool steel. This resulted in a gearing that was almost indestructible. Considering the labor involved, Ben Meeks's monthly production, for instance, was about seven reels, and these would sometimes bring sixty or seventy dollars apiece. Customers didn't ask the price in those days—they ordered and were charged what the builder thought it was worth. The best a sporting goods dealer could hope for was a 10 percent discount, and the order was filled when the "manufacturer" was in the mood.

An old reel exhibited at the World's Fair in Chicago in 1893 stamped "Meek and Milam" was actually of 1844 vintage; the pillars are still of the Snyder plan, as is the narrow spool. The improvements are a collar on the crank, sliding buttons for the click and drag, and, for the first time, a bent or U-shaped click spring formed from a piece of watch spring. With exception of the ornamentation, this reel closely resembles the Hardman in general form.

Ben Meek wearied of his watch trade, and in 1883 he headed for Louisville, Kentucky, where he started a reel business once again. His indecision can probably be explained by the fact that Ben was never an angler. Of all our Kentucky reel-makers, this autocratic master knew little about fishing and couldn't care less. He formed a partnership with his two sons, and together they created a new departure in the gearing of reels, which is called the "spiral gear." This consisted of cutting the teeth of the wheel and pinion diagonally instead of horizontally. The space between the teeth at their base was rounded instead of being made flat or square. But even more significant was the fact that the Meeks started building reels in an organized fashion. Here is what the *Tri-Weekly Kentucky Yeoman* of November 21, 1882, had to say in an article on Benjamin F. Meek:

> *He proposes, we learn, to make his reels entirely of wrought metal, no casting or drawn wire being used, and the machinery will be as perfect as that of an astronomical instrument. For this purpose he has provided himself with machinery of the most improved pattern, most of it being invented by himself, and made under his immediate direction at Waltham, Massachusetts, by the American Watch Tool Company. This, which is costly and intricate, will run by a gas engine, which he is now engaged in putting up. But such is the nature of the works that the greater part has to be done by hand, and Mr. Meek says that there will not be a piece that will not receive*

his touch. . . . He will not be able to turn out reels before the first of February, but after that time he will endeavor to supply the demands. We commend Mr. Meek as in every respect worthy of the respect and confidence of the people of Louisville, and as to his reels, they will commend themselves.

Meek made reels for the next sixteen years, and by the time he died in 1901, he had made some of the most important contributions toward the development of modern bait-casting reels. His use of spiral gears instead of spur gears and the introduction of jeweled pivot bearings reduced wear, resulting in a smooth-running reel. The tiniest weight would set a Meek spool in motion. E. J. Martin of Rockville, Connecticut, started making braided-silk casting lines in 1884, so the delicate sensitivity of Meek reels was brought to full flower. Ben cashed in his chips just as the game ended; bait-casting rods had been growing shorter all the time—now they used 5-foot bamboo sticks and cast Dowagiac minnows in "Kalamazoo" style. The overhead, or Kalamazoo, cast was the dawn of a new era, and the end of the Kentucky reelmaker. Bait casting became immensely popular, and mass production methods became absolutely essential.

The Talbots, Gayles, Noels, the Sages, and many other itinerant watchmakers had burned the midnight oil in the backrooms of Kentucky shops. However, none of these men made significant changes in the multiplying reel. A Wisconsin firm, Wheeler and McGregor, made a device for lever-winding the line—which Ben Meek perfected for them. Their original design is still embodied in the level-wind devices of today. But the old-time reel makers would have none of it; the bluegrass artists stuck to their Kentucky pattern right down to the very last. These were great reels, and while none of them are made now, the modern bait-casting reel owes its existence to the watchmakers of Frankfort, Louisville, and Paris, Kentucky. Some of their reels are still being fished with; it's possible that there's one in your attic.

So George Snyder did not declare a war, change a money system, or build a rocket to the moon. But students of angling who learned to cast before the age of spinning mark his name well. Like sinners in sackcloth we sniff the dry roses of regret—not only has the Kentucky reel vanished, but now a geometrized, streamlined, nonrevolving cone is dissolving the ranks of bait casters. Things have gotten to a state where a mere stripling of a child can throw a plug to the other side of the lake. There is no more apprenticeship to serve, no more backlashes to philosophize over, no purring of a carefully balanced spool—and these moderns don't even smell of oil. How can they?

[241]

Few people know where to squirt at the uncannily correct self-contained reels of spinning. But take heart, good friend, my old Kentucky reel was a way of living rather than a manufactured product, and may you and I be granted no worse an inheritance while we walk under the sun.

29

CAME A REVOLUTION

Fishing with a famous fisherman can be an unpleasant experience—particularly if your companion is self-conscious and vain about his reputation. Competitiveness infects the morning like a virus, and by noon you wished you had stayed in bed. But Al McClane is different—particularly if you're fishing on what he considers to be home waters. Since he has fished almost everywhere in the world, most places qualify as McClane's "home waters." Therefore, as host, he feels it his responsibility to do all he can to see that you get good fishing. Of course, short of catching the fish himself, no man can guarantee another success. Yet even if the fishing is slow, A. J. has a rich and varied store of angling anecdotes that make the hours fly.

Many of these stories relate to his friendship with Charles Ritz. The bond between Europe's greatest fly fisherman and his American counterpart is intricate and substantial. Just one indication of their closeness: Al McClane is the only person Ritz tolerates calling him "Charley." Just after World War II, when McClane was still a struggling writer/film maker, Ritz helped him find inexpensive lodgings in Paris and taught him several of his favorite recipes, an interest Al expanded over the years into his present title as *Officier Commandeur* in the *Confrérie des Chevaliers du Tastevin*, a world renowned wine and food society, and upcoming publication of his *Encyclopedia of Sea Food*. In appreciation Al dedicated *The American Angler* (1951) to his friend and *pêcheur exceptionnel*, Charles Ritz, and helped Charles find an American publisher for *Pris sur le Vif*. Today *A Fly Fisher's Life* has gone through several American and English editions.

Whenever a mutual friend is with Albert or Charles, but not with them both together, an inordinate amount of time is spent by the one extolling the virtues of his missing counterpart. The first time I met Ritz at his Paris hotel, his initial inquiry was into the health and well-being of Al and Patti McClane. When Al found I had recently returned from France, he asked if I had seen Monique and *le grand Charles*—and he didn't mean DeGaulle.

While compiling this anthology of McClane's best writings, I knew it would be incomplete without some story involving the two men. As you read what follows, remember that the year is 1948 and that Europeans have a devotion to angling gimmicks that far exceeds our own. The only important difference between then and now is that the Risle, once *the* incomparable Norman chalk stream, has been ruined by the residues of a processing plant.

GWR

CAME A REVOLUTION

We watched the open water near the bank very closely. Minutes passed. Two hours passed. I had yet to see my first trout. I had traveled 3,000 miles to make a movie on chalk-stream fishing—and here we were, belly down, nose out, looking for one of the characters.

This peculiar situation came about last summer after I had interviewed Charles Ritz to get some dope on the parabolic rod. Charles mentioned at the time that a movie on the chalk streams of northwestern France would be a valuable addition to the *Field & Stream* Library—"but it really can't be done; the trout are much too shy." Not only was this an understatement (for the movie took thirty days to make), but at the time it sparked an idea. The film library had always needed a good instructive picture on dry-fly fishing, and what better setting could there be than the classic streams on which fly fishing was born? There was only one hitch—chalk-stream trout are caught by tossing the line into the next county, and to meet the limitations of a camera we had to develop a system or a method of fishing that would keep the action within a forty- or fifty-foot radius.

"Leave us study the matter on hand by stalking a few trout. I think, when you see them eat, everything will be simple. I have picked the most colossally difficult river you ever saw—the fish are epicures. They have read all the best books on fishing. They have eyes like a wohol."

"You mean owl?"

"Yes, and they are wonderfully impossible to catch."

"Impossible?"

"Yes, you will have a wonderful time. I'm sure we will not catch a movie."

"But how much longer must we lie here?"

"Shhh. Here he comes!"

The dark form glided slowly upward, then, scarcely making a ripple, just pushed the tip of his nose above the surface and quietly sucked in a floating dun. Gradually dropping back and downward in the slow current, the trout looked carefully from right to left, from left to right. Satisfied that nothing edible had escaped him, the fish slipped into the weeds.

"There's a typical chalk-stream trout. He's like a fat man living in a cafeteria."

I tried to brush the nettles off my nose, push Charley's rod butt out of my eye, and lift my stomach off the grass long enough to shake the ants out of my waders.

"You'll see," he continued as we crawled upstream, "the river is lousy with food. The weeds are full of snails, shrimps, nymphs, and all that stuff. Most of all—it's lousy with fish. When you see the mayflies hatch, you will go wonderfully crazy. The water just boils!"

"I am already wonderfully crazy from these lousy French ants."

"These are nothing. Ants—pooh! When you stand up, they will fall in your socks and you can trample them to death. In France we have no black-flies."

"That's good."

Twice as we crawled forward my hands dropped in bottomless tunnels, just an arm's width in diameter, which left me momentarily balanced on my chin. "I hope the creatures who live in these holes have a gentle disposition."

"Shh. Look up there."

Clearing an opening under some bushes, I stuck my head out and took a good look.

The Risle is a beautiful river throughout its length. It meanders between gentle hills, touching the feet of ancient Norman châteaus. Crossing farmlands, it reaches thick stands of poplar and willow before a long run to the North Sea. The name "chalk stream" is derived from the calcareous clay bottom, typical of those streams that were part of the ocean centuries ago. Sea urchins, shellfish, and other fossilized remains of marine life are commonly found in shallow water.

The trout that live in these waters offer a sport that cannot be paralleled by any other type of fishing. They are wise to the point of distinction, they feed in the most impossible places—in pockets as big as a teacup, and channels no wider than this page—they can make the most expert angler look, feel, and act awkward. Because of the weeds the oxygen content of the water is high, food of all types extremely abundant, and the trout are in perfect condition—small heads and thick bodies.

A close approach is impossible, drag on the line because of the necessity for cross-stream shots a certainty. In short, it is the finest school in the world for a dry-fly angler. There is no protective current or cover to screen the angler's errors.

The stretch I was looking at was a long piece of crystal-clear water bordered by tules, barbed wire, and sun-bleached cows. It was like many other sections of the river, but with one important difference—the weeds did not grow to the surface. There was fully two feet of open water above the swaying vegetation; from bank to bank it was a smooth run. Several large trout were feeding in midstream. Telltale bubbles floated down, following the soft, dignified suck of trout that would heft two pounds or more.

"You may have the first trout. I will retreat and uncollapse my collapsible landing net. I will also uncollapse my collapsible fishing chair and our collapsible fish cage. By that time you should have the trout at the bank, and if all these devices have worked I shall net the trout for you."

"Thank you, Charles, but I'd much prefer that you catch the first trout, as my suspenders collapsed from too much crawling. In addition, I'm no longer capable of reaching the perpendicular position required by local custom"—and I crawled off to the shade of a friendly willow.

[246]

If you have never had the opportunity of fishing a chalk stream, particularly a difficult river like the Risle, the need for odd implements such as stools, cages, and all the claptrap associated with the game may seem like overindulgence on the part of the angler. But when you get down to brass tacks, there's much to be said for "gadget" fishing. Take the fish cage, for instance.

Nobody ever kills a trout on the Risle. The cage, which has a one-way hinged cover, will hold six or eight good-sized fish. The angler keeps the fish caged—in the water—and at various points along the river deposits the contents in a larger wooden live-box. When the day's fishing is finished, he can pick out those trout that meet the requirements of his appetite, show off the rest, if he's so inclined, then open the door and let them free. In support of the "careful handling—high survival rate" dictum, there is rarely a fish lost, even after this considerable shoving around.

The stool will make a better fisherman out of anyone. In Europe, where the streams are comparatively small and hard-fished, you are expected to pick a stretch of water and stay with it. If you run up and down the river à la Beaverkill you accomplish nothing. A fast pace will flush anglers from the bushes, sour the cows, and send the trout scurrying for cover. The sod banks are as hollow as a drum, and a careless foot will kill the fishing for hours. On the other hand, if you plunk your stool in a likely spot and garner enough willpower to wait for the trout to show his dorsal, much can be learned in the interim.

The trout that Charley was going after were steady feeders, methodical food collectors that loafed about just under the surface. This type of fish is much preferred to the infrequent riser, or those trout caught in the act of "bulging," "tailing," or "smutting." Trout in the bulging and tailing categories may appear to the unsophisticated observer to be the honest fish taking winged insects of some kind or other, but the truth of the matter is they're grabbing a quick meal below the surface. The smutting fish is the common nuisance that confines his feeding to insects so tiny that they defy imitation. Books have been written devoted to the smutters—but no one really catches them. Only by accident.

The half-crouched angler rose cautiously on his knees, rod cocked, carefully coiled line on the grass at his feet. When it comes to the smooth beauty of effortless fly casting, Charley is hard to beat. The yellow line flicked skyward in the blink of an eye, lengthening in fast pulls as he extended about fifty feet at a tangent to the target. In the clear, shadowless waters of a chalk stream even the motion of a high-flying line might easily put the fish down.

Not only was the cast directed away from the trout, but because of their position twenty or twenty-five feet more of line was required to reach them. Confident that his rod had reached its pulling load, he leaned hard against the bamboo on the next cast and with a quick shift of his wrist sent the speeding line upstream where it was checked over the target, dropping lightly to the water. The *fly* was sucked under in a tiny bubble, the deliberate, slow rise of a completely duped trout.

Chalk-stream trout are not ordinarily hard fighters. The fish spend their lives in an almost motionless element where an abundance of food produces the laziest brown trout in the world. Occasionally one will jump and take out a few yards of line, but more often the hooked trout will bore down into a bed of watercress and there, grabbing the weeds with his teeth, defy extraction. Or else the fish will swim under a weed bed, giving the angler no alternative but to try pulling up the stream bottom. Either way you lose.

The system developed by connoisseurs is known as "aquaplaning." The instant the trout is hooked his head is turned shoreward, and with a high-held rod the fish is skidded along the surface and into the net. At least that is the theory.

The first thing Charley's trout did was to jump, and the old maestro was completely disconcerted. Instead of being aquaplaned, the fish—a good 2-pounder on a 3X tippet—became airborne by the tip jerk at the peak of his jump and sailed fully five feet over the surface. Gaining this slack, the fat brown torpedoed into a weed bed, and action ceased.

"I find your tactics very unusual, Mr. Ritz—in fact, I think you are a lousy fisherman."

"Patience. My trout is still hooked; he is merely chewing weeds. I will wait him out."

"While you are waiting you may uncollapse this collapsible landing net, as I have squeezed, pushed, pulled, and shaken every part of its anatomy."

With the snap of a bullwhip the net opened one-third of its length in one plane and in a ghostly fashion extended another third in another plane, and with a dying gasp clicked itself in complete rigor mortis, the flaxen strings dropping from an odd-shaped frame.

"But this net is for egg-shaped fish."

"Do not cast aspersions on my equipment. It took me two years to design this net. The frame was shaped thus to fit inside the third extension. You'll notice what a long handle I've attained."

"I notice. But there are many strings missing from the bottom of the bag. Perhaps we should just swat the trout over the head with the handle when he gets close to the bank."

"Wait. Here comes my fish."

The trout, free from the pressure of a bending rod, was not certain whether it was still hooked or not. This game of possum frequently gets results. The angler lowers his rod, keeping the line slack, and after a period of several minutes the fish gets restless and moves back into open water, or under another weed bed.

The art of chalk-stream fishing is paced at a slow tempo. Like two chess players, the participants are allotted periods of silence to plan the next move. The "bingo" atmosphere of fast-water fishing is remote.

The trout moved leisurely toward the surface, lifting the leader free of the weed bed. The long dragging line which had been playing against the brittle chara suddenly pulled against the fish's jaw, turning him downstream in an erratic run. Half diving and half surfacing, the black-faced trout gave in to the rod's pressure and swam directly into the outstretched net.

"Two and a half pounds easy. Beautiful, no?"

"Beautiful, yes, but your style was pathetic. I don't see how we are going to make a movie on chalk-stream fishing if you're going to crawl in the grass throughout the picture. We must wade in the water, smoke pipes, wear red shirts and deal with fish that struggle for hours. It's all in the script I brought from New York."

"Pooh! You have ants in your waders. We will be here five years before we find enough stupid trout to make a movie. Nobody has ever waded in the Risle."

"Then we're going to revolutionize chalk-stream tactics. The cameraman has to stand up, in back of you, in front of you, in front of the trout, between both of you—in fact, he will climb all over the place. So you might just as well rehearse upright. Let's examine the stream above: I suspect that the heavy weed sections will be easier to work. I once fished a difficult stream in Austria by plowing through the weeds and fishing the pockets; perhaps we can devise a similar approach."

"This will ruin my reputation, kill the sales on my stool and landing net,[1] and cause me to write another book on flyfishing—if it works. *Allons!*"

My first shot was from a high bank, a knob of a hill that offered a screen of tules, putting me about ten feet above the level of the stream. A deep channel barely two feet in width sliced between heavy weed beds slightly across and about sixty feet upstream from where I stood. Three good fish

---

[1] Charles Ritz, an incurable gadgeteer, invented or pioneered the development of many items of fishing tackle, not the least of which was the parabolic rod. However, few people know that he was, also, in the shoe business on the Rue St. Honoré where he invented the après-ski boot.

were pocketed in this run. The audible *slurp, slurp* of steady risers made me confident of a quick kill.

The cast was perfect. By checking the line high in the air, the forebelly of the taper touched the water first, cushioning the arrival of the point and then the leader. A classical stylist might prefer his cast the other way around —fly first, followed by leader, then line. This is not only a nuisance to execute, but throws the fly down hard, scaring any trout worthy of the name into hiding.

The Light Cahill dropped with barely a dimple, and as it drifted back a heavy pale-colored fish turned and quietly mouthed the feathers. I struck hard and fast—a safe and proper reaction when fishing a long line. Before I realized what had happened the trout pirouetted into the roof of a dense weed bed and stood, nose down, with his tail out of water. We had arrived at an impasse on the first move. The tail flickered back and forth, then stopped. Apparently the trout was enjoying the situation.

"Why don't you wade out and put salt on it?"

Under the circumstances there wasn't much to do but wade out and grab the fish by the tail. I did.

"Now that I am in the lousy stream, I will fish this run according to plan."

"Wonderful! You fish and I will make use of my collapsible ear plugs to fool the mosquitoes while I take a snooze. Wake me up when you return."

Chalk-stream fishing is ordinarily accomplished by stalking only rising fish. The rule is to toss out three casts only, rest him, and try again. There's no doubt in my mind that this is the soundest approach when there's a good hatch of flies on the water and the area can be covered from the bank.

The stretch of water I stepped into, however, was fully a hundred feet in width, and the only fishy-looking pockets were along the far bank. In fact, the weeds were so thick that the only place to fish was a foot-wide channel with ninety-nine feet of weed beds on the other side of the river. The water was about hip-deep, and past experience indicated that I could wade to within several yards of the channel as long as I stayed in the grass and didn't move around too much.

Several large trout swam blindly into my legs. I could feel the tap and then the squirming as the fish became oriented in some unseen channel below the weeds. Provided none of these trout headed for the far bank, prospects looked pretty good. Two large trout were feeding under a scraggly bush straight ahead.

About twenty feet from the channel I stopped and waited the duration of a cigarette for the disturbance to settle. A woodpecker banging in high key took time out to look me over, then went back to his drilling. Slightly downstream two small trout were consistently rising against what had once been the foundation of a bridge, probably licking larvae off the coarse cement. While watching their antics I heard the sucking pop of a good fish at close range. A fat black trout had moved from his sunless tunnel under the bush slightly upstream from me and was now weaving in the feeble current about twenty-five feet away.

I began scratching desperately at every tactic I had catalogued, but my hand was too nervous to take orders. A small olive came waltzing downstream, and the big nose barely broke the surface. The fly disappeared with barely a ripple.

Considering how narrow the channel was, there seemed to be only one course open—to cast a right hook (how, I couldn't remember), keeping the line on top of the weeds and causing the leader and fly to swing over the fish without drag. To lay the line directly up the channel was out of the question. I'd have to wade right up the alley.

The first two casts were beautiful left hooks. Cautiously flipping the fly back off the weeds, I undershot the next cast and executed a right that put the fly right on his nose. At that precise instant another olive came flitting off the weed bed and sailed downstream barely an inch away from the Cahill. The trout turned, and sucked in the olive.

A half hour and six flies later, I broke out a package of 5X tippets. I had sunk almost ten inches in the stream bottom from standing in the same spot for so long. "As any dope can plainly see, this is not easy," I thought. "I have matched the trout olive-for-olive, my nerves are shattered, and I am talking to myself."

The next cast was a very poor right hook that put the fly over the rim of the weed bed. The little Cahill was seized in that split second between loss of motion and drift by a heavy, mettlesome fish. Taking the initiative, the fish immediately turned and bolted downstream, following the open water all the way!

The frail arched rod quivered with every tug. Changing tactics, the trout raced into a weed bed below me and began a long contest of sweat-and-worry. Giving all the line I dared, I struggled out of the river and trotted along the bank to get below my quarry. The brown scooted out of the weeds and continued downstream, which still left me bringing up the rear.

I stumbled along, retrieving line, until I had out little more than my twelve-foot leader. Each time the trout stopped I coaxed him close to finish the job, but after four or five passes the fish made a new spurt that tore off more line. The leader was too light to really pressure the fish.

I decided to get back into the water and sneak up on him if possible.

Naturally I assumed that the water was still the same depth twenty yards downstream. It wasn't. I stood my ground in bloated waders with hopes the fish would soon tire.

"You look very silly. I see now why we need pipes. You could put one in your mouth and imitate a submarine," Charley broke in.

"I thought I left you sleeping."

"I was, but one of my collapsible ear plugs collapsed when you galloped downstream. Do you have a trout on?"

"Yes, but I'm waiting him out. Why don't you come over to my side of the stream with your collapsible net—I'm catching a record fish."

"Personally, I will stay here. I cannot help but say that I see no improvement in your system over mine, unless the cameraman works in a diving bell."

"Do not make jokes. I have solved the problem. This fish is an exception. I let him run only to have the satisfaction of playing a fish American style. Be silent a moment. I feel my victim working loose."

The trout broke free of the weeds, but the leader caught, holding him in the open turned slightly on one side. I moved in and grabbed the fish in back of the head and waded for the far bank.

"I once sent a trout like that to a taxidermist, and when he was finished it looked like an ax handle. The corpse had gained four inches. Your trout looks like my taxidermist."

"This is a beautiful fish. I'm going to send that old tarpon in my New York office to Ted Trueblood and hang this trout in its place. Let us collapse our collapsible stool, cage, net, and ear plugs, and return whence we came. Tomorrow I want you to go to Paris and hire a collapsible cameraman, as I think we can make a movie."

30

THE *FIELD & STREAM* HAT TRICK

A. J. McClane has so many talents, skills, and credentials, only temperament and personal choice have kept him from running a publishing house, a tackle company, a university, an army division, or a first-class hotel. Instead his career has been devoted to angling, good food, and the company of interesting people. Anything that interferes with these three essentials of life is not to be tolerated. Of course, young outdoor editors don't start out in such full control of their destinies. In the beginning they must be polite and patient (if sometimes puzzled) with their superiors. They must write countless blurbs and captions they'd just as soon not write. And they must spend untold hours cutting, pasting, and doing much else reminiscent of those days they received gold stars for good work in second grade. But the light of freedom at the end of the tunnel keeps many of them at it. In The Field & Stream Hat Trick," A. J. looks back with a smile on some of his early days of trial by fire.

This story first appeared in the seventy-fifth anniversary issue of Field & Stream. Besides giving us a sample of A. J.'s considerable talents as a raconteur, the article offers us a brief look at one of the last of the great independent magazine owners. Men like Eltinge F. Warner ruled the publishing world from the turn of the century to just after World War II when communications conglomerates began buying them out in a search for corporate empire. Names like Frank A. Munsey, John A. McGuire, and Henry R. Luce (the latter creating a conglomerate of his own) are rich with associations of this bygone era, and Warner more than holds his own with the best of them.

He bought control of Field & Stream in 1908 after the death of co-founder John P. Burkhard. Warner then built up the magazine's circulation in part by expanding his other business interests, including an executive position in two motion-picture companies from 1916 to 1924, publisher of Smart Set (edited by H. L. Mencken and George Jean Nathan) from 1914 to 1926, and head of a magazine chain after 1933. Warner was a crack shot, a devoted fisherman, and an energetic crusader on behalf of wildlife conservation. He hired another crusader, former federal warden Ray Holland, to be his editor-in-chief, and beefed up the staff with such outstanding writers as Corey Ford, Robert Ruark, and Ed Zern. In some quarters he is best remembered today as the man who introduced the tango to Paris with Miss Irene Castle.

"The Hat Trick" skims lightly over the three decades A. J. McClane has been with Field & Stream. His career certainly represents one of the greatest associations between an editor and a magazine in the history of outdoor writing. In addition, it's appropriate we close with this story, for not only does it have us exit laughing in the best traditions of the magazine, it leaves us sighing with relief that E. F. Warner had the good sense to rehire A. J. after firing him the same day he was hired!

GWR

THE *FIELD & STREAM* HAT TRICK

Eltinge F. Warner was the publisher of *Field & Stream* when I delivered my pale white body to Madison Avenue in 1947. The office looked like a taxidermist's shop. The fact that he hired me in the morning, fired me before lunch (because I took a coffee break across the street), and rehired me in the afternoon was prophetic.

For a long time he couldn't remember my name, but then he identified John Steinbeck as that guy down South who owns the bird dog—so it was nothing personal. E. F. was a dapper little trapper who somehow reminded me of a Groucho Marx with the spending habits of a J. Paul Getty. Expense money was kept in a piggy bank by our treasurer, Elmer Chambers, so we always knew when E. F. was going on a trip. "Chaim-burrs!" he'd bellow. All the mounted heads on the wall would shudder. Even those not on the wall.

I don't recall *why* we went grouse hunting, but E. F. enlisted those editors and friends who were breathing or ambulant and marched us over the Catskills. E. F. took the lead, puffing on his cigar like a steam engine straining at a bunch of empty boxcars. His gnat's-eye shooting was legendary. He bopped every bird that was idiot enough to flush, and by nightfall back at the lodge he was ready to take the whole staff on. Me, I was first on his list.

His voice had the solemn tone used by Pat O'Brien at half time when he struts into the Notre Dame locker room to announce this one is for the Gipper. "McClane, you are . . . well, you are remarkable. I *watched* you. I told our host here that you have the fastest reflexes I've ever seen in any man." The name was right, but he had me mixed up with Lefty Page. I fired only two shots all day and knocked down a pair of innocent pine boughs. "I'd like this gentleman to see just how fast you react." The put-on was great.

"I'm going to place this fifty-cent piece on the table and cover it with my hat. Now, I want you to stand at the ready with your hand about a foot over the hat, and when I pull it away, hit that coin as fast as you can. I've bet our friend here *five dollars* that your hand will cover it before he sees it." E. F. whipped the hat away and I slammed my palm over the coin. Our host had the beady-eyed expression of a mouse learning to be a rat. "I saw it, E. F., I saw it. Just caught a glimpse," he tutted. Honest Ben Turpin. Pencils and a tin cup he needs.

"Well, he's tired. Been a long day. Whadda you say, double-or-nothing? I can always take it out of McClane's salary." *Yuk-yuk.*

I was ready now. Oh, I was ready! Me with the fastest reflexes. I cocked my hand over the hat and when E. F. started his motion, I damn near knocked the table down. The egg exploded in my face. It squished upward like a fountain between my splayed fingers. Nobody told me that our publisher was a sleight-of-hand artist who could palm an egg as quickly as he changed a rate card.

I should have been suspicious. Whenever he stoked a cigar, which was about ninety-five times a day, he would pull a wooden match out of his pocket—already lit. E. F. rolled his stogie around and stared at me. "Well, now you look like a *Field & Stream* editor." Like I said, the guy was prophetic.

*

I wrote my first article in 1941 which was published by *Outdoor Life*. I did a bit of free-lancing while in college, and in 1944 I received a letter from *Field & Stream* suggesting a job interview. The only problem was that my mail was being delivered to a foxhole in Normandy. As a patriot I had a strong urge to go home and do something for the war effort. My chaplain read the letter and said in the voice used by Pat O'Brien when he turned his collar backwards and walked into the death cell, "Let's pray together, son." He had run out of slips.

Anyhow, in 1947, thanks to Ted Trueblood, who wisely went back to Idaho, I inherited his scissors and paste pot plus a couple of rusty fishhooks. I phoned the news to dear mother who cried, "But what will you do?"

"Fish."

"What kind of work is that? We had such hopes for you, son. . . ."

For. twenty-three years I've been trying to think of an answer. The title "Fishing Editor" is a bit misleading. In this enlightened age of radio and TV talk shows, other people have made some suggestions. Like the day I arrived late at a Los Angeles studio and was greeted by a public-relations man who trotted me into what looked like the broom closet. The sheet on top of his clipboard read: "McClane, *Field & Stream*, World Champion Fly Caster." As I recall, Johnny Dieckman held the title at the time—and I never did—but before I could object, I was practically shoved in the lap of some yo-yo sitting at a microphone. He wore a mohair shirt, pursed lips, and open-toed sandals. This cutie couldn't even read.

"Lay-dees and gennel-min, today we are going to talk with the world's champion fly catcher." *Oi vay*, I could feel that egg sliding down my nose. "Can you tell our audience, Mr. McClane, just how you *catch* those little darlings?"

"*Bluh, blah*. Fly paper?"

Then there was the former Hollywood actress with a talk show who refused to talk before the show. No warm-up. Her P.R. man said it was a rule because it resulted in a more informal interview. Wendy Barrie's slogan was, "Be A Good Bunny"—whatever the hell that meant. Hugh Hefner hadn't cornered the market yet.

"And now bunnies," she cooed, "Sitting next to me is the Fashion Editor of *Field & Stream* who is going to tell us what's *au courant* in the out-of-doors." The hat was on the table.

"*Bluh, blah*. Hobnail boots?"

*

The classic was one that never appeared on camera. My wife and I were flying down to Washington, D. C., to visit General Walter Bedell Smith, who was then Director of the Central Intelligence Agency. We were going to spend the weekend bass fishing in Virginia. It was a rainy night over Dulles Airport, and air traffic was stacked clear back to Baltimore. The pilot announced that we'd hold for about an hour and a half. I no sooner slouched back in my seat than I could feel the plane going down. Fast. I didn't even see the seat-belt sign go on. We rolled to a halt and the pilot and copilot popped out like jacks from a box to wish everybody goodnight. What a way to run an airline, I thought. They probably let the stewardesses make the landing.

When Patti and I stepped off the ramp, a tough-looking character in a trench coat grabbed me by the arm and said, "This way." Before I could have a heart attack, he steered me into a black limousine with Patti meekly following. There sat "Beedle" polishing his mahogany tackle box.

"Cripes, I thought you'd never get here."

"Get here? We beat everybody down."

"Sure," said Beedle, "I told the tower there is a Russian spy on board accompanied by a blonde."

*

Fishing with Beedle was never dull. When he was Commander of the First Army, we were frequent visitors at A. F. Wechsler's mountain retreat —a 10,000-acre estate that straddles the Neversink and Bushkill Rivers. The Bushkill is a pretty little stream that meanders through heavy forest. It becomes club water about halfway down after it leaves the Wechsler property. Occasionally we'd meet a club member who strayed into Wechsler's water, but it was a tacit agreement that if anybody got lost, the respective owners wouldn't push the panic button.

[257]

For a long time we politely ignored that top pool of the club section. We'd fish to where the Bushkill Club posters began, then stand around admiring the trout rising on the other side of a single barbed-wire strand. Just about dark one evening, Beedle rationalized that we more or less had an invitation to fish the club water and anyhow, a big brownie was working on mayflies in midstream and to present the fly properly, one of us had to get below the wire to be in position. We both volunteered. I don't think we'd been in that pool five minutes when all hell broke loose.

First it was sirens. It sounded like thirty police cars. Which it was. Then horns started to blow. Then powerful lights—obviously spotlights—sweeping the treetops.

"Geez, these guys mean business!" said Beedle. "Let's get the hell outta *here*." We floundered up a muddy bank and headed across the wire, reeling in our lines as we ran. We could hear people shouting. "Let's advance as far upstream as we can," commanded the General, always the tactician. "Nobody will know we were *near* the place."

Judging by the number of voices echoing along the Bushkill, the entire First Army knew where we were. Beedle plowed through the bushes and I followed. Before long we were surrounded. Flashlights closed in from all directions. We stood there blowing like two beached whales. The woods were full of cops and Wechslers (and *that* is a formidable family).

The first state trooper to reach us was a big guy who pointed his light in our faces. "Which one of you is General Smith?" A brilliant question.

"I am," said Beedle in that basso profundo tone saved for dress parades.

"Sir." The trooper snapped to attention. "I have the honor of informing you that President Truman announced your appointment as Director of the Central Intelligence Agency, and you are to proceed to Washington at once. Sir."

Now you'd think Harry would have sent Beedle a coded message by pigeon or quietly dropped a CIA agent in the Bushkill by parachute. That brown trout was 5 pounds if it was an ounce! I'll say one thing—he took it like a true general. All he said under his breath was (delete expletive).

*

One of the things that changed at *Field & Stream* after Eltinge F. Warner's tenure was our emphasis on travel. With the airline boom of the fifties, angling really became an international sport. To keep apace, editors had to abandon the wilds of Madison Avenue, and it was inevitable in these politically unstable times that some of us would arrive in the right place at the wrong time. I have fished in seventy-one countries and as a result inadvertently attended various revolutions. I had one lucky streak in which four trips produced three revolts and one earthquake. Jolly old Hugh Grey, the editor then, knew how to boost a feller's morale.

"Blow up any countries lately?" *Har-de-har*. Then there was the shouted office joke so everybody could yuk-yuk. "Who's McClane's travel agent? I want to remember not to use him."

I was fishing for tarpon when the spear hit the fan in the Congo, which is hardly worth recounting here, as it was nothing more than an exercise in survival. My photographer, Louis Renault, who was later killed in a helicopter crash, went north across the border and I got stuck in Leopoldville. But our trip to Havana—that was pure E. F. With so many people taking free rides to Cuba these days, Fidel Castro has things better organized now. However, we went before the Bearded One returned stray airplanes. Naturally, *Field & Stream* scoops 'em all.

Vic Barothy had a famous houseboat operation based at the Isle of Pines in Cuba. Every time I tried to get down to his place, some priority trip came along, but we corresponded regularly. Sooner or later we'd get together.

The last week in December of 1958 was a good time for me. Don Carter had a DC-3 available; he invited the president of our company, Edgar T. Rigg, General Paul Berrigan, myself, and our respective wives, and we headed for Cuba on what the travel agencies call "a glorious Caribbean vacation."

The Havana tower wouldn't clear us to the Isle of Pines. When we landed in Havana I noticed a pair of P-47's sitting on the strip doing run-ups and slung under their wings were 500-pounders. Batista's people obviously didn't know what to do with us. Fidel was taking the town in a matter of hours, or so they thought, and what arrives but a private plane and an American general with a bunch of ding-a-lings headed for one of his key targets— Isla de Pinos. The American Embassy had said that Castro was in the hills of Oriente. That's what *they* knew.

After a lot of palaver, they impounded the plane and sent us to the Nacional Hotel. It wasn't exactly the liveliest place in town, but the Cubans made it interesting. What do you do with eight people carrying thirty pieces of baggage so you can keep tabs on 'em? *Oi vay*. The hat trick.

We'd get up in the morning and haul all our baggage down to the lobby. Cuban taxis were about the size of a sardine can, so you could spend an hour stuffing spaces only to learn that you need two more cabs for the leftovers. Then we'd go to the airport where Batista's functionary said we could leave on a commercial flight. Unload. Wrong airport. Reload. Right airport. Unload. No airplane. Wait ten hours. Back to the hotel. Unload. Haul the baggage back to the rooms. My discs were slipping. By the third day, the cab drivers had our routine down pat. They'd even invite their friends to watch. Sallie Carter had a constructive suggestion: "Why don't we throw it all in the bay?"

The only thing that broke the monotony was that once they let us get on a plane which circled Havana and came back again. I was playing hopscotch in the terminal when I chanced upon an American sitting by himself looking very glum. Maybe he had some news of the outside world. I hopped in his direction.

"My name's McClane," I said, extending my well-calloused baggage hand.

"No," he said. "*No!*" Well, I've been fooled before, I thought.

"I'm Vic Barothy!"

*

Don Carter, who is a fine sportsman from Dallas, Texas, was a director of our company for ten years, and we shared many a trip together all over the world. If meeting Vic Barothy at the Havana airport was coincidental, what happened on an Alaskan safari I took with Carter borders on the ludicrous.

We had flown into the Katmai Monument area with Johnny Walatka and from there puddle-jumped into more remote areas to the northwest. Walatka is one of the fabled angling pioneers in that country and a first-class pilot. It was no fault of his that the flaps stuck at full on the Norseman shortly after takeoff and it was pure skill that saved the day. We were climbing from a lake through a mountain pass with fog coming in behind us, and it was a cinch we weren't going to get over the hump with the flaps dragging air. Johnny elected to go down fast somewhere before we ran out of water to land on.

It was, as they say, a long landing on a short lake. We ended up nudging a gravel bar at a river mouth. I jumped out to help Johnny grab the floats. The fog was so thick we could hardly see each other. While I was grunting at the pontoon, out of the soup walks a woman. She was at least six feet tall and dressed like Daniel Boone. Her opener was unforgettable.

"Did you ever hear a tit?" she asked.

"*Bluh, blah*," I answered, true to form. She whistled beautifully. Johnny stood there with his mouth open while she did the mating call of the tufted titmouse. Up to our knees in ice water, 400 miles from nowhere, and whom do we meet? A bird imitator. She finally ran out of notes.

"Would you like a cup of tea?" she inquired as though we casually stopped by for a crumpet. After securing the Norseman, we all followed her off into the fog, and sure enough, there was an abandoned sourdough's cabin. The otherwise bare room looked like a Peerless Camera Shop, with motion-picture equipment stacked all over the place. Her husband was a roly-poly

[260]

guy with a Smith Brothers' beard who stared at us blankly. He sat in one corner with his back to the wall. Our hostess grabbed a blackened gallon can and, sitting in the opposite corner, balanced it on her knees and began guzzling tea. There was no sign of food in the cabin.

"They're bushwacky," said Johnny. As things turned out, we had found two of Walt Disney's photographers who were lost. They were making a wildlife film and wandered too far from their pickup point. When I think of all the vast, empty miles Johnny could have set down in, well, it makes a believer out of me.

*

Field & Stream made a number of motion pictures in the forties and early fifties. We did these in cooperation with RKO-Pathé and the National Film Board of Canada. Those that I appeared in were routine scripts except for one that I'd rather forget.

I don't remember who got the bright idea that my co-star would be a fox. When I arrived on location at Crescent Lake in Florida, our director, Bob McCahon,[1] had a regular menagerie in the back of a van which he'd rented from one of those roadside Jungle Jim attractions. Although Florida has its share of alligators, bears, wildcats, egrets, and various other wildlife, the cameraman[2] wanted absolute control over his subjects. Why go running around a swamp looking for an alligator when you bring one along and take his picture at will? The idea didn't appeal to me.

"But baby, we don't have *time*. Get *with* it, kiddo. These animals are *trained*. I want you to meet your co-star Spudsy." I looked in the box and all I could see was bared teeth. *Oi vay.* He even smelled bad.

Exactly why anybody, other than the village idiot, would go fishing with a fox in the boat is beyond me. So I played the role of the village idiot. The first thing the fox did was bite me. In fact, for three weeks, that's about all the miserable cur could think of. To the knees I was one mass of Band-Aids. I learned that if you make any quick motion near a fox—like changing the position of your foot—you've had it. Blood. Worse yet, on my wedding anniversary, friend wife came to visit and she wouldn't even stay in the same room with me.

"You smell," she accused me. I didn't notice it. Fox aroma is so potent that after a while you don't smell it. You wear it.

[1] Now an independent producer, McCahon began his career with the World War II documentary *Fighting Lady*.

[2] The chief cameraman was Arthur J. Ornitz, one of Hollywood's outstanding director/cinematographers of the present day with such film credits as *The Anderson Tapes, Boys in the Band, A Thousand Clowns,* and *The Goddess.*

Anyhow, the picture dragged along to the climactic scene. The script (written on the back of a greasy menu every night) called for a long shot of me poling a skiff down a narrow creek with the fox in the bow looking like a furry Jim Bridger leading me through the wilderness. You know, the devoted doggie bit. At this point, the villain symbol, a huge alligator, was to come sliding down the embankment in an effort to slaughter My Friend Spudsy. How they were going to cue a 15-foot-long alligator and aim him straight puzzled me. But keep the faith. Hollywood can do anything. Yes sir-ee!

"Mr. Snowden, our animal trainer, assures me that he can perform on cue," said Mr. McCahon.

"It's really simple. I'll uncrate the 'gator on the bank and throw my coat over his head. If a 'gator can't see, he won't move," revealed Mr. Snowden. "When I pull my coat away, he'll dive in the water." *Oi vay*. A coat trick now.

"How will you get the 'gator out of the water?" I asked stupidly.

"We'll tie a rope on a hind leg. It won't be obvious in the film." Pure genius, that's what.

When the camera crew was ready, they signaled me to go. By this time I had learned that foxes have a passion for Coca-Cola and Swiss cheese sandwiches because Spudsy gobbled my lunch one day. So to keep him in the bow, I rubbed Swiss cheese all over the gunwale and sprinkled it with Coke. The beast was slathering on his chin.

When the skiff reached a point opposite the camera, out of the corner of my eye I saw Snowden step up and whip the coat away. Talk about reflexes! When a 15-foot-long 'gator swings his tail, it's as potent as a buzz saw. The tripod disappeared. That 'gator wasn't about to go in the water. He scrunched around and bolted for the camera crew, jaws snappin' and tail a-wavin'. I'll say one thing for Snowden. That boy hung on to the rope. He looked heroic skidding on his butt through the buck-brush while the 'gator chased Bob McCahon.

On the very last day of shooting, Spudsy escaped. The fox had learned to move the sliding door on the top of his crate. Bob Snowden reported it to the police and local newspapers thought it was a good page-two story— you know: "Fox Film Star Disappears." Personally, I was glad to see him go. Patti was making me take bubble baths three times a day, and I was beginning to get waterlogged.

*

One year, when *Field & Stream* was doing a joint promotion with United

Aircraft on round-the-world fishing,[3] I flew more than 100,000 miles on commercial airlines and uncountable miles in bush planes. Trout fishing was just getting its start in South America, so I got the bright idea to rent a plane in Santiago, Chile, and fly to Tierra del Fuego, fishing as many remote spots as possible. Old buddy Captain Don MacArthur, now of Braniff Airlines, was going to do the actual flying while I logged a few hours along the way under his expert tutelage. I had to learn the fundamentals in self-defense. We rented a light, single-engine crate with a fuselage that waggled like Raquel Welch's behind. Don, who *habla español* like a Castilian fishmonger, asked the man if he had made an engine overhaul recently.

"What did he say?"

"He said, don't worry. If it ever gave full power, the whole airplane would fall apart."

By the time we reached Puerto Montt on the Chilean side of the Cordillera, I was more interested in flying than fishing. But this place scared me. The Andean ridge rises abruptly to 11,660 feet ENE of Puerto Montt in the direction of San Carlos de Bariloche on the Argentine side—which was where we were headed. A Chilean Air Force pilot said we'd find a pass at a lower elevation near Lago Mascardi. Maybe we'd have enough ceiling. *Quién sabe?*

Anyhow, the Stinson and I put on a display of mutual confidence and got each other off the ground. We climbed to 5,000 feet when Don said the engine temperature was running hot and to level off. My cold hands were sweating on the yoke.

"There should be a strong thermal somewhere around here," Don said. Thermal, schmermal. I asked him to take over. "Naw, you're doing fine. Watch the altimeter. If it jumps, make a tight circle." We had sashayed around for ten minutes when Don briefly spotted a bird gliding to starboard. "Get over him," he instructed. I eased to the right, looking for the bird, and suddenly the altimeter spun as we went up the Andean elevator. We almost reached 8,000 feet, and the temperature was dropping back to normal. Then something out of a horror movie was staring me in the face through the port window. It disappeared.

"Geez, what was that?" I screamed.

"What was what?" asked old buddy looking in the other direction.

"*Bluh, blah,*" said I, getting my horizon lopsided. Then the damfool bird

[3] This resulted in *100 Best Fishing Spots in the World,* a soft-cover book that sold over ¼ million copies.

came straight out of the sun. A South American vulture—the condor has a wingspan of ten feet or more and this one had a *lot* more. It loomed in front of us like a 747 on crash course. The condor whooshed over the prop at twelve o'clock, banked, and came back to study MacArthur.

"Looka the length of his middle toe," said Don. All I can see is a mean, flat, naked head with wattles like a turkey hanging on the end of a long bare neck and talons capable of carrying away grown sheep, and MacArthur is admiring its middle toe. We were still circling in the grip of the thermal, so the crazy bird had no trouble buzzing the plane with hardly a wing beat. I suppose the condor finally decided, after drooling all over us, that the only part worth eating was inside the Stinson and he didn't have a can opener. When last seen the show-off was climbing to 16,000 feet.

*

Over the years I've met some kinky guides. Like the old man in the Gulf of Tehuantepec who fished commercially. There wasn't much floating equipment around, and though his boat hardly inspired confidence, he agreed to take me out as long as he could keep the fish. The ship didn't have outriggers, so I mounted two rods in the aluminum tubes that passed for gimbals on the stern. Sailfish were all over the place and before long we had a double on.

His boat was absolutely unmaneuverable. The lines tangled, then the fish switched directions and untangled. It became evident that the old man was a real thinker. He shouted something at his thirteen-year-old son who donned a cork life jacket, which, judging by the holes in it, was a reject from the Titanic. Then he shoved my rod in the kid's hands and threw him overboard. *Olé. Oi vay*. A true Brother of the Jungle Cock. Junior bobbed toward the horizon like a crippled duck.

"Sharks? *Tiburón?*" I croaked. He shrugged, like who worries?

"I have five sons, señor." When we retrieved the kid the fish was still on.

*

Then there was Guillermo. He was truly unique. It will take more than a minute to explain him. In 1957, at the invitation of the Venezuelan Government, we spent many weeks doing exploratory fishing in the Orinoco watershed and offshore from La Guaira to Isla de Margarita. Dictator Marcos Pérez Jiménez was in office at the time (seeking to improve his image) and SN, or Secret Police, was headed by Pedro Estrada. Estrada was one of the bully boys who plucked people's fingernails with pliers and generally assassinated anybody who voted "no." Or thought "no," because nobody voted.

I didn't know a cotton-pickin' thing about local politics and when the

Minister of Interior, Dr. Vallenilla Lanz, handed me a bunch of papers with stamps all over them, I figured it was a collection of fishing licenses. The government had George Bass's boat, the Sambo, freighted down for coastal fishing because there wasn't any local craft available at the time. The swift-running Sambo required high octane fuel, and to rate that in a Venezuelan port we had to register the boat as an airplane. One of the papers *proved* it was an airplane—as any pump attendant would plainly see when we pulled up to a dock. The hat trick. But with a revolution in the wind, such details become important.

I guess somebody forgot to tell the SN that a couple of gringos would be tooling up and down the coast in a boat/airplane and roaming around the countryside carrying shotguns. Anyhow, George and I split up after Isla de Margarita, and Patti and I took our guide Guillermo on to San Cristobal in the western interior. I had a funny feeling that we were being shadowed, and when we reached San Cristobal, I was sure of it. Patti pulled back the drapes in our hotel room and outside on the lawn stood a little guy in—you guessed it—a trench coat. He had a gray fedora pulled down over his eyes and looked about as inconspicuous as W. C. Fields at a Las Vegas temperance drive.

"Who is he?" asked Patti.

"Not a friendly. Call Guillermo and ask him to come here."

"Guillermo went shopping," she said.

"Shopping?"

"He went to Cúcuta."

"That's in Colombia." I know my geography.

"So, it's just over the border."

We stayed in the San Cristobal area about a week, fishing the Río Uribante by day and returning to the hotel at night. The little man stuck like glue except when we took off in the boat. Guillermo put a ring-a-ding cousin in charge and went shopping every day. Some guide. He must be a fashion editor for Consumer Reports.

"Did you ever notice how fat Guillermo looks sometimes?" asked Patti. "It's funny, he's really a skinny guy."

"Who sees him? The only time he shows up is for chow." That evening I saw Guillermo waddle into the lobby. He was a veritable Latin Sidney Greenstreet. Yet when he came to the table, he was skinny as a rail. Maybe I needed new glasses.

"You got boo-leets for dees gun, señor?" he asked.

"Which gun?"

"A man in dee bus axed me where you kip dee boo-leets . . . ees all."

At least the SN hadn't frisked the station wagon. But my funny bone told me that something would happen soon.

We were nailed at a roadblock on the way back to Caracas. Roadblocks in that area were, and probably still are, a way of life. This is the main route for smuggling contraband into Venezuela. There was an endless clutter of cars ahead of us and soldiers waving tommy guns were stalking the road shoulder making a random check. I had sweaty armpits. Guillermo was shaking like a hound dog.

The military didn't say anything. They just yanked the doors open and waved us out. It was obvious that they had no sense of humor. I handed them our passports which they didn't look at. Then I produced some of the papers Dr. Lanz had given me. Maybe a fishing license would impress them. No dice. Naturally, the little man in the gray fedora arrived, and they started to empty the station wagon in the middle of the road. One of the soldiers barked something at Guillermo, who was vibrating so bad now that I thought he'd come unbolted. He proceeded to strip.

To this day I've never figured out how any man, even a skinny male, can wear eight suits. Progressive sizes maybe? But eight suits he took off before he got to the buff. When they opened his duffel, what appeared to be another fifty suits were tossed on the road. A suit smuggler! Guillermo stood naked as a jaybird in a rag nest waiting to hear the gun go off.

"I have more papers in my bag," announced Patti, hoping to delay his execution. "Maybe we have a permit for smuggling." What a kook! She proceeded to empty her purse, which is always a fascinating operation. Even the tommygunners shook their heads in disbelief. Somewhere among all her junk, Patti found more of Dr. Lanz's handiwork, which she passed around like a Salvation Army worker handing out biblical tracts. One of them, which didn't even have a stamp on it, and began "To Whom It May Concern" practically caused a panic.

Everybody saluted everybody, our gear was dusted off and repacked. They even put a suit back on Guillermo, who looked stunned. The magic signature on that document was "Pedro Estrada," the fingernail plucker. We rated a platoon-strength escort, sirens included.

*

Well, I've left out a lot of things that E. F. predicted, some of them not even printable in a family publication, but having survived almost one-third of *Field & Stream*'s anniversaries, I can look down on my yolk-stained shirt and say the moral to the hat trick is not the fact that you get egg on your face—but how well you wear it.

I'm sure that's what E. F. had in mind.

[266]